The SCRABBLE®
Brand Games
WORD GUIDE

By Jacob Orleans and Edmund Jacobson

Formerly titled
The Scrabble Word Guide

A GD/PERIGEE BOOK

Perigee Books
are published by
The Putnam Publishing Group
200 Madison Avenue
New York, New York, 10016

Formerly titled
The Scrabble Word Guide

SCRABBLE® is the registered trademark
of Selchow & Righter Company for its line of word games
and entertainment services.

ISBN 0-399-50817-1
First Perigee printing, 1982
Four previous Grosset & Dunlap printings
Printed in the United States of America
3   4   5   6   7   8   9

INTRODUCTION

This book is a convenient source to check the spelling of over 30,000 words selected especially for playing SCRABBLE brand word games. In addition, specific lists help you to use the games' high-scoring letters and alert you to many-vowel and uncommon words. Glancing over these listings before you play may allow you to come up with a word at a crucial time. You don't have to know the meanings of these unusual words, but it will help you to remember them if you do. All of them may be found in *Funk & Wagnalls New College Standard Dictionary,* 1953 edition, from which this selection was compiled, with the permission of the publishers.

To make the master list compact, regular plurals of words, parts of verbs formed by adding such endings as -ed or -ing, or words formed by adding -ly, -ness, -ment, -able, -er have been excluded. We have, however, included unusual plural endings and other irregularly formed words.

Some common words, such as *so, dot,* and *car,* have also been omitted. No book short of an unabridged dictionary could possibly list every word allowed in play.

In most SCRABBLE brand word games, you will be using mainly shorter words, but words even nine or ten letters long can be made by adding to existing words. For example, the word *ponderable* is built up from the shorter words: *pond, ponder, era,* and *able.*

We trust that the comprehensive and selected word listings in this book will be a great help to you in your games.

THE BIG FOUR

The letters J, Q, X, and Z are the "Big Four" in word game play. Their values are eight and ten times that of the vowels. Since they occur rarely by comparison with most of the other letters, it is important to know as many as possible of the words listed below in which they are used. The words are arranged by the number of letters. Words containing two of the high value letters are in heavier type.

Words Containing the Letter J

3 Letters
haj
jab
jag
jam
jar
jaw
jay
jee
jet
jib
job
jog
jot
joy
jug
jus
jut
raj

4 Letters
ajar
guja
hadj
haje
haji
hajj
jack
jade
jady
jail
jamb
jape
jarl
jazz
jean
jeep
jeer
jerk
jess
jest
jibe
jill
jilt
jinn
jinx
jive

joad
join
joke
jole
jolt
jowl
juba
jube
juju
jump
junk
jura
jury
just
jute
raja
soja

5 Letters
banjo
bijou
eject
ejido
enjoy
fjord
hadji
hajji
jabot
jacal
jacko
jacky
jaggy
jakes
jalap
jambe
japan
jaspe
jaunt
jazzy
jebel
jehad
jemmy
jenny
jerky
jerry
jetty
jewel
jihad

jimmy
jinni
jinny
jirky
jocko
joint
joist
jolly
joram
jorum
jougs
joule
joust
judge
jugal
juice
juicy
julep
jumbo
jumpy
junco
junta
jupon
jural
jurat
juror
jutty
major
mujik
rajah
sajou
slojd
thuja

6 Letters
abject
abjure
acajou
adjoin
adjure
adjust
banjos
bijoux
cajole
cajput
canjar
crojik
deject
donjon

enjoin
frijol
hadjee
hejira
inject
injure
injury
jabber
jaboty
jacana
jackal
jacket
jackey
jackie
jadish
jadite
jaeger
jaguar
jangle
jepery
jarabe
jarfly
jargon
jarina
jasper
jaunty
jejune
jennet
jerboa
jereed
jerkin
jerrid
jersey
jessed
jetsam
jetton
jigget
jiggle
jigsaw
jingal
jingko
jingle
jinnee
jitter
jockey
jocose
jocund
joggle
joseph

jostle
jounce
jovial
joyful
joyous
jubate
jugate
juggle
jumble
jujube
jungle
jungly
junior
junket
jurant
jurist
moujik
muzjik
object
reject
rejoin
svaraj
swaraj
unjust
wejack

7 Letters
abjurer
adjourn
adjudge
adjunct
adjurer
basenji
cajeput
canjiar
conjoin
conjure
disject
disjoin
ejector
frijole
jacinth
jackbox
jackdaw
jackleg
jackpot
jaconet
jadeite

jaggery
jalapin
jambeau
jargoon
javelin
jejunum
jeofail
jewfish
jingall
janitor
jasmine
jealous
jessant
jewelry
jinglet
jobbery
jocular
joinder
joinery
jollity
jonquil
journal
journey
joyless
jubilee
jugular
jujitsu
juniper
junkman
juridic
juryman
jussive
justice
justify
majesty
mojarra
pajamas
perjure
perjury
project
rejoice
sapajou
sejeant
sjambok
sojourn
subject
subjoin
traject

Words Containing the Letter Q

3–4 Letters
qua, quad, quag, quay, quid, quip, quit, **quiz**, quod

5 Letters
equal, equip, fique, pique, quack, quaff, quail, quake, qualm, quart, quash, quean, queen, queer, quell, querl, quern, query, quest, queue, quick, quiet, quill, quilt, quint, quipu, quire, quirk, quirl, quirt, quish, quite, quoin, quoit, quota, quote, quoth, roque, squab, squad, squat, squaw, squib, squid, toque, tuque, usque

6 Letters
acquit, aequum, aquose, barque, basque, bisque, caique, cinque, cirque, claque, clique, cliquy, coquet, equate, equity, liquid, liquor, maquis, masque, mosque, opaque, piquet, pulque, quaere, quagga, quaggy, quahog, quaint, qualmy, quanta, quarry, quarte, quarto, **quartz**, quaver, queasy, quench, **quezal**, quince, quinic, quinin, quinsy, quirky, quiver, quohog, quorum, risque, roquet, sacque, sequel, squail, squall, squama, square, squash, squawk, squeak, squeal, squill, squint, squire, squirm, squirt, toquet, torque, unique

7 Letters
acquire, aliquot, aquaria, aquatic, aqueous, bequest, bouquet, briquet, brusque, cacique, cliquey, coequal, conquer, coquina, cumquat, enquire, enquiry, equable, equator, equerry, esquire, flanque, inquest, inquire, inquiry, **jonquil**, lacquer, liquefy, marquee, marquis, masquer, oblique, obloquy, obsequy, oquassa, parquet, pasquil, pasquin, picquet, piquant, quadrat, quadric, quaffer, qualify, quality, quamash, quantic, quantum, quarrel, quartan, quarter, quartet, quassia, quassin, quavery, quayage, querist, quester, **quetzal**, quibble, quicken, quiddle, quietus, quillai, quilter, quinary, quinate, quinine, quinnat, quinoid, quinone, quintal, quintan, quintet, quitter, quittor, quondam, racquet, relique, request, requiem, require, requite, ronquil, rorqual, sequela, sequent, sequoia, siliqua, silique, squabby, squalid, squally, squalor, squalus, squamae, squashy, squatty, squeaky, **squeeze**, squelch, squilla, squinch, squirmy, unequal

Words Containing the Letter X

2–3 Letters
ax, axe, box, **fix**, fox, kex, lax, lex, mix, nix, ox, pax, pox, pyx, sax, sex, six, tax, vex, vox, wax, **zax**

4 Letters
apex, axil, axis, axle, axon, coax, coxa, crux, eaux, exit, flax, flex, flux, foxy, hoax, ibex, ilex, ixia, **jinx**, lynx, minx, moxa, next, onyx, oryx, oxen, oxid, oxim, pixy, sext, taxi, taxy, text, xyst

5 Letters
addax, admix, affix, annex, ataxy, axial, axile, axiom, axled, axman, axone, beaux, borax, boxen, boxer, braxy, buxom, calyx, cimex, codex, cylix, exact, exalt, excel, exert, exile, exist, expel, extol

extra	vixen	excess	oxygon	anxiety	extreme	peroxid
exude	waxen	excite	oxymel	anxious	fixture	perplex
exult	xebec	excuse	paxwax	apyrexy	flexile	phalanx
flaxy	xenia	exempt	phenix	axillae	flexion	phoenix
galax	xenon	exhale	pickax	axillar	flexure	pickaxe
helix	xerus	exhort	plexes	axolotl	fluxion	pretext
hexad	xylan	exhume	plexor	bandbox	foxbane	pyrexia
hexyl	xylem	exodus	plexus	bauxite	foxfire	pyrexic
hyrax	xylic	exotic	pollex	biaxial	foxfish	radixes
index	xylol	expand	praxis	boxhaul	foxhole	rheotax
infix	xylyl	expect	prefix	boxwood	foxhunt	salpinx
ixtle		expend	prolix	bureaux	foxskin	sandbox
kylix	6 Letters	expert	reflex	cachexy	foxtail	saxhorn
latex	adieux	expire	reflux	carapax	foxtrot	saxtuba
laxly	admixt	export	scolex	chevaux	foxwood	sexless
malax	afflux	expose	sexfid	coaxial	hexadic	sextant
maxim	ataxia	extant	sextan	coexist	hexagon	sextile
mixer	ataxic	extend	sextet	complex	jackbox	simplex
murex	axilla	extent	sexton	conflux	laxness	sixfold
nixie	axseed	extort	sexual	context	lexical	sixteen
noxal	biaxal	fixate	spadix	coxcomb	lexicon	soapbox
oxbow	bijoux	fixity	sphinx	dextral	mailbox	synaxis
oxeye	bombyx	flaxen	storax	dioxide	maxilla	taxable
oxide	boxcar	flexor	suffix	exactly	maximal	taxicab
oxime	calxes	galaxy	surtax	examine	maximum	taxitic
oxlip	caudex	hallux	syntax	example	maxwell	tectrix
phlox	climax	hatbox	syrinx	exclaim	mixable	textile
proxy	coaxal	hexane	taxine	exclude	mixible	textual
pulex	coccyx	hexone	taxite	execute	noxious	texture
pyxie	commix	icebox	thorax	exhaust	overtax	toxemia
pyxis	convex	larynx	toxine	exhibit	oxazine	toxemic
radix	cortex	laxity	turnix	expanse	oxidase	toxical
relax	cruxes	luxate	tuxedo	expiate	oxidate	trioxid
remex	dexter	luxury	vertex	explain	oxidize	triplex
silex	dioxid	matrix	vortex	explode	oxyacid	xanthic
sixth	diplex	maxima	xylene	exploit	oxynora	xanthin
sixty	duplex	maxixe	xyloid	explore	oxyntic	xerosis
toxic	efflux	meninx	xylose	expound	oxysalt	xerotic
toxin	elixir	orexis	xyster	express	oxytone	xiphoid
unfix	exceed	oxalic		expunge	paradox	xylidin
unsex	except	oxalis	7 Letters	extract	pemphix	
varix		oxygen	anthrax			

Words Containing the Letter Z

3–4 Letters				5 Letters		
adz	fez	ooze	zebu	amaze	braze	fuzee
adze	fizz	oozy	zein	azoic	colza	fuzil
azo	friz	oyez	zero	azote	cozen	fuzzy
azym	fuze	quiz	zest	azure	craze	gauze
buzz	fuzz	raze	zeta	azyme	crazy	gauzy
coz	gaze	size	zinc	bazar	croze	glaze
cozy	haze	sizz	zip	bezel	dizen	graze
czar	hazy	tzar	zoa	blaze	dozen	hazel
daze	jazz	whiz	zoic	bonze	enzym	huzza
doze	laze	zala	zone	booze	fizzy	jazzy
dozy	lazy	zany	zoom	bortz	frizz	kazoo
faze	maze	zax	zoon	braza	furze	lazar
	mazy	zeal	zyme		furzy	maize

mazer	ablaze	frowzy	wheeze	apprize	ebonize	seizure
mezzo	amazon	frozen	wizard	azimuth	elegize	squeeze
mirza	assize	gazebo	zaffar	azotize	emblaze	stylize
mizen	azalea	guzzle	zaffir	azurite	frazzle	swizzle
nozle	azonic	hazard	zaffre	azygous	frizzle	trapeze
ouzel	azotic	huzzah	zanana	azymous	frizzly	tzarina
ozena	azymic	huzzay	zapate	bazooka	fuzzily	zacaton
ozone	bazaar	izzard	zareba	benzene	gazelle	zaptiah
plaza	benzin	mazily	zealot	benzine	gazette	zaptieh
prize	benzol	mazoid	zebeck	benzoic	gizzard	zareeba
razee	benzyl	mizzen	zechin	benzoin	grizzle	zealous
razor	bezant	mizzle	zenana	benzoyl	grizzly	zebrass
seize	bezoar	mizzly	zendik	bezique	horizon	zebrine
sezin	blazer	muzhik	zenith	bizarre	itemize	zebroid
sizar	blazon	muzjik	zephyr	blowzed	lazaret	zebrula
sized	blazor	nozzle	zeugma	bonanza	lazarly	zebrule
sizer	blowzy	nyanza	zinced	brazier	matzoon	zecchin
sozin	borzoi	ozaena	zincky	britzka	matzoth	zedoary
spitz	brazen	ozenic	zinnia	bromize	mazurka	zemstvo
suzin	brazil	ozonic	zipper	buzzwig	mestiza	zeolite
topaz	breeze	panzer	zircon	canzone	mezuzah	zestful
vizir	breezy	piazza	zither	canzoni	mitzvah	zincate
vizor	bronze	podzol	zodiac	capsize	muezzin	zincify
waltz	bronzy	puzzle	zombie	chintzy	obelize	zincing
winze	buzzer	quartz	zonary	citizen	outsize	zincite
wizen	chintz	quezal	zonate	coenzym	oxazine	zincked
zamia	coryza	razzia	zonula	cognize	oxidize	zincous
zayin	cozily	rezone	zonule	cozener	ozaenic	zingara
zebec	crazed	seizor	zoonal	crazier	ozonide	zittern
zebra	crozer	sizzle	zorila	crazily	ozonize	zoisite
zibet	dazzle	sleazy	zounds	crozier	ozonous	zooidal
zinic	eczema	sneeze	zygoma	cruzado	pectize	zoology
zinky	evzone	snooze	zygote	cyanize	peptize	zoonomy
zloty	fizgig	sozine	zymase	czardom	pretzel	zooster
zombi	fizzle	stanza	zymose	czarina	quetzal	zootomy
zonal	foozle	syzygy		czarism	realize	zygosis
zooid	frazil	teazel	*7 Letters*	diazine	rhizoid	zymogen
zoril	freeze	touzle		diazole	rhizoma	zymosis
zymic	frenzy	tweeze	agonize	dozenth	rhizome	zymotic
	frieze	tzetze	alcazar	drizzle	scherzi	zymurgy
6 Letters	frizer	vizard	analyze	drizzly	scherzo	
		vizier				

WORDS WITH MANY VOWELS

One Consonant	audio	fie	ocean	*Many Vowels*	apogee	bureau
aalii	aura	gee	oleo	acacia	aquose	calorie
adieu	beau	idea	olio	aculei	arena	cause
aerie	bee	ilia	out	aerial	areola	cease
agee	boa	inia	pea	alienee	arete	ceria
agio	boo	ixïa	pie	alive	aside	cilia
ague	cooee	io	queue	aloof	ataxia	ciliae
aim	eat	iota	raia	alulae	audile	cooer
aloe	eau	lea	roue	ameer	avail	cookie
amia	eerie	lee	tie	anemia	aviate	donee
area	emeu	miaou	too	anuria	aureous	dulia
aria	epee	moo	unau	aorta	aureus	eaten
asea	etui	oaf	wee	aoudad	aurora	eerily
	fee	oii	woo		axial	elate

elide
elite
elope
emeute
enate
enema
epopee
epopoeia
etwee
fiancee
galeae
giaor

guaiac
heaume
hoodoo
hoopoe
hoopoo
house
idiom
idiot
iguana
ileac
ileitis
imbue

initial
inure
ionic
iota
irate
iris
lease
leave
mania
melee
ocean
oleate

olein
olive
onion
oogone
oolite
oomiak
opera
opiate
oribi
oriel
oriole
ouabain

ovaria
ovoli
ovolo
paean
paeon
palea
paleae
payee
peace
pease
peewee
piano

piece
quaere
radii
radio
ragee
ramee
ramie
ratio
reeve
riata
rodeo
seine

seize
siege
sieur
sieve
souari
suede
taboo
taenia
taiga
unique
unite
woodsi

Words Ending in "A"

aloha
alumna
aorta
area
aroma
asthma
aurora
balboa
balsa
banana
cala
camera
canna
cantata
charta
china
cicada
cinema
cobra
cocoa
coda
cola
coma
comma

conga
corona
crania
dicta
diorama
diploma
dogma
donna
drama
duenna
edema
enema
enigma
era
fiesta
fistula
flora
folia
fuchsia
gala
gamma
ganglia
hula
hurra

hydra
ilia
inia
insula
iota
jerboa
juba
junta
ka
kabbala
kana
kola
la
lacuna
lama
larva
mama
manna
mamma
manila
media
mica
moa
mocha

olla
omega
opera
ora
ova
pagoda
papa
parka
pascha
pasha
patella
patina
pelota
persona
phobia
piazza
pica
pika
pinna
plasma
platina
plaza
pleura
pneuma

proa
puma
punka
pupa
quanta
quota
raia
raja
retina
rhumba
rostra
rota
rotunda
rumba
saga
saliva
salvia
schema
sepia
shea
sienna
sierra
siesta

sigma
silica
soda
sofa
solaria
soya
spa
spectra
stadia
stamina
stanza
strata
tea
tapioca
testa
tiara
tibia
toga
trauma
tuba
tuna
ulna
ultra

urea
uremia
uria
uva
uvea
uvula
vacua
via
visa
vista
viva
vodka
volva
vomica
whoa
xenia
yea
yoga
yucca
zanana
zebra
zeta
zinnia

Words Ending in "B"

absorb
adverb
aplomb
bib
blab
blob
bomb
cab
climb
club
cob
cobweb
comb
coxcomb
crib

crumb
cub
curb
daub
drab
drub
dub
dumb
entomb
enwomb
fib
fob
garb
glib
gob

grab
grub
herb
hob
hub
intomb
jamb
jib
kerb
knob
lamb
limb
lob
mob
nab

nabob
neb
nib
nub
numb
orb
pleb
plumb
rhubarb
rib
rob
scab
scrub
shrub
slab

slob
snob
snub
sob
stab
stub
succumb
superb
swab
tab
throb
thumb
tomb
tub
verb

web
womb

adsorb
alb
ardeb
carob
coulomb
drib
fub
gamb
gib
iamb
kab

kerb
mib
resorb
reverb
rhomb
rhumb
scarab
sib
sibb
slub
squib
stilb
stob
swob

Words Ending in "F"

Ending in one f	fief	kef	relief	thereof	enfeoff	raff
alef	ganef	kerf	reproof	thief	feoff	rebuff
aloof	ganof	khalif	roof	turf	fluff	ruff
beef	grief	kief	scarf	waif	griff	scoff
brief	gulf	leaf	scurf	wharf	gruff	scruff
calf	half	lief	self	woof	guff	sheriff
chef	hereof	loof	serf		huff	skiff
chief	herself	massif	serif	*Ending in two f's*	infeoff	sniff
clef	himself	motif	shadoof		luff	snuff
coif	hoof	naif	shaduf	buff	muff	staff
corf	if	oaf	sheaf	cliff	off	stiff
deaf	ingulf	of	shelf	cuff	playoff	stuff
dwarf	itself	pelf	shereef	doff	pontiff	tariff
engulf	kalif	proof	sherif	draff	puff	tiff
	keef	reef	surf	duff	quaff	tuff
						whiff

Words Ending in "I"

aalii	chili	gyri	nidi	peri	soldi	tipi
abri	cirri	hamuli	nielli	pili	soli	titi
agni	coati	houri	nilgai	quillai	solidi	tori
agouti	cocci	iambi	nimbi	rabbi	sori	torsi
ai	corgi	indri	nisi	rabboni	souari	tragi
alibi	cormi	jinni	nuclei	radii	splenii	tripoli
alkali	crotali	kadi	nylghi	ragi	spumoni	tumuli
alumni	dromoi	kaki	oboli	rami	stelai	tutti
ani	effendi	kali	ocelli	ravioli	stimuli	urari
asci	emboli	kepi	octopi	reguli	sulci	vagi
aurei	epi	khaki	oii	safari	swami	virelai
bonaci	etui	krubi	okapi	salami	syllabi	volvuli
borzoi	foci	litchi	onagri	salmi	tali	wadi
bronchi	fungi	loci	oribi	saluki	tarsi	wapiti
cacti	genii	loculi	ourebi	scenari	taxi	woorali
calami	ghetti	lungi	pali	scherzi	thalami	woorari
calli	gingeli	mallei	palpi	scirrhi	thalli	yogi
caroli	glutei	miladi	pappi	scudi	ti	zombi
carpi	grigri	mufti	papyri	serai	timpani	

Words Ending in "O"

also	compo	gusto	junco	oleo	rhino	thoro
altho	congo	hallo	kazoo	olio	rodeo	tiro
alto	curio	halo	keno	outdo	rondo	to
azo	dingo	hello	kino	outgo	sago	too
bilbo	ditto	hero	largo	patio	salvo	torso
bingo	duo	ho	limbo	pedro	shako	two
bolo	echo	hobo	lingo	pengo	shoo	tyro
bongo	ergo	hollo	loco	pepo	silo	umbo
bubo	faro	hoo	loo	piano	soldo	undo
burro	folio	igloo	loto	polo	solo	verso
cameo	fordo	inro	lotto	potto	taboo	video
canto	forgo	into	mango	pro	tango	vireo
cello	fresno	jacko	milo	radio	taro	wahoo
chico	fro	jocko	misdo	ratio	tempo	whoso
cisco	go	jumbo	motto	recto	tho	woo
coco						zero

Words Ending in "U"

babu	congu	iglu	litu	pareu	sabicu	tinamou
baku	coypou	jujitsu	manitou	parvenu	sajou	tolu
beau	coypu	juju	manitu	perdu	sapajou	tonneau
bureau	dhu	kudu	menu	pilau	sou	turacou
caribou	fichu	landau	miaou	quipu	tabu	unau
catechu	gnu	leu	nylghau	rondeau	thou	virtu
congou	habu	lieu	ormulu	rouleau	thru	zebu

UNUSUAL WORDS

aalii	cultch	fipple	jacana	nth	quern	snits
abb	cumin	fitch	jacko	nub	quetzal	soja
addax	cylix	flanch	jakes	nurl	quipu	soke
ai	dhoti	fletch	jarl	obol	quirl	sprag
alb	dhow	flitch	jocko	od	quod	squama
amock	dhu	foh	joram	oii	quoin	stilb
amyl	dirndl	fub	juju	orc	raphe	stob
ankh	diss	fubsy	ka	oryx	resh	sump
awn	doit	fyke	kad	osar	ret	swage
azo	dowle	fylfot	kaiak	oxeye	rhaphe	swart
babu	drachm	gamb	keef	oxim	rhea	swiple
basenji	draffy	gar	kef	pah	rhein	swot
bel	drib	gecko	kerf	palpi	riley	sybo
bice	drongo	glume	kex	parn	roc	tain
bilbo	duad	graul	kibe	pawl	rotch	targ
bleb	dubh	greige	knop	peag	rotl	tenrek
bongo	dyad	grigri	krubi	peepul	ruth	tink
bortz	ecad	haaf	kudu	phat	rynd	titi
bot	edh	haak	lakh	phot	ryot	tolu
bott	eft	habu	leet	pili	samp	toph
braxy	eikon	hadj	lehr	pipal	sapajou	trasko
brut	ejido	haj	lehua	placebo	scaup	umbo
bubo	ekka	haje	leu	podzol	scend	unau
buhl	emyd	haji	lev	pome	schuit	ut
burke	enfeoff	hajj	marl	potto	schwa	valkyr
burl	ens	hogan	marly	pugh	scurf	vomito
cala	ensky	hoicks	maw	puisne	sedum	wejack
canjar	epi	hoopoo	mel	pulkha	shaduf	winze
chico	epopee	ictus	mho	punka	shawm	wych
cimex	epopoeia	infeoff	mib	puy	shend	xylyl
cisco	epopt	inkle	mir	pyoid	shiv	xyst
col	eth	ipomea	mirk	pyx	sid	yftria
coly	etui	ism	mneme	pyxis	sjambok	yupon
corf	feoff	istle	moa	quag	skeg	zanana
corgi	feu	ixia	mol	quagga	skua	zax
coz	fey	ixtle	mot	quean	slojd	zemstvo
crambo	fid	izzard	moxa	querl	slub	zoon
crojik	fique	jaboty	nixie			

THE SCRABBLE® BRAND GAMES MASTER WORD LIST

aalii	abhor	abrasive	acacia	accouter	acicula	acrodrome
aardvark	abhorrent	abrastol	academic	accredit	aciculae	acrogen
aardwolf	abidal	abreact	academism	accresce	acicular	acrogenic
aba	abidance	abreast	academy	accrete	aciculate	acrolein
abaci	abide	abri	acajou	accretion	acid	acrolith
aback	ability	abridge	acaleph	accretive	acidic	acromia
abacus	abiosis	abroach	acalephan	accroach	acidify	acromial
abacuses	abiotic	abroad	acalephe	accrual	acidity	acromion
abaft	abject	abrogate	acanthi	accrue	acidosis	acronic
abalone	abjection	abrupt	acanthial	accumbent	acidotic	acronical
abandon	abjective	abruption	acanthine	accuracy	acidulate	acropetal
abase	abjure	abscess	acanthion	accurate	acidulent	acropolis
abash	ablactate	abscind	acanthoid	accursed	acidulous	acrospire
abate	ablation	abscissa	acanthous	accusal	acierate	across
abatis	ablative	abscond	acanthus	accuse	aciform	acrostic
abattis	ablaut	absence	acardia	accustom	acini	acrotism
abattoir	ablaze	absent	acardiac	ace	aciniform	acrylic
abaxial	able	absentee	acariasis	acedia	acinose	act
abaxile	ablegate	absentism	acarid	acentric	acinous	actinal
abb	abloom	absinth	acaroid	acerate	acinus	actinia
abbacy	abluent	absinthe	acarpous	acerb	acline	actinian
abbatial	ablush	absolute	acaudal	acerbate	aclinic	actinic
abbatical	ablution	absolve	acaudate	acerbity	acme	actinical
abbess	ably	absolvent	acaules	acerose	acne	actinism
abbey	abnegate	absonant	acauline	acervate	acnode	actinium
abbot	abnormal	absorb	acaulose	acervulus	acock	actinoid
abbotcy	abnormity	absorbent	acaulous	acescence	acolyte	action
abbotship	aboard	abstain	accede	acescent	aconite	activate
abdicate	abode	absterge	accent	acetamide	aconitine	active
abdicable	abolish	abstinent	accentual	acetate	aconitum	activity
abdomen	abolition	abstract	accept	acetic	acorn	actor
abdominal	aboma	abstruse	acceptant	acetify	acoumeter	actress
abduce	abomasum	absurd	access	acetonate	acoustic	actual
abducent	abominate	absurdity	accessary	acetone	acoustics	actuality
abduct	aboon	abulia	accession	acetonic	acquaint	actualize
abduction	aboral	abulic	accessory	acetonize	acquest	actuarial
abeam	aborigen	abundance	accidence	acetose	acquiesce	actuary
abecedary	aborigin	abundant	accident	acetous	acquire	actuate
abed	aborigine	abune	accite	acetum	acquit	actuation
abele	abort	abuse	acclaim	acetyl	acquittal	acuate
abelmosk	abortion	abusive	acclimate	acetylene	acrasia	acuity
abelmusk	abortive	abut	acclivity	acetylic	acre	aculeate
aberrance	aboulia	abutilon	acclivous	ache	acreage	aculei
aberrancy	aboulic	abutment	accolade	achene	acred	aculeus
aberrant	abound	abuttal	accompany	achenia	acrid	acumen
abet	about	abysm	accord	achenial	acridine	acuminate
abettal	above	abysmal	accordant	achenium	acridity	acuminous
abeyance	abradant	abyss	accordion	achieve	acrimony	acushla
abeyancy	abrade	abyssal	accost	achromic	acrobat	acute
abeyant	abrasion	abyssic	account	achromous	acrobatic	acyclic

adactylia
adage
adamant
adamite
adamsite
adapt
adaptive
adays
add
addax
addend
addenda
addendum
adder
addict
addiction
addictive
addition
additive
addle
address
addressee
adduce
adducent
adduct
adduction
adductive
adeem
adelphous
ademption
adenoid
adenoidal
adenology
adenoma
adept
adequacy
adequate
adfected
adhere
adherence
adherency
adherent
adhesion
adhesive
adhibit
adiabatic
adiantum
adieu
adieus
adieux
adipic
adipocere
adipoma
adipomata
adipose
adiposis
adipous

adjacence
adjacency
adjacent
adjective
adjoin
adit
adjourn
adjudge
adjunct
adjure
adjust
adjustive
adjutage
adjutancy
adjutant
adjuvant
admeasure
adminicle
admirable
admiral
admire
admissible
admission
admissive
admissory
admit
admix
admixt
admixture
admonish
admonitor
adnascent
adnate
adnation
adnoun
adnominal
ado
adobe
adopt
adoption
adoptive
adoration
adore
adorn
adown
adrenal
adrift
adroit
adscript
adsorb
adsorbate
adsorbent
adularia
adulate
adulation
adulatory
adult

adultery
adulterer
adulthood
adumbral
adumbrant
adumbrate
adunc
aduncous
adust
advance
advantage
advection
advent
adventive
adventure
adverb
adverbial
adversary
adverse
adversity
advert
advertent
advertise
advertize
advice
advise
advisory
advocacy
advocate
advowee
advowson
adynamia
adynamic
adyta
adytum
adz
adze
aedeagus
aedaeagus
aedes
aedile
aedoeagus
aeneous
aeneus
aequum
aerarian
aerate
aeration
aerial
aerialist
aeriality
aerie
aeried
aeriform
aerify
aerobe
aerobia

aerobic
aerocurve
aerodyne
aerogen
aerogram
aerograph
aerolite
aerolith
aerolitic
aerologic
aerology
aeromancy
aerometer
aerometry
aeronaut
aeronef
aerophore
aerophyte
aeroplane
aeroscope
aeroscopy
aerosled
aerosol
aerostat
aerotaxis
aery
afar
affable
affair
affect
affection
affective
afferent
affiance
affiant
affidavit
affiliate
affined
affinity
affirm
affirmant
affix
affixture
afflation
afflatus
afflict
affluence
affluent
afflux
afforce
afford
afforest
affray
affricate
affright
affront
affuse

affusion
afghan
afield
afire
aflame
afloat
afoot
afore
aforehand
aforesaid
aforetime
afoul
afraid
afresh
afreet
afrit
aft
after
aftermath
aftermost
afternoon
afterpain
aftertime
afterwale
afterward
aftmost
again
against
agalloch
agama
agamic
agamous
agape
agar
agaric
agate
agateware
agatize
agave
agee
ageless
agency
agent
agential
ageratum
ageusia
ageustia
agger
aggrade
aggravate
aggregate
aggress
aggressin
aggrieve
aghast
agile
agility

aging
agio
agiotage
agist
agitate
agitation
aglet
aglow
agminate
agnail
agnate
agnatic
agnation
agni
agnomen
agnomina
agnominal
agnostic
agnus
ago
agog
agon
agones
agonic
agonist
agonistic
agonize
agony
agouti
agouties
agoutis
agouty
agrafe
agraffe
agraph
agrapha
agraphia
agraphic
agrarian
agree
agrestic
agrimony
agriology
agrology
agrologic
agromania
agronomic
agronomy
aground
ague
agueweed
aguish
ah
aha
ahead
aheap
ahem

ahimsa
ahold
ahoy
ahull
ahungered
ai
aid
aide
aiglet
aigret
aigrette
ail
ailanthic
ailanthus
aileron
ailment
aim
aimless
ain
air
aircraft
airhole
airless
airlock
airlog
airometer
airplane
airport
airpost
airproof
airstream
airstrip
airtight
airway
airworthy
airy
aisle
ait
aitch
aitchbone
aithe
ajar
akimbo
akin
akinesia
akinesic
akinesis
ala
alae
alabamine
alabaster
alack
alackaday
alacrity
alan
aland
alant

alanin
alanine
alar
alare
alarm
alarmism
alarmist
alary
alas
alaska
alate
alb
alba
albacore
albata
albatross
albeit
albertite
albescent
albinic
albinism
albino
albite
albitical
albornoz
albuginea
album
albumen
albumin
albumose
alburnum
alcaide
alcalde
alcayde
alcazar
alchemic
alchemist
alchemize
alchemy
alchymy
alcohol
alcoholic
alcove
aldehyde
alder
alderman
aldose
ale
aleatory
alee
alef
alegar
alehouse
alembic
aleph
alert
aleurone

aleuronic
alevin
alewife
alewives
alexia
alexin
alfaki
alfalfa
alfaqui
alfaquin
alfileria
alforge
alforja
alfresco
alga
algebra
algebraic
algedonic
algae
algerine
algid
algidity
algoid
algology
algometer
algometry
algor
algorism
algorithm
algous
alguazil
alias
alibi
alibility
alible
alidad
alidade
alien
alienable
alienage
alienate
alienee
alienism
alienist
alif
aliform
alight
align
alike
alikeness
aliment
alimental
alimony
aline
aliped
aliphatic
aliquant

aliquot
alist
alit
alive
alizarin
alizarine
alkahest
alkalemia
alkali
alkalic
alkalies
alkalify
alkalin
alkaline
alkalis
alkalize
alkaloid
alkalosis
alkane
alkanet
alkene
alkyl
alkyne
all
allantoic
allantoid
allantoin
allantois
allay
allege
allegoric
allegory
allegro
alleluia
alleluiah
allergen
allergic
allergin
allergy
alleviate
alley
alliance
alligator
allision
allium
allocable
allocate
allocatur
allodia
allodial
allodium
allogamy
allomorph
allonym
allopath
allopathy
allophane

alloplasm
allosome
allot
allotrope
allotropy
allottee
allow
allowance
alloy
alloyage
allspice
allude
allure
allusion
allusive
alluvia
alluvial
alluvian
alluvion
alluvious
alluvium
alluviums
ally
allyl
allylic
alma
almacen
almacenes
almah
almanac
almandine
almandite
almemar
almighty
almner
almond
almoner
almonry
almost
alms
almsdeed
almshouse
almsman
almswoman
almuce
almud
almude
aloe
aloes
aloetic
aloetical
aloft
aloha
aloin
alone
along
alongside

aloof
aloofly
alopecia
aloud
alow
alp
alpaca
alpenglow
alpha
alphabet
alphosis
alphyl
alpine
alpinist
already
alsike
also
alt
altar
altarage
alter
alterant
altercate
alternate
altho
althorn
although
altigraph
altimeter
altimetry
altiscope
altitude
alto
altrical
altrices
altricial
altruism
altruist
aludel
alula
alulae
alular
alum
alumin
alumina
alumine
aluminize
aluminous
aluminum
alumna
alumnae
alumni
alumnus
alumroot
alumstone
alunite
alveary

alveolar
alveolary
alveolate
alveolus
alvine
always
alyssum
am
amain
amalgam
amanita
amanous
amaracus
amaranth
amaroid
amaryllis
amass
amateur
amative
amatol
amatorial
amatory
amaurosis
amaurotic
amaze
amazon
amazonite
ambage
ambagious
ambary
ambassage
ambassy
amber
ambergris
amberoid
ambery
ambient
ambiguity
ambiguous
ambit
ambition
ambitious
ambivert
amble
amblyopia
amblyopic
amblyopy
ambo
ambones
ambos
ambroid
ambrosia
ambrosial
ambrosian
ambrotype
ambry
ambsace

ambulacra
ambulance
ambulant
ambulate
ambuscade
ambuscado
ambush
ameba
amebae
amebas
amebic
amebean
amebiasis
ameboid
ameer
amelcorn
amen
amenable
amenably
amend
amende
amends
amenity
ament
amentia
amerce
americium
amethyst
ametropia
ametropic
amia
amiable
amianthus
amic
amicable
amice
amicrobic
amid
amide
amidic
amidin
amidogen
amidol
amidships
amidst
amine
amino
amir
amiss
amitosis
amitotic
amity
ammeter
ammine
ammonal
ammonia
ammoniac

14

ammonite amply analgetic ancon anhydrous annulary anthelia
ammonium ampoule analgia ancone ani annulate anthelion
amnesia ampul analog anconal anigh annulet anthelix
amnesic ampule analogic anconeal anight annulose anthem
amnestic ampulla analogist ancoral anights annulus anthemia
amnesty ampullae analogize and anil anodal anthemio
amnia ampullar analogous andante anile anode anther
amnion amputate analogue andesite anilin anodic anthesis
amnionate amreeta analogy andiron aniline anodize anthodia
amnionic amrita analysand andradite anility anodyne anthodiui
amniotic amuck analyses androgen animal anoint anthoid
amniote amulet analysis androgyny animalism anolyte anthology
amock amuse analyst android animalist anomalous anthotaxy
amoeba amusive analytic androidal animality anomalism anthozoai
amoebic amygdule analytics anecdote animalize anomaly anthozoic
amoeboid amyl analyze anecdotal animate anon anthrax
amok amylase anamnesis anecdotic animation anonym antiar
amoke amylene anamnia anele animative anonymous antibody
amole amylic anandria anemia animism anonymity antic
among amylogen anandrous anemic animist anopheles anticked
amongst amyloid ananthous anemology animistic anorak anticking
amoral amyloidal anapest anemone animosity anorexia antichlor
amorality amylopsin anapestic anemosis animus anorectic antidim
amorally amylose anaphase anenst anion anorexy antidotal
amoretto amylum anaphora anent anise anorthite antidote
amorini an anaplasty anergia aniseed anosmia antigen
amorino ana anaptotic anergic anisette anosmic antigene
amorist anabaena anarch anergy anker another antigenic
amorous anabas anarchic aneroid ankerite anoxemia antilogy
amorphism anabases anarchism aneurism ankh ansa antimask
amorphous anabasis anarchist aneurysm ankle ansae antimere
amort anabatic anarchy anew anklet answer antimeric
amortize anabiosis anarthria angaria ankus ant antimonic
amotion anabiotic anastroph angary ankush anta antimony
amount anabolic anatase angel ankylose antacid antimony.
amour anabolism anathema angelhood ankylosis antae antinode
amove anabranch anathemas angelic ankylotic antalgic antinomy
amperage anadem anatomic angelica anlace antalkali antipathy
ampere anaerobe anatomist angelical anlage antarctic antiphon
ampersand anaerobia anatomize angelus anlas ante antiphony
amphibian anaerobic anatomy anger annal antecede antipodal
amphibion anaglyph anatropal angina annalist antechoir antipode
amphibole anagoge anatto angle annat antedate antipole
amphiboly anagogic annatto anglepod annates antefix antipyic
amphigory anagogy ancestor anglesite annatto antefixa antiquary
amphioxus anagram ancestral angleworm anneal antefixae antiquate
amphipod anal ancestry angry annex antefixal antique
amphipode analcime anchor angstrom annexive antelope antiquity
amphiscii analcite anchorage anguine annotate antenatal antiscii
amphiuma analect anchoress anguish announce antenna antiserum
amphora analecta anchorite angular annoy antennula antitoxic
amphorae analects anchoret angulate annoyance antennule antitoxin
amphoral analectic anchovy angustate annual antepast antitrade
amphoric analeptic anchusa anhelous annually anterior antitrust
ample analgen anchusin anidrosis annuitant anteroom antitypy
amplify analgene ancient anhydrate annuity antes antitype
amplitude analgesic ancipital anhydride annul antetype antitypic
           analgesia ancillary anhydrite annular antevert antivenin

antler	aphasic	apolog	appose	arbor	areole	armlet
antonym	aphasy	apologia	apposite	arboreal	areometer	armor
antrorse	aphelia	apologist	appraisal	arboreous	arethusa	armorial
anuran	aphelian	apologize	appraise	arboretum	argala	armory
anuresis	aphelion	apologue	apprehend	arborous	argent	armozeen
anuretic	aphemia	apology	appressed	arbuscle	argental	armozine
anuria	aphemic	apomictic	apprise	arbuscule	argentate	armpit
anuric	apheresis	apomixis	apprize	arbute	argentic	army
anurous	apheretic	apophasis	approach	arbutean	argentine	arnica
anury	aphesis	apophyge	approbate	arbutus	argentite	arnatto
anus	aphetic	apophysis	approve	arc	argentol	arnotto
anvil	aphid	apoplexy	appulse	arcade	argentous	aroid
anviltop	aphides	aport	appulsion	arcanum	argil	aroideous
anxiety	aphis	apostasy	apricot	arcature	argillous	aroma
anxious	aphonia	apostate	apron	arch	argillite	aromatic
any	aphonic	apostil	apronful	archaic	arginine	aromatize
anybody	aphorism	apostille	apronless	archaical	argol	arose
anyhow	aphorist	apostle	apropos	archaism	argon	around
anyone	aphorize	apostolic	apse	archaist	argonaut	arousal
anything	aphotic	apothece	apsidal	archaize	argosies	arouse
anyway	aphrodite	apothecia	apsides	archangel	argosy	arow
anywhere	aphyllose	apothegm	apsis	archducal	argot	arpeggio
anywise	aphyllous	apothem	apt	archduchy	argotic	arquebus
aorist	aphylly	appal	apteryx	archduke	argue	arrack
aoristic	apian	appall	aptitude	archery	argument	arraign
aorta	apiarian	appanage	apyretic	archetype	argus	arrange
aortae	apiarist	apparatus	apyrexia	archfiend	argute	arrant
aortas	apiary	apparel	apyrexial	archicarp	aria	arras
aortal	apical	apparency	apyrexy	archil	arid	arrasene
aortic	apices	apparent	aquaplane	archimage	aridity	array
aoudad	apicial	apparitor	aquaria	archiplasm	ariel	arrayal
apace	apiculate	appeal	aquarium	architect	arietta	arrear
apagoge	apiculus	appear	aquariums	archival	ariette	arrearage
apagogic	apiece	appease	aquatic	archive	aright	arrest
apanage	apiology	appeasive	aquatical	archivist	aril	arret
apart	apish	appelable	aquatint	archivolt	arillate	arris
apartheid	apivorous	appelant	aquatinta	archon	arillode	arrival
apartment	aplanatic	appellate	aqueduct	archway	ariose	arrive
apatetic	aplasia	appellee	aqueous	arciform	arise	arrogate
apathetic	aplastic	appellor	aquiform	arctic	arisen	arrow
apathy	aplomb	append	aquilegia	arcuate	arista	arrowhead
apatite	apnea	appendage	aquiline	arcuation	aristate	arrowroot
ape	apnoeal	appendix	aquose	ardeb	aristol	arrowwood
apeak	apnoeic	appertain	arabic	ardency	ark	arrowy
aperient	apocarp	appetence	arability	ardent	arm	arroyo
aperitive	apocopate	appetency	arable	ardor	armada	arsenal
aperiodic	apocope	appetite	araceous	arduous	armadillo	arsenate
apert	apod	appetize	araneous	are	armament	arseniate
apertural	apodal	applaud	arapaima	area	armature	arsenic
aperture	apodan	applause	araroba	areal	armband	arsenical
apery	apodictic	apple	araucaria	areaway	armchair	arsenide
apetalous	apodosis	appliance	arbalest	areca	armet	arsenite
apex	apogamic	applicant	arbiter	areic	armful	arsenous
apexes	apogamous	applique	arbitress	arena	armhole	arsine
aphanite	apogamy	apply	arbitrage	areology	armiger	arses
aphanitic	apogeal	appoint	arbitral	areola	armigero	arsis
aphasia	apogean	appointee	arbitrary	areolar	armillary	arson
aphasiac	apogee	apportion	arbitrate	areolate	armistice	art

arterial
arteritis
artery
artful
arthritic
arthritis
arthropod
arthroses
arthrosis
artichoke
article
articular
artifact
artifice
artificer
artillery
artisan
artist
artiste
artistic
artistry
artless
arty
arum
arval
arytenoid
as
asarum
asbestos
asbolin
ascarid
ascend
ascendent
ascension
ascensive
ascent
ascertain
ascetic
ascetical
asci
ascidian
ascidioid
ascidium
ascites
ascitic
ascitical
ascocarp
ascorbic
ascospore
ascot
ascribe
ascus
asdic
asepsis
aseptic
asexual
ash

ashamed
ashcake
ashcan
ashen
ashery
ashine
ashlar
ashler
ashlaring
ashman
ashore
ashtray
ashy
asialia
aside
asinine
asininity
ask
askance
askew
aslant
asleep
aslope
asocial
asp
asparagus
aspect
aspen
asper
asperate
aspergill
asperity
aspermous
asperse
aspersion
aspersive
asphalt
asphaltic
asphodel
asphyxia
asphyxial
asphyxy
aspic
aspirant
aspirate
aspire
aspirin
aspis
asquint
ass
assagai
assail
assailant
assassin
assault
assay
assemble

assembly
assent
assert
assertion
assertive
assertory
assess
asset
assiduity
assiduous
assign
assignee
assist
assistant
assize
associate
associes
assoil
assonance
assonant
assort
assuage
assuasive
assume
assumpsit
assurance
assure
assurgent
astasia
astatic
aster
asterial
asterisk
asterism
astern
asternal
asteroid
asthenia
asthenic
asthma
asthmatic
astir
astonish
astound
astraddle
astragal
astrakhan
astral
astrand
astray
astrict
astride
astringe
astrology
astronomy
astrut
astucious

astute
astutious
astylar
asunder
aswim
aswoon
asylum
asymmetry
asymptote
asyndetic
asyndeton
at
atalaya
ataman
atamasco
ataunt
atavic
atavism
atavist
atavistic
ataxia
ataxic
ataxy
ate
atelic
atelier
ateliosis
athanasia
athart
atheism
atheist
atheistic
atheling
atheneum
athetosis
athirst
athlete
athletic
athletics
athort
athwart
atilt
atlantean
atlantes
atlas
atmology
atmometer
atmometry
atoll
atom
atomic
atomical
atomicity
atomism
atomist
atomistic
atomize

atomy
atonal
atonality
atone
atonic
atonity
atony
atop
atria
atrichous
atrip
atrium
atrocious
atrocity
atrophic
atrophous
atrophy
atropine
atropism
attach
attache
attack
attain
attainder
attaint
attar
attemper
attempt
attend
attendant
attent
attention
attentive
attenuant
attenuate
attest
attic
attire
attitude
attorney
attract
attrahens
attrahent
attribute
attrite
attrited
attrition
attune
atwain
atwirl
atypic
atypical
auburn
auction
audacious
audacity
audible

audibly
audience
audient
audile
audio
audiogram
audiophone
audit
audition
auditive
auditory
augen
augend
auger
aught
augite
augitic
augment
augur
augural
augurial
augury
august
auk
auklet
aunt
auntie
aunty
aura
aural
aurate
aureate
aurei
aureola
aureole
aureolin
aureous
aureus
auric
auricle
auricula
auriculae
auricular
auriform
auriscope
auriscopy
aurist
aurochs
aurora
auroral
aurorean
auroric
aurous
aurum
auscultate
auspex
auspicate

auspice
auspices
auspicial
austenite
austere
austerity
austral
autacoid
autarchic
autarchy
autarky
authentic
author
authoress
authorian
authority
authorize
autism
autistic
autoboat
autobus
autoclave
autocracy
autocrat
autocycle
autodyne
autogamy
autogenic
autogeny
autogiro
autograph
autoharp
automat
automata
automatic
automaton
autonomic
autonomy
autopsy
autoptic
autosomal
autosome
autotomy
autotoxin
autotoxic
autotoxis
autotruck
autotype
autotypic
autotypy
autumn
autumnal
autunite
auxiliary
auximone
avail
avalanche

17

avant	awesome	azymous	backwater	baldhead	bandy	bard
avarice	awful	**B**	backwoods	baldpate	bane	bare
avast	awhile		bacon	baldric	baneberry	bareback
avatar	awhirl	babassu	bacteria	baldrice	baneful	barefoot
avaunt	awing	babbitt	bacterial	bale	bang	barege
avenge	awkward	babble	bacterin	baleen	bangle	baresark
avens	awl	babe	bacterine	balefire	bani	bargain
avenue	awless	babirusa	bacterium	baleful	banian	barge
aver	awlwort	baboo	bacterize	balisaur	banish	bargeman
average	awn	baboon	bacteroid	balk	banister	barghest
averse	awned	baboonery	baculine	balkanize	banjo	baric
aversion	awnless	baboonish	bad	balky	banjos	barilla
avert	awning	babu	bade	ball	banjoist	barite
avian	**awny**	babuism	badge	ballad	banjorine	baritone
aviarist	awoke	babushka	badger	ballade	bank	barium
aviary	awry	baby	badinage	ballast	bankbook	bark
aviate	ax	babyhood	badman	ballerina	banknote	barkeep
aviation	axe	babyish	badminton	ballet	bankpaper	barkless
aviator	axial	baccate	**baffle**	balistic	bankrupt	barky
aviatress	axil	**bacchanal**	baffy	balistics	banksia	barley
aviatrice	axile	**bacchant**	bag	**balloon**	banner	barm
aviatrix	axilla	bacchante	bagass	ballot	banneret	barmaid
avicular	axillae	bacchic	bagasse	balm	bannock	barmy
avid	axillar	bacchical	bagatelle	balmacaan	banquet	barn
avidity	axillary	bacciform	baggage	balmoral	banquette	barnacle
avifauna	axiom	bachelor	**baggy**	balmy	banshee	barnstorm
avifaunal	axiomatic	bacillar	bagman	balneal	bant	barnyard
avigation	axis	bacillary	bagnio	balsa	bantam	barogram
aviso	axle	bacillus	bagpipe	balsam	banter	barograph
avocado	axletree	back	baguet	balsamic	bantling	barometer
avocados	axeman	backbite	baguette	baluster	banyan	barometry
avocation	axman	backboard	baguio	bambini	baobab	baron
avocatory	axolotl	backbone	bagworm	bambino	baptism	baronage
avocet	axon	backcross	bah	bamboo	baptismal	baroness
avocette	axone	backdrop	bail	ban	baptistery	baronet
avoid	axseed	backfall	bailey	banal	baptistry	baronetcy
avoidance	ay	backfire	bailiff	banality	baptize	baronial
avoset	aye	backhand	bailiwick	banana	bar	barony
avouch	ayahuasca	backhouse	bailsman	band	barathea	baroque
avow	ayin	backlash	bait	bandage	barb	baroscope
avowal	azalea	backlog	baize	bandana	barbarian	barouche
avowry	azedarach	backmost	bakehouse	bandanna	barbaric	barque
avulsion	azimuth	backrope	bakery	bandbox	barbarism	barrack
avuncular	azimuthal	backset	bakeshop	bandeau	barbarity	barracoon
await	azo	backside	baksheesh	bandeaux	barbarous	barracuda
awake	azoic	backsight	baku	banderol	barbate	barrage
awaken	azonic	backslide	bakuin	banderole	barbecue	barranca
award	azote	backstage	balalaika	bandicoot	barbel	barranco
aware	azoth	backstay	balance	bandit	barberry	barratry
awash	azotic	backstop	balas	banditry	barbet	barrel
away	azotize	backstrap	balata	bandog	barbette	barren
awe	azure	backswept	balboa	bandoleer	barbican	barret
aweing	azurite	backsword	balcony	bandolier	barbicel	barretor
aweary	azygous	backwall	bald	bandoline	barbital	barretry
aweather	azym	backward	baldachin	bandore	barbitone	barrette
aweigh	azyme	backwards	baldaquin	bandstand	barbule	barricade
aweless	azymic	backwash	baldface	bandwagon	barcarole	barrier

barrister	bastinade	beacon	bedaub	beeves	believe	benzol
barroom	bastinado	bead	bedazzle	beewolf	belittle	benzoline
barrow	bastion	beadhouse	bedbug	befall	bell	benzoyl
bartender	bat	beadle	bedeck	befell	bellbird	benzyl
barter	batch	beadledom	bedevil	befit	bellboy	bequeath
bartizan	bate	beadroll	bedew	befog	belle	bequest
barye	bateau	beadwork	bedfellow	befool	belleek	berate
baryta	bateaux	beady	bedight	before	bellhop	berberin
barytes	batfish	beagle	bedim	befriend	bellicose	berberine
barytone	batfowl	beak	bedizen	befoul	bellman	bereave
basal	bath	beam	bedlam	befuddle	bellow	bereft
basalt	bathe	beamish	bedlamite	beg	bellwort	beret
basaltic	bathetic	beamy	bedmaker	began	belly	berg
bascule	bathhouse	bean	bedmate	beget	bellyache	bergamot
base	batholite	beancaper	bedpost	begat	bellyband	beriberi
baseball	batholith	beano	bedquilt	beggar	belong	beriberic
baseboard	bathos	bear	bedspring	beggardom	belove	berime
baseburner	bathrobe	bearberry	bedstand	beggary	below	berlin
baseless	bathroom	bearcat	bedtime	begin	belt	berline
baselevel	bathtub	beard	bedwarmer	begird	beluga	berm
baseman	batik	beargrass	bedplate	begohm	belvedere	berme
basement	batiste	bearish	bedraggle	begone	bema	bernicle
basenji	baton	bearskin	bedrid	begonia	bemata	berry
bash	batrachian	bearwood	bedrock	begot	bemean	berseem
bashaw	batsman	beast	bedroll	begotten	bemire	berserk
bashful	batt	beat	bedroom	begrudge	bemoan	berth
basic	battalion	beaten	bedside	beguile	bemuse	bertha
basicity	batten	beatific	bedsore	begum	bench	berthage
basidial	battery	beatify	bedspread	begun	benchmark	beryl
basidium	battle	beatitude	bedstaff	behalf	benchroot	berylline
basify	batty	beau	bedstaves	behave	bend	beryllium
basil	bauble	beaus	bedstead	behavior	beneath	beseech
basilar	baudekin	beauish	bedstraw	behead	benedict	beseem
basilary	baulk	beauteous	bedward	beheld	benefic	beset
basilica	bauson	beautiful	bedwards	behemoth	benefice	beshow
basilican	bauxite	beautify	bee	behest	benefit	beside
basilisk	bawd	beauty	beebread	behind	bengaline	besides
basin	bawdry	beaux	beech	behold	benight	besiege
basinet	bawdy	beaver	beechen	beholden	benign	besmear
basion	bawl	bebeerine	beechdrops	behoof	benignant	besmirch
basis	bay	bebeeru	beechmast	behoove	benignity	besom
bask	bayadere	becalm	beechnut	behove	benison	besot
basket	bayard	became	beef	beige	benne	besought
basketry	bayberry	because	beefing	being	bennet	bespangle
basophile	bayman	beccafico	beefsteak	bel	bent	bespatter
basque	bayonet	bechamel	beefy	belabor	benthic	bespeak
bass	bayou	bechance	beehive	belated	benthonic	bespoke
basset	baytree	beck	beeline	belay	benthos	bespread
bassinet	baywood	becket	been	belch	benumb	best
basso	bazaar	beckon	beer	beldam	benzene	bestead
bassoon	bazar	becloud	beery	beldame	benzidin	bestial
basswood	bazooka	become	beestings	beleaguer	benzidine	bestially
bast	bdellium	bed	beeswax	belemnite	benzin	bestiary
bastard	be	bedchair	beeswing	belfry	benzine	bestir
bastardy	beach	bedcover	beet	belga	benzoate	bestow
baste	beachhead	bedframe	beetle	belie	benzoic	bestowal
bastille	beachy	bedgown	beetree	belief	benzoin	bestrew

bestride	biconcave	bile	biolysis	bisexual	blade	blindworm
bestrode	biconvex	bilection	biolytic	bishop	bladebone	blink
bet	bicorn	bilestone	biometry	bishopric	blain	bliss
beta	bicorne	bilge	bionomic	bismuth	blame	blister
betaine	bicornous	bilgekeel	bionomics	bismuthal	blameful	blistery
betake	bicron	bilgy	bionomist	bismuthic	blameless	blithe
betatron	bicuspid	biliary	bioplasm	bison	blanch	blithely
betel	bicuspis	bilinear	biopsic	bisque	bland	blizzard
betelnut	bicycle	bilingual	biopsy	bister	blandish	bloat
bethel	bicyclic	bilious	bioscope	bistort	blank	blob
bethink	bicyclical	biliteral	bioscopic	bistoury	blankbook	block
bethought	bicyclist	bilk	bioscopy	bisulcate	blanket	blockade
betide	bid	billhook	biosphere	bisulfate	blare	blockhead
betimes	bidden	billboard	biota	bisulfide	blarney	blockish
betoken	bidactyl	billet	biotic	bisulfite	blase	blocklike
betony	bidarka	billfish	biotical	bit	blaspheme	blockline
betook	bidarkee	billfold	biotin	bitch	blasphemy	blocky
betray	biddy	billhead	biotite	bite	blast	blond
betroth	bide	billiards	biotitic	bitstock	blastema	blonde
betrothal	bidentate	billion	biotope	bitt	blasthole	blood
between	biennial	billionth	biotype	bitten	blastula	bloodless
bevel	bier	billon	biotypic	bittern	blastulae	bloodline
beverage	bifacial	billow	biparous	bitumen	blastular	bloodroot
bevy	bifarious	billowy	bipartite	bivalence	blatancy	bloodshed
bewail	bifid	billy	biped	bivalency	blatant	bloodtest
beware	bifidate	bilorate	bipedal	bivalent	blather	bloodwood
bewilder	bifidity	bilocular	biphenyl	bivalve	blaze	bloodworm
bewitch	bifilar	bimanous	bipinnate	bivalvous	blazon	bloodwort
bey	biflex	bimanual	biplane	bivalvular	blazonry	bloody
beylict	bifocal	bimensal	bipod	bivouac	bleach	bloom
beylik	bifold	bimonthly	bipolar	biweekly	bleachery	bloomery
beyond	bifoliate	bimotored	biradial	biyearly	bleak	bloomy
bezant	biform	bin	birch	bizarre	bleakish	bloop
bezel	bifurcate	binary	birchen	blab	blear	blossom
bezique	bifurcous	binate	bird	black	bleary	blossomy
bezoar	big	bination	birdcall	blackball	bleat	blot
biangular	bigamic	binaural	birdgrass	blackbird	bleb	blotch
biannual	bigamous	bind	birdhouse	blackboy	blebby	blotchy
bias	bigamy	bindery	birdie	blackcap	bled	blouse
biases	bigaroon	bindweed	birdlime	blackcock	bleed	blow
biasses	bigarreau	bine	birdseye	blackdamp	blemish	blowfish
biaxal	biggin	bing	birdsfoot	blacken	blench	blowfly
biaxial	bighorn	bingo	birdsnest	blackface	blend	blowgun
bib	bight	binnacle	bireme	blackfish	blende	blowhole
bibb	bignonia	binocle	biretta	blackgum	blendous	blown
bibcock	bigot	binocular	birth	blackhaw	blendy	blowpipe
bibelot	bigotry	binomial	birthday	blackhead	blennioid	blowsy
biblical	bijou	binominal	birthmark	blackish	blenny	blowtorch
biblicist	bijoux	binuclear	birthroot	blackjack	bless	blowtube
bibulous	bijugate	bioassay	birthwort	blackleg	blet	blowy
bicameral	bijugous	biogen	bis	blacklist	blew	blowzed
bice	bilabial	biogeny	biscuit	blackmail	blight	blowzy
biceps	bilabiate	biography	bisect	blackpoll	blind	blubber
biche	bilander	biologic	bisection	blackwill	blindage	blubbery
bicipital	bilateral	biologism	bisector	blackwood	blindfish	blucher
bicker	bilbo	biologist	bisectrix	bladder	blindfold	bludgeon
bicolor	bilboes	biology	biserrate	bladdery	blindpig	blue

bluish
blueball
bluebell
blueberry
bluebird
bluebook
bluecap
bluecoat
bluecurls
bluefish
bluegill
bluegum
bluejack
bluenose
blueprint
bluestone
bluet
blueweed
bluewood
bluff
blunder
blunge
blunt
blur
blurry
blurb
blurt
blush
blushful
bluster
blustery
blustrous
boa
boar
board
boardwalk
boarfish
boarhound
boarish
boast
boastful
boat
boatage
boatbill
boatman
boatswain
bob
bobbin
bobbinet
bobcat
bobolink
bobsled
bobstay
bobtail
bobtailed
bobwhite
bock

boddle
bode
bodement
bodice
bodied
bodiless
bodkin
bodyguard
bog
boggish
bogbean
bogey
boggle
boggy
bogie
bogle
bogus
bogwood
bogy
bohea
boil
boiler
bolar
bolary
bold
boldface
bole
bolero
boletus
bolide
bolivar
bolivars
bolivia
boll
bollard
bollworm
bolo
bolograph
bolometer
bolshevik
bolster
bolt
boltel
bolthead
boltonia
boltrope
bolus
bomb
bombard
bombardon
bombast
bombastic
bombazine
bombe
bombproof
bombshell
bombsight

bombycid
bombic
bombyx
bonaci
bonanza
bonasus
bond
bondage
bondmaid
bondman
bondwoman
bondsman
bondstone
bondslave
bonducnut
bone
bonedust
bonehead
bonemeal
boneset
boneyard
bonfire
bongo
bonhommie
bonito
bonnet
bonny
bonus
bony
bonze
boo
booby
boodling
book
bookish
bookland
bookmaker
bookman
bookplate
bookworm
boom
boomerang
boon
boor
boorish
boost
boot
bootblack
bootee
booth
bootjack
bootleg
bootless
bootlick
booty
booze
boracic

boracite
borage
borate
borax
border
bordure
bore
boreal
boredom
boric
boride
born
borne
borneol
bornite
boron
borough
borrow
bort
borty
bortz
borzoi
boscage
boskage
boschbok
boshbok
boschvark
boshvark
bosh
bosk
bosky
bosket
bosquet
bosom
boss
bossy
bossism
boston
bosun
bot
bota
botanic
botanical
botanist
botanize
botany
botch
botchery
botchy
botfly
both
bother
botone
botonee
botony
botryoid
botryose

bots
bott
bottle
bottom
bottomry
botulism
boucle
boudoir
bouffe
bough
bought
bougie
bouillon
boulder
boule
boulevard
bounce
bound
boundary
bounden
boundless
bounty
bouquet
bourdon
bourg
bourgeois
bourgeon
bourn
bourne
bourrelet
bourse
bouse
bout
bovine
bow
bowel
bower
bowerbird
bowfin
bowhead
bowknot
bowl
bowlder
bowline
bowman
bowpin
bowshot
bowsprit
bowstring
bowtie
bowyer
box
boxberry
boxcar
boxen
boxhaul
boxthorn

boxwood
boy
boyar
boyard
boycott
boyhood
boyish
brabble
braccate
brace
bracelet
brachial
brachiate
brachia
brachium
bracken
bracket
brackish
bract
bracteal
bracteate
bracteole
bractlet
brad
brag
braggart
bragget
braid
brail
braille
brain
brainfag
brainless
brainpan
brainstem
brainy
braise
braize
brake
brakeage
brakeman
brakesman
braky
bramble
brambly
bran
branch
branchia
branchiae
branchial
brand
brandish
brandy
branle
branny
brant
brantail

brash
brashy
brass
brassard
brassie
brassiere
brassy
brat
brattice
brattle
bravado
bravadoes
bravados
brave
bravery
bravo
bravura
brawl
brawn
brawny
braxy
bray
brayera
braza
braze
brazen
brazier
brazil
breach
breachy
bread
breadline
breadnut
breadriot
breadroot
breadth
break
breakage
breakbone
breakfast
breakneck
bream
breast
breastpin
breath
breathe
breathy
breccia
bred
breech
breeches
breeching
breed
breeze
breezy
bregma
bregmata

bregmate	briquette	brooklet	bucket	bulla	bur	bushgoat
brehon	brisance	brookweed	bucketful	bullate	burble	bushel
brethren	brisk	broom	buckeye	bullbat	burbot	bushrider
breve	brisket	broomy	buckhorn	bulldog	burden	bushwhack
brevet	brisling	broomcorn	buckhound	bulldozer	burdock	bushy
brevetcy	bristle	broomrape	buckle	bullet	bureau	busk
breviary	brit	broth	bucko	bulletin	bureaus	buskin
brevier	britannia	brothel	buckram	bullfight	bureaux	buskit
brevity	brittle	brother	bucksaw	bullfinch	buret	busman
brew	britska	brougham	buckshee	bullfrog	burette	bust
brewage	britzka	brought	buckshot	bullhead	burg	bustard
brewery	britzska	brow	buckskin	bullion	burgage	bustic
brewis	broach	browband	buckthorn	bullish	burgee	bustle
briar	broad	browbeat	bucktooth	bullneck	burgeon	busy
briard	broadbean	brown	buckwheat	bullock	burgess	busybody
briarwood	broadbill	brownish	bucolic	bullpen	burgher	but
briary	broadbrim	brownie	bud	bullpout	burglar	butadiene
bribe	broadcast	browntail	buddle	bullring	burglary	butane
bribery	broaden	browse	buddleia	bullweed	burgoo	butanol
brick	broadish	brucine	budge	bully	burgrave	butanone
brickbat	broadleaf	bruise	budget	bullyboy	burial	butcher
brickkiln	broadside	bruit	budgetary	bullyrag	burin	butchery
brickwork	broadtail	brumal	buff	bullytree	burke	bute
brickyard	brocade	brume	buffalo	bulrush	burl	butler
bricole	brocatel	brumous	buffet	bulwark	burlap	butlery
bridal	broccoli	brunet	buffoon	bum	burlesque	butment
bride	broch	brunette	buffy	bumble	burley	butt
bridesman	brochure	brunt	bug	bumblebee	burly	butte
bridewell	brocket	brush	bugbane	bumboat	burn	butterbur
bridge	brogan	brushwood	bugbear	bumkin	burnet	buttercup
bridle	brogue	brushy	bugeye	bump	burnish	butterfat
bridoon	broil	brusk	buggy	bumpkin	burnoose	butterfly
brief	brokage	brusque	bugle	bumptious	burnt	butterine
briefcase	broke	brut	bugleweed	bumpy	burr	butternut
briefless	broken	brutal	buglight	bun	burrdrill	buttery
brier	broker	brutality	bugloss	bunch	burro	buttock
briery	brokerage	brutalize	bugseed	buncombe	burrow	button
brierwood	broma	brute	buhach	bund	burrstone	buttony
brig	bromal	brutify	buhl	bundle	burry	buttress
brigade	bromate	brutish	build	bung	bursa	buttweld
brigadier	brome	bryology	built	bungalow	bursal	butyl
brigand	bromic	bryonin	bulb	bungee	bursar	butylene
bright	bromide	bryony	bulbar	bungle	bursarial	butyrate
brighten	bromine	bryophyte	bulbiform	bunion	bursary	butyric
brill	bromism	bubal	bulbil	bunk	burse	butyrin
brilliant	bromize	bubaline	bulbel	bunkhouse	burseed	buxom
brim	bronchi	bubble	bulbous	bunkie	bursiform	buy
brimful	bronchia	bubo	bulbul	bunkmate	bursitis	buzz
brimstone	bronchial	bubonic	bulge	bunky	burst	buzzard
brindle	bronchus	buccal	bulgy	bunt	burthen	buzzwig
brine	bronco	buccaneer	bulimia	buntline	burton	by
brinish	bronze	buck	bulimic	buoy	burweed	bye
bring	bronzy	buckaroo	bulk	buoyage	bury	bygone
brink	brooch	buckbean	bulkage	buoyance	busby	bylaw
briny	brood	buckberry	bulkhead	buoyancy	bush	bypast
briolette	broody	buckboard	bulky	buoyant	bushboy	byre
briquet	brook	buckwagon	bull	buprestid	bushbuck	byroad

22

byssus
bystander
bywater
byway
byword
bywork
byzant

C

cab
caba
cabal
cabala
cabalism
cabalist
caballine
cabana
cabane
cabaret
cabas
cabbage
cabin
cabinet
cable
cablegram
cablet
cabman
caboched
caboose
caboshed
cabotage
cabriole
cabriolet
cacao
cachalot
cache
cachectic
cachepot
cachet
cachexia
cachexy
cacholong
cachou
cacique
cackle
cacodemon
cacodyl
cacodylic
cacoethes
cacology
cacophony
cacti
cactus
cactuses
cacumen
cacuminal
cad

caddish
cadaster
cadastral
cadaver
cadaveric
caddie
caddis
caddy
cade
cadelle
cadence
cadency
cadent
cadenza
cadet
cadetship
cadetcy
cadette
cadge
cadgy
cadmium
cadre
caducean
caducei
caduceus
caducity
caducous
caesarian
caesarist
caesural
cafe
caffeic
caffeine
cafeteria
caftan
cage
cagy
caique
cairn
cairned
cairngorm
caisson
caitiff
cajaput
cajeput
cajole
cajolery
cajun
cake
cakewalk
cala
calabar
calabash
caladium
calamanco
calamary
calami

calamine
calamint
calamite
calamity
calamus
calash
calathi
calathus
calcanea
calcaneum
calcaneus
calcar
calcarate
calcaria
calceate
calces
calcic
calcific
calciform
calcify
calcimine
calcine
calcinize
calcite
calcitic
calcium
calcspar
calctufa
calctuff
calculate
calculous
calculus
caldera
caldron
calendal
calendar
calender
calends
calendula
calenture
calescent
calf
caliber
calibrate
calices
calicle
calico
calicoes
calicos
caliginous
caligraphy
calipash
calipee
caliper
caliph
calisaya
calix

calk
calla
callboard
callboy
calliope
callitype
callose
callosity
callous
callow
calli
callus
calluses
calm
calmative
calomel
caloric
calorie
calorific
calory
calotte
caloyer
caltrap
caltrop
calumet
calumny
calvaria
calvarium
calvary
calve
calvities
calx
calxes
calyces
calycinal
calycine
calycle
calypso
calypter
calyptra
calyx
cam
camail
camas
camber
cambist
cambium
cambric
came
camel
cameleer
camelish
camellia
cameo
camera
camerae
cameral

cameraman
cameras
camion
camise
camisole
camlet
camomile
camp
campaign
campanero
campanile
campanula
campfire
camphene
camphire
camphogen
camphol
camphor
camphoric
campion
camshaft
camwood
can
canaille
canal
canalage
canalize
canape
canard
canary
canaster
cancan
cancel
cencelli
cancer
cancerate
cancerous
cancroid
candent
candid
candidacy
candidate
candle
candlenut
candlepin
candor
candy
candytuft
cane
canebrake
canella
canephora
canescent
cangue
canicular
canikin
canine

canions
canister
canities
canjar
canjiar
canker
cankery
canna
cannabin
cannel
cannelure
cannery
cannibal
cannikin
cannon
cannonade
cannoneer
cannonry
cannot
cannula
cannular
cannulate
canny
canoe
canon
canonic
canonical
canonist
canonize
canonries
canonry
canonship
canopy
canorous
cant
cantabile
cantaloup
cantar
cantata
cantdog
canteen
canter
cantharis
canthus
canticle
cantle
canto
canton
cantonal
cantor
cantus
canvas
canvass
cany
canyon
canzone
canzonet

canzoni
cap
capable
capably
capacious
capacity
caparison
cape
capelin
capeline
caper
capeskin
capias
capiases
capillary
capita
capital
capitally
capitate
capitol
capitula
capitular
capitulum
capon
caponiere
caporal
capot
capote
capric
capriccio
caprice
capriform
capriole
caproic
capsaicin
capsicum
capsize
capstan
capstone
capsular
capsulate
capsule
captain
captaincy
caption
captious
captivate
captive
captivity
captor
capture
capuche
capuchin
caput
car
carabid
caracal

caracara	cardsharp	carp	casein	catalyst	catty	cavity
carack	care	carpal	casemate	catalytic	catwalk	cavort
caracole	careen	carpale	casement	catalyze	caucus	cavy
carafe	careenage	carpalia	caseose	catamaran	cauda	caw
caramel	career	carpel	caseous	catamenia	caudad	cay
carangoid	careerist	carpellum	casern	catamount	caudae	cayman
carapace	carefree	carpenter	caseworm	cataplasm	caudal	cease
carapacic	careful	carpentry	cash	cataplexy	caudate	ceaseless
carapax	careless	carpet	cashaw	catapult	caudated	ceca
carat	caress	carpetbag	cashbook	cataract	caudex	cecal
carate	caret	carpology	cashew	catarrh	caudexes	cecum
caravan	caretaker	carpi	cashier	catarrhal	caudices	cedar
caravel	cargador	carpus	cashmere	catbird	caudle	cedarbird
caraway	cargo	carrack	cashoo	catblock	caught	cedarn
carbamic	caribe	carrageen	casino	catboat	caul	cede
carbazole	caribou	carrell	cask	catbrier	cauldron	cedilla
carbide	caried	carreta	casket	catcall	caules	cedula
carbine	caries	carriage	casque	catch	caulicle	ceiba
carbineer	carillon	carriole	cassareep	catchfly	cauliform	ceil
carbinol	carina	carrion	cassation	catchment	cauline	ceiling
carbolate	carinal	carrom	cassava	catchpole	caulis	celadon
carbolic	carinate	carronade	casse	catchword	caulk	celandine
carbolize	cariole	carrot	casserole	catchy	caulome	celebrant
carbon	carious	earroty	cassia	catechism	caulomic	celebrate
carbonado	cariosity	carry	cassimere	catechist	causal	celebrity
carbonate	carline	cart	cassock	catechize	causalgia	celerity
carbonic	carload	cartage	cassowary	catechu	causality	celery
carbonis	carman	carte	cast	catechuic	causation	celesta
carbonize	carmelite	cartel	castanet	category	causative	celestial
carbonyl	carmine	cartilage	caste	catenary	cause	celestine
carbora	carminic	cartogram	castellan	catenate	causerie	celestite
carboxyl	carnage	carton	castelry	cater	causeway	celiac
carboy	carnal	cartoon	castigate	caterwaul	caustic	celibacy
carbuncle	carnalist	cartouche	castle	catfall	caustical	celibate
carburet	carnalite	cartridge	castlery	catfish	cauterant	cell
carburize	carnation	cartulary	castor	catgut	cauterism	cella
carcajou	carnelian	cartwheel	castoreum	catharsis	cauterize	cellar
carcanet	carnify	caruca	castrate	cathartic	cautery	cellarage
carcass	carnival	carucage	casual	cathead	caution	cellaret
carcel	carnivora	carucate	casualism	cathedra	cautious	cellist
carcinoma	carnivore	caruncle	casualist	cathedral	caval	cello
carcinus	carnosity	carvacrol	casualty	catheter	cavalcade	celloidin
card	carnotite	carve	casuist	cathexis	cavalier	cellular
cardamom	carob	carvel	casuistic	cathode	cavalla	cellule
cardamon	caroche	carven	casuistry	cathodic	cavally	cellulose
cardamum	carol	caryatid	cat	catholic	cavalry	cellulous
cardboard	caroli	caryopses	catabasis	cation	cavan	celt
cardcase	carolus	caryopsis	catabatic	catkin	cavatina	celtium
cardia	caroluses	cascabel	catabolic	catlike	cave	cement
cardiac	carom	cascade	cataclysm	catling	caveat	cementite
cardiacal	carotene	cascaron	catacomb	catmint	cavern	cementum
cardialgy	carotid	case	catalase	catnap	cavernous	cemetery
cardigan	carotidal	casease	catalepsy	catnip	cavesson	cenobia
cardinal	carotte	caseate	catalo	catoptric	cavetto	cenobite
cardioid	carousal	caseation	catalog	cattalo	caviar	cenobitic
carditis	carouse	casefy	catalpa	cattle	cavicorn	cenobium
cardoon	carousel	caseic	catalysis	cattleman	cavil	cenoby

cenotaph	cere	chairman	chape	chauffer	chevron	chink
cense	cereal	chaise	chapeau	chaunt	chew	chinkapin
censer	cerebella	chalaza	chapeaux	chausses	chewink	chinky
censor	cerebra	chalazae	chapel	chazan	chi	chinook
censorial	cerebral	chalcid	chaperon	cheap	chiasm	chintz
censual	cerebrate	chalder	chaperone	cheapen	chiasma	chintzy
censure	cerebric	chaldron	chaplain	cheat	chiasmal	chip
census	cerebrin	chalet	chaplet	chebec	chiasmic	chipmunk
cent	cerebrum	chalice	chapman	check	chiasmus	chipper
cental	cerecloth	chaliced	chapter	checkmate	chibouk	chippy
centare	cered	chalk	char	checkrein	chic	chirm
centaur	cerement	chalkitis	charabanc	checkroom	chicane	chiromant
centaury	ceremony	chalky	character	checkrow	chicanery	chiropody
centavo	cereus	challenge	charade	cheddite	chick	chiropter
centenary	ceria	challie	charbon	cheek	chickadee	chirp
center	cerise	challis	charcoal	cheeky	chickaree	chirr
centerbit	cerite	chalumeau	chard	cheep	chicken	chirre
centesimi	cerium	chalybite	charge	cheeper	chickpea	chirrup
centesimo	cernuous	chamber	charily	cheer	chickweed	chirrupy
centigram	cero	chambray	chariot	cheerful	chicle	chisel
centile	cerograph	chameleon	charity	cheerless	chico	chit
centime	ceros	chamfer	charivari	cheery	chicory	chitin
centiped	cerotic	chamfrain	chark	cheese	chid	chitinous
centipede	cerotype	chamois	charka	cheesy	chidden	chiton
centner	cerous	champ	charkha	cheetah	chide	chivalric
cento	certain	champac	charlatan	chef	chief	chivalry
centra	certainty	champacol	charlock	chela	chieftain	chivaree
centrad	certify	champagne	charlotte	chelae	chiffon	chive
central	certitude	champaign	charm	chelate	chigger	chlamydes
centric	cerulean	champak	charnel	cheliform	chignon	chlamys
centrical	cerumen	champerty	charpal	chemical	chigoe	chloral
centriole	ceruse	champion	charpoy	chemise	chilblain	chlorate
centroid	cerusite	chanar	charqued	chemism	child	chloric
centrum	cervical	chance	charry	chemist	childbed	chloride
centumvir	cervices	chanceful	chart	chemistry	childhood	chlorine
centuple	cervine	chancel	charta	chemurgic	childing	chlorite
centurial	cervix	chancelor	chartless	chemurgy	childish	chlorosis
centurion	cesious	chancelry	chary	chenille	childless	chlorotic
century	cesium	chancery	chase	chenopod	childlike	chlorous
ceorl	cespitose	chancre	chasm	cherish	children	chock
ceorlish	cessation	chancroid	chasmal	cheroot	chile	chocolate
cephalad	cession	chancrous	chasse	cherry	chili	choice
cephalic	cesspit	chandelle	chassepot	chert	chiliad	choir
cephalin	cesspool	chandler	chasseur	cherub	chiliarch	choiral
cephalous	cesta	chandlery	chassis	cherubic	chiliasm	choke
ceraceous	cestode	change	chaste	cherubim	chiliast	chokebore
ceramic	cestoid	changeful	chasten	cherubs	chill	chokedamp
ceramics	cestus	channel	chastise	chervil	chime	choky
ceramist	cetane	chanson	chastity	chess	chimer	cholagog
cerastes	chacma	chant	chasuble	chest	chimera	cholecyst
cerate	chafe	chantage	chat	chestnut	chimere	cholemia
ceratodus	chaff	chantey	chateau	cheval	chimeric	choler
ceratoid	chaffinch	chantry	chateaux	chevalet	chimney	cholera
cercaria	chaffy	chaos	chatelain	chevalier	chin	choleric
cercarial	chagrin	chaotic	chatoyant	chevals	china	choline
cercarian	chain	chaotical	chattel	chevaux	chinaware	chondrify
cerci	chainman	chaparral	chatter	cheviot	chinch	chondroid
cercus	chair	chapbook	chatty	chevon	chine	chondroma

choose	chub	cinchona	citreous	class	cliency	clothe
chop	chubasco	cinchonic	citric	classic	client	clothier
chophouse	chubby	cincture	citrin	classical	clientage	cloture
chopine	chuck	cinder	citrine	classify	cliental	cloud
choplogic	chuckhole	cindery	citron	classis	clientele	cloudland
choppy	chuckle	cinema	citrous	classmate	cliff	cloudless
choragi	chuffie	cinematic	citrus	classroom	climatal	cloudlet
choragic	chuffy	cineraria	cittern	clastic	climate	cloudy
choragus	chug	cinerator	city	clatter	climatic	clough
choral	chukker	cinereous	cityfied	clausal	climax	clout
chord	chum	cingula	cityward	clause	climactic	clove
chordal	chummy	cingulate	civet	claustral	climb	cloven
chore	chump	cingulum	civic	clausura	clime	clover
chorea	chunk	cinnabar	civicism	clavate	clinch	clovetree
choreal	chunky	cinnamic	civics	clavated	cline	clown
choria	church	cinnamon	civil	clavecin	cling	clownery
choriamb	churchman	cinnamyl	civilian	clavicle	clinic	clownish
choric	churl	cinque	civility	clavicorn	clinical	clownism
chorion	churlish	cion	civilize	clavier	clinician	cloy
chorist	churn	cipher	civism	claviform	clinique	club
chorister	churr	cipolin	clabber	claw	clink	clubfoot
choristic	chute	circinate	clack	clay	clinquant	clubgrass
choroid	chutney	circle	clad	claybank	clintonia	clubhand
chorology	chyle	circlet	cladode	clayey	clip	clubhaul
chortle	chylous	circuit	clag	claymore	clique	clubmoss
chorus	chyme	circuity	claim	claytonia	cliquey	cluck
chose	chymify	circular	claimant	clean	cliquish	clue
chosen	chymosin	circulate	clam	cleanse	cliquy	clump
chough	chymous	circus	clamant	clear	clistase	clumpish
chow	cibol	cirque	clambake	clearance	clitoris	clumpy
chowder	ciboria	cirrate	clamber	clearcut	clivers	clumsy
chresard	ciborium	cirri	clammy	clearweed	cloaca	clung
chrism	cicada	cirriped	clamor	clearwing	cloacal	clupeid
chrismal	cicadae	cirrous	clamorous	cleat	cloak	clupeoid
chrisom	cicadas	cirrus	clamp	cleavage	cloakroom	cluster
christen	cicatrice	cirsoid	clamshell	cleave	cloche	clustery
chroma	cicatrix	cirsotomy	clamworm	cleckin	clock	clutch
chromate	cicatrize	cisalpine	clan	cledonism	clockwise	clutter
chromatic	cicely	cisco	clang	clef	clockwork	clypeate
chromatin	cicero	cissoid	clangor	cleft	clod	clypei
chrome	cicerone	cist	clank	clematis	cloddish	clypeus
chromic	cicerones	cistern	clannish	clemency	cloddy	clyster
chromism	ciceroni	cistus	clanship	clement	clog	coach
chromite	cichlid	citadel	clansman	clench	cloggy	coachman
chromium	cider	cital	clap	clepsydra	cloisonne	coact
chromo	cigar	citation	clapboard	clergy	cloister	coaction
chromogen	cigaret	citatory	claque	clergyman	cloistral	coactive
chromous	cigarette	cite	clarence	cleric	clon	coadjutor
chronaxia	cilia	cithara	clarendon	clerical	clone	coadunate
chronaxie	ciliary	cither	claret	clerisy	clonic	coagency
chronaxy	ciliate	cithern	clarify	clerk	clonicity	coagent
chronic	cilice	citied	clarinet	clerkship	clonus	coagula
chronical	cilicious	citified	clarion	cleveite	close	coagulant
chronicle	ciliolate	citizen	clarionet	clever	closet	coagulate
chrysalid	cilium	citizenry	clarity	clevis	closure	coagulin
chrysalis	cimices	citral	clary	clew	clot	coagulum
chthonian	cimex	citrange	clash	cliche	clotty	coal
chthonic	cinch	citrate	clasp	click	cloth	coalesce

coalfish	cockfight	cogitate	collapse	colossi	comma	complin
coalhole	cockhorse	cognac	collar	colossus	command	compline
coalition	cocking	cognate	collard	colostrum	commandry	complot
coalpit	cockle	cognation	collaret	colotomy	commence	compluvia
coalsack	cocklebur	cognition	collargol	colt	commend	comply
coalti	cockloft	cognitive	collate	colter	commensal	compo
coaming	cockmatch	cognizant	collation	coltish	comment	component
coarctate	cockney	cognize	collative	coltsfoot	commerce	compony
coarse	cockneyfy	cognomen	colleague	colubrine	commerge	comport
coarsen	cockpit	cognomens	collect	colugo	commingle	compose
coast	cockroach	cognomina	colleen	columbiad	comminute	composite
coastal	cockscomb	cogon	college	columbine	commissar	compost
coastward	cockshead	cogway	collegial	columbite	commit	composure
coastways	cockspur	cogwheel	collegian	columbium	committal	compote
coastwise	cocksure	cohabit	collet	columella	committee	compound
coat	cockswain	cohere	collide	column	commix	comprador
coati	cocktail	coherence	collie	columnar	commode	compress
coatless	coco	coherency	collier	columned	commodity	comprisal
coax	cocoa	coherent	colliery	columnist	commodore	comprise
coaxal	cocoanut	cohesion	colligate	colure	common	compute
coaxial	cocobolo	cohesive	collimate	coly	commonage	computist
cob	cocograss	cohobate	collinear	colyone	commoner	comrade
cobalt	coconut	cohort	collinsia	colza	commons	comradery
cobaltic	cocoon	cohosh	collision	coma	commotion	con
cobaltite	cocotte	cohune	collocate	comal	commove	conation
cobaltous	coction	coif	collodion	comate	communal	conative
cobble	cod	coiffure	collodium	comatose	commune	conatural
coble	coda	coign	colloid	comatous	communion	conatus
cobnut	coddle	coil	colloidal	comatula	communism	concave
cobra	code	coin	collop	comatulid	communist	concavity
cobweb	codeia	coinage	colloquy	comb	community	conceal
cobwebby	codein	coincide	collotype	combat	communize	concede
cobwork	codex	coinsure	collotypy	combatant	commutual	conceit
cocain	codices	coir	collude	combative	commutate	conceited
cocaine	codicil	coition	collusion	combine	commute	conceive
cocainism	codify	coitus	collusive	combust	comose	concenter
cocainize	codling	coke	collyrium	comby	comous	concept
cocci	codpiece	col	colocynth	come	compact	concern
coccoid	codress	cola	cologne	comedian	compadre	concert
coccus	coenzym	colander	colon	comedo	companion	concerted
coccygeal	coenzyme	colanut	colonic	comedones	company	concerto
coccyges	coequal	colcannon	colonel	comedy	compare	conch
coccyx	coerce	colchicum	colonelcy	comely	compart	concha
cochineal	coercion	colcothar	colonial	comet	compass	conchoid
cochlea	coercive	cold	colonist	cometary	compeer	concierge
cochleae	coeternal	coldframe	colonitis	cometic	compel	concise
cochlear	coeval	cole	colonize	comfit	compend	concision
cochleate	coexist	coleslaw	colonnade	comfiture	compendia	conclave
cock	coextend	colessee	colony	comfort	compete	conclude
cockade	coffee	colessor	colophon	comfrey	competent	concoct
cockaded	coffer	coleus	colophony	comic	compile	concord
cockateel	cofferdam	colewort	color	comical	complain	concordat
cockatiel	coffin	colic	colorado	comitatus	complaint	concourse
cockatoo	coffle	colicky	colorful	comitia	complect	concrete
cockboat	cog	colin	colorific	comitial	complete	concubine
cockcrow	cogency	colitis	colorist	comitium	complex	concur
cocker	cogent	collage	colorless	comity	complexus	concuss
cockerel	cogitable	collagen	colossal		compliant	condemn

condense
condign
condiment
condition
condole
condone
condor
conduce
conducent
conducive
conduct
conduit
condylar
condyle
condyloid
condyloma
cone
conepate
conepatl
coney
confer
conferee
conferva
conferval
confess
confest
confetti
confidant
confide
confident
configure
confine
confirm
confirmee
confiture
conflate
conflict
conflux
confluent
confocal
conform
confound
confrere
confront
confuse
confusion
confute
conga
conge
congeal
congener
congenial
conger
congeries
congest
conglobe
congo
congou

congress
congreve
congruent
congruity
congruous
congu
conic
conical
conid
conidial
conidium
conifer
coniferin
coniine
conium
conjoin
conjoint
conjugal
conjugate
conjugant
conjunct
conjure
conjury
connate
connation
connaught
connect
connive
connivent
connotate
connote
connubial
conoid
conoidal
conoidic
conquer
conquest
conquian
conscious
conscript
consensus
consent
conserve
consider
consign
consignee
consist
consocies
console
consomme
consonant
consonous
consort
conspire
constable
constancy
constant
constrain

constrict
construct
construe
consul
consular
consulate
consult
consume
contact
contagia
contagion
contagium
contain
contemn
contempt
contend
content
contented
contest
context
continent
continua
continual
continue
continuum
contort
contour
contract
contralti
contralto
contrary
contrast
contrite
contrive
control
contumacy
contumely
contuse
contusive
contusion
conundrum
convector
convene
convent
converge
converse
convert
convex
convexity
convey
convict
convince
convivial
convoke
convolute
convolve
convoy
convulse

cony
coo
cooee
cooey
cook
cookery
cookey
cookie
cooky
cool
coolant
cooler
coolish
coolie
coom
coomb
coon
cooncan
coontie
coop
cooper
cooperage
cooperate
coopery
coopt
cooptate
coordinal
coot
cooter
cop
copaiba
copaiva
copal
copalm
cope
copeck
copepod
copepodan
copestone
copious
copped
copper
copperas
coppice
copra
copremia
copraemia
copremic
coprolite
coprology
copse
copula
copular
copulate
copy
copybook
copycat
copygraph

copyhold
copyist
copyright
coquet
coquetry
coquette
coquille
coquina
coquito
coracle
coracoid
coral
coralline
coralite
coralloid
corallum
coralroot
corban
corbeil
corbel
cord
cordage
cordate
cordial
cordiform
cordite
cordoba
cordon
cordovan
corduroy
cordwain
cordwood
cordy
core
coreless
coreopsis
coreplasty
corf
corgi
coriander
coria
corium
cork
corkage
corkscrew
corkwood
corkiness
corky
corm
cormi
cormorant
cormus
corn
cornbread
corncob
corncrib
cornea
corneal

cornel
cornelian
corneous
corner
cornet
cornetcy
cornfield
cornice
cornmeal
cornus
cornute
cornuted
corny
corody
corol
corolla
corollate
corollary
corona
coronach
coronal
coronary
coroner
coronet
corpora
corporal
corporale
corporate
corporeal
corposant
corps
corpse
corpsman
corpulent
corpus
corpuscle
corrade
corral
corrasion
correct
correlate
corridor
corrival
corrode
corrodent
corrody
corrosion
corrosive
corrugant
corrugate
corrupt
corsage
corsair
corselet
corset
corslet
cortege
cortex

cortical
corticate
cortices
córticose
corticous
cortin
corundum
coruscate
coruscant
corvee
corves
corvet
corvette
corvine
corymb
corymbose
corymbous
coryphei
corypheus
coryza
cosecant
coseismal
coscismic
cosher
cosinage
cosine
cosmetic
cosmic
cosmism
cosmist
cosmogony
cosmology
cosmorama
cosmos
coss
cosset
cost
costa
costae
costal
costate
costive
costmary
costume
cot
cotangent
cote
cotenancy
cotenant
cotenure
coterie
cothurn
cothurnal
cothurni
cothurnus
cotidal
cotillion
cotillon

cotta
cottae
cottas
cottabus
cottage
cottager
cotter
cottier
cottise
cottised
cotton
cottony
cotyledon
cotyloid
couch
couchant
coucher
couching
cougar
cough
could
coulee
coulisse
couloir
coulomb
coulter
coumaric
coumarin
coumarine
council
councilor
counsel
count
counter
countess
countless
countrify
country
county
coup
coupe
coupee
couple
couplet
coupon
courage
courant
courante
couranto
courier
courlan
course
court
courteous
courtesan
courtesy
courtezan
courtier

courtleet
courtlike
courtly
courtroom
courtship
courtyard
cousin
cousinry
couteau
couteaux
coutel
couvade
covalence
covalent
cove
covenant
cover
coverage
coverall
coverlet
coverlid
covert
coverture
covet
covetous
covey
coving
cowage
cowalker
coward
cowardice
cowbane
cowbell
cowberry
cowbind
cowbird
cowboy
cower
cowfish
cowhage
cowherb
cowherd
cowhide
cowl
cowlick
cowlstaff
cowman
cowpea
cowpilot
cowpox
cowrie
cowry
cowskin
cowslip
cowtree
coxa
coxalgia
coxalgic

coxcomb
coxcombry
coxswain
coy
coyish
coyote
coyotillo
coypou
coypu
coz
cozen
cozenage
cozy
craal
crab
crabby
crabgrass
crabstick
crack
crackle
cracknel
cradle
craft
craftsman
crafty
crag
cragged
craggy
cragsman
crake
cram
crambo
cramp
crampfish
crampon
cranberry
cranch
crandall
crane
cranebill
cranefly
crania
cranial
craniate
cranium
crank
crankcase
crankle
crankpin
crannied
crannog
cranny
crape
crapefish
crappie
craps
crapulent
crapulous

crapy
crash
crasis
crass
crate
cravat
crave
craven
craw
crawfish
crawl
crayfish
crayon
craze
crazed
crazy
creak
creaky
cream
creamcups
creamer
creamery
creamy
crease
creasy
create
creatine
creation
creative
creatural
creature
creche
credence
credenda
credendum
credible
credit
credo
credulity
credulous
creed
creek
creel
creep
creepy
cremate
cremation
crematory
cremocarp
crenate
crenated
crenation
crenature
crenel
crenelate
crenelle
crenulate
creodont

creosol
creosote
crepe
crepitant
crepitate
crept
crepuscle
crescendo
crescent
cresol
cress
cresset
cressy
crest
crestless
cresyl
cresylate
cresylic
cretic
cretin
cretinism
cretonne
crevasse
crevice
creviced
crew
crewel
crib
cribbage
cribbite
cribbiter
cribble
cribwork
crick
cricket
cricoid
cried
crime
criminal
criminate
crimp
crimpage
crimpy
crimson
cringe
cringle
crinite
crinkle
crinoid
crinoidea
crinoline
crinum
cripple
crises
crisis
crisp
crispate
crispated

crissal
crissum
cristate
cristated
criteria
criterion
critic
critical
criticism
criticize
critique
crizzling
croak
croaky
crocein
crochet
crocin
crock
crockery
crocket
crocodile
crocoite
crocus
croft
crofter
crojik
cromlech
cromorna
crone
crony
crook
crookback
crooked
crookneck
crool
croon
crop
croquet
croquette
crore
crosier
cross
crossbar
crossbill
crossbow
crossbred
crossbun
crosscut
crossfire
crossfoot
crosshair
crosshead
crossjack
crosslet
crossroad
crossruff
crosstree
crossway

crosswise
crotali
crotaline
crotalus
crotch
crotched
crotchet
crotchety
croton
crouch
croup
croupe
croupier
croupous
croupy
crouton
crow
crowbar
crowberry
crowd
crowfoot
crown
crownless
crownlet
crowquill
croze
crozer
crozier
cruces
crucial
cruciate
crucible
crucifer
crucifix
cruciform
crucify
crude
crudity
cruel
cruelty
cruet
cruise
cruller
crumb
crumble
crumbly
crumby
crump
crumpet
crumple
crunch
crunodal
crunode
crupper
crura
crural
crus
crusade

cruse
cruset
crush
crust
cruster
crustose
crusty
crutch
crutched
crux
cruxes
cruzado
cruzeiro
cry
cryogen
cryogenic
cryolite
cryomete.
cryoscope
cryoscopy
cryostat
crypt
cryptic
cryptical
cryptogam
cryptonym
crystal
crystallic
crystule
ctenoid
cuarenta
cub
cubage
cubature
cubbish
cubbyhole
cube
cubic
cubical
cubicle
cubicula
cubicular
cubiculum
cubiform
cubism
cubist
cubit
cubital
cuboid
cuboidal
cuckold
cuckoldy
cuckoldry
cuckoo
cucullate
cucumber
cucurbit
cucurbite

cud
cudbear
cuddle
cuddy
cudgel
cudweed
cue
cuerpo
cuff
cuirass
cuish
cuisine
culch
culet
culets
culettes
culinary
cull
cullender
cullet
cullion
cullis
cully
culm
culmen
culminal
culminate
culotte
culottes
culpa
culpable
culprit
cult
cultch
cultigen
cultivate
cultrate
cultrated
cultural
culture
culturist
culver
culverin
culvert
cumber
cumbrance
cumbrous
cumin
cumquat
cumshaw
cumulate
cumuli
cumulous
cumulus
cunctator
cuneal
cuneate
cuneated

cuneatic
cuneus
cuneiform
cuniculus
cunner
cunning
cup
cupbearer
cupboard
cupcake
cupel
cupful
cupidity
cupola
cuppy
cupreous
cupric
cuprite
cuprious
cupshake
cupule
cur
curacy
curara
curare
curari
curarize
curassow
curate
curative
curator
curb
curbstone
curculio
curculios
curcuma
curcumin
curcumine
curd
curdle
curdly
curdy
cure
cureless
curettage
curette
curfew
curialism
curialist
curie
curiegram
curio
curiosity
curious
curium
curl
curlew
curlicue

curlycue
currant
currency
current
curricle
curriery
curry
currish
currycomb
curse
cursive
cursorial
cursory
curt
curtail
curtain
curtate
curtation
curtesy
curtilage
curtsey
curtsy
curule
curvate
curvated
curvation
curvature
curve
curvet
curvity
cusec
cushat
cushaw
cushion
cushiony
cusk
cusp
cusped
cuspated
cuspidal
cuspidate
cuspid
cuspidor
cusso
custard
custodial
custodian
custody
custom
customary
customer
custodes
custos
custumal
cut
cutaneous
cutaway
cutback

cutch
cutchberry
cute
cutgrass
cuticle
cuticula
cuticular
cutin
cutinize
cutlas
cutlass
cutler
cutlery
cutlet
cutpurse
cuttie
cuttle
cutwater
cutworm
cyanamid
cyanamide
cyanate
cyanic
cyanide
cyanin
cyanine
cyanize
cyanogen
cyanopia
cyanopsia
cyanopsis
cyanotic
cyanotype
cyanuric
cybotaxis
cycad
cyclamen
cycle
cyclic
cyclical
cyclist
cyclogiro
cycloid
cycloidal
cyclone
cyclonic
cyclorama
cyclosis
cyclotron
cygneous
cygnet
cylinder
cylindric
cylix
cyma
cymae
cymatia
cymatium

cymbal
cymbalist
cymbling
cyme
cymene
cymlin
cymling
cymol
cymogene
cymograph
cymoid
cymometer
cymophane
cymoscope
cymose
cymous
cynic
cynical
cynicism
cynophobe
cynosure
cypher
cypress
cyprinid
cyprinoid
cypsela
cyst
cystic
cystous
cystidium
cystine
cystitis
cystitome
cystocarp
cystocele
cystoid
cystolith
cystotomy
cytase
cytaster
cytogenic
cytologic
cytology
cytolysin
cytolysis
cytolytic
cytometer
cytophagy
cytophil
cytoplasm
cytoplast
czar
czardom
czarevna
czarina
czaritza
czarism

D

dab
dabble
dabchick
dace
dachshund
dacite
dactyl
dactylate
dactylic
dactylion
dactylium
dad
daddy
dado
dadoes
daduchi
daduchus
daffodil
daft
dag
dagger
daggle
daglock
dahlia
dahoon
daily
daimio
daimyo
dainty
dairy
dairymaid
dairyman
dais
daisied
daisy
dakerhen
dale
dalesman
dalet
dalles
dalliance
dally
dalmatic
dalton
dam
damage
damar
damascene
damaskeen
damask
dame
damewort
damiana
dammar
dammer
damn

damnation	datolite	death	decide	deed	defray	delimit
damnatory	datum	deathbed	decidua	deedful	defrock	delineate
damnify	datura	deathblow	deciduous	deedless	defrost	deliriant
damp	daub	deathcup	decigram	deem	deft	delirious
dampen	daubery	deathful	decile	deemster	deftness	delirium
dampish	daubry	deathless	deciliter	deep	defunct	deliver
damsel	dauby	deathlike	decillion	deepmost	defy	delivery
damson	daughter	deathmask	decimal	deepen	degas	dell
dance	daunt	deathy	decimate	deer	degauss	delouse
dandelion	dauntless	debacle	decimeter	deerberry	degrade	delphinic
dander	dauphin	debar	decimetre	deerfly	degree	delta
dandify	dauphine	debark	decipher	deergrass	degum	deltaic
dandle	davenport	debase	decision	deerhound	degust	deltoid
dandruff	davit	debate	decisive	deerlet	degustate	delude
dandy	daw	debauch	decistere	deerskin	dehisce	deluge
dandyish	dawdle	debauchee	deck	deerweed	dehiscent	delusion
dandyism	dawn	debenture	deckle	deface	dehorn	delusive
danewort	day	debility	declaim	defalcate	dehydrate	delusory
danger	daybook	debit	declare	defame	deicide	delve
dangerous	daybreak	debonair	declinable	default	deictic	demagog
dangle	daydream	debonaire	decline	defeat	deific	demagogue
dank	dayfly	debouch	declivity	defeatism	deifical	demagogic
dankish	daylight	debris	declutch	defeatist	deiform	demagogy
danseuse	daylily	debt	decoct	defecate	deify	demand
dap	daylong	debtor	decoction	defect	deign	demandant
daphne	dayspring	debut	decode	defection	deipotent	demarch
dapple	daystar	decade	decollate	defective	deism	deme
dare	daytime	decadence	decolor	defend	deistic	demean
daredevil	daze	decadent	decompose	defendant	deistical	demeanor
dareful	dazzle	decagon	decorate	defense	deity	dement
daric	deacon	decagonal	decorous	defensive	deject	dementia
daring	deaconry	decagram	decorum	defer	dejecta	demerit
dark	deaconess	decalcify	decoy	deference	dejection	demersed
darken	dead	decaliter	decrease	deferent	dekagram	demesne
darkish	deadbeat	decameter	decree	defiance	dekaliter	demigod
darkle	deaden	decamp	decrement	defiant	dekalitre	demijohn
darkroom	deadeye	decanal	decrepit	deficit	dekameter	demilune
darksome	deadfall	decane	decretal	defilade	dekametre	demise
darling	deadhead	decant	decretive	defile	dekastere	demission
darn	deadhouse	decapod	decretory	define	delaine	demit
darnel	deadlight	decapodal	decry	definite	delate	demitasse
dart	deadline	decare	decuman	deflate	delation	demiurge
dartars	deadlock	decastere	decumbent	deflation	delay	demivolt
dartle	deadly	decathlon	decuple	deflect	dele	demiwolf
dartrous	deadman	decay	decurion	deflector	deleble	democracy
dash	deadmarch	decease	decurrent	deflex	delible	democrat
dashboard	deadwood	decedent	decurve	deflexion	delectate	demolish
dasheen	deaf	deceit	decury	deflexure	delegacy	demon
dashy	deafen	deceitful	decussate	deflorate	delegant	demoniac
dastard	deal	deceive	dedalous	deflower	delegate	demonian
dastardy	dealt	decemvir	dedans	defluxion	delete	demonic
dasyure	dealfish	decemviri	dedicate	defoliate	deletion	demonism
data	dean	decency	deduce	deforce	delft	demonist
dataria	deanery	decent	deducive	deforest	delicacy	demonize
datary	deanship	decenter	deduct	deform	delicate	demotic
date	dear	decern	deduction	deformity	delicious	demotics
dateless	dearborn	deciare	deductive	defoul	delict	demount
dative	dearth	decibel	dee	defraud	delight	dempster

demulcent	dependent	derringer	deter	dewberry	dialyses	dichroism
demur	depict	derris	deterrent	dewclaw	dialysis	dichroite
demure	depiction	derry	deterge	dewdrop	dialytic	dichromic
demurrage	depicture	dervish	detergent	dewlap	dialyze	dicker
demurral	depilate	descant	determine	dewy	diameter	dickey
demy	depilator	descend	detersion	dexter	diametral	dicky
den	depilatory	descent	detersive	dexterity	diametric	diclinous
denarii	deplete	describe	detest	dexterous	diamine	dicliny
denarius	depletion	descry	dethrone	dextrous	diamond	dicrotal
denary	depletive	desecrate	detinue	dextrad	diandrous	dicrotic
denature	depletory	deseret	detonate	dextral	dianoetic	dicrotism
denazify	deplore	desert	detorsion	dextrin	dianthus	dicrotous
dendrite	deploy	desertion	detour	dextrine	diapason	dicta
dendritic	deplumate	deserve	detract	dextrose	diaper	dictate
dendroid	deplume	desiccate	detrain	dey	diaphony	dictation
dendron	depolarize	design	detriment	dharna	diaphonic	diction
denehole	depone	designate	detrition	dhoti	diaphragm	dictum
dengue	deponent	desinence	detritus	dhooti	diaphyses	dictynid
denial	depopulate	desipient	detrital	dhoora	diaphysis	did
denigrate	deport	desirable	detruck	dhourra	diarchy	didactic
denim	deportee	desire	detrude	dhow	diarist	didactics
denitrate	deposal	desirous	detrusion	dhu	diarrhea	didapper
denitrify	depose	desist	detrusive	diabase	diarrheal	diddle
denitrize	deposit	desk	deuce	diabasic	diarrheic	didrachma
denizen	depot	desman	deuteric	diabetes	diary	didym
denote	deprave	desmid	deuterium	diabetic	diaspore	didymium
denounce	depravity	desmidian	deuteron	diablerie	diastase	didymous
dense	deprecate	desmoid	deuton	diablery	diastasic	die
density	depredate	desolate	devaluate	diabolic	diastatic	dieback
dent	depress	despair	devalue	diabolism	diaster	diecious
dental	deprive	despatch	develop	diabolist	diastole	diereses
dentate	depth	desperado	devest	diabolize	diastolic	dieresis
dentation	depurant	desperate	deviate	diabolo	diathermy	dieretic
dentel	depurate	despise	deviation	diachylon	diathesis	diesis
denticle	depute	despite	deviatory	diacid	diathetic	diestock
dentiform	deputize	despoil	device	diaconal	diatom	diet
dentil	deputy	despond	devil	diaconate	diatomic	dietary
dentinal	deraign	despot	devilfish	diacritic	diatomite	dietetic
dentine	derail	despotic	devilish	diactinic	diatonic	dietetics
dentist	derange	despotism	devilkin	diadem	diatribe	dietetist
dentistry	derby	despotize	devilry	diagnose	diazine	dietician
dentition	derelict	despumate	deviltry	diagnosis	diazole	differ
dentoid	deride	dessert	devilwood	diagonal	diazonium	different
denture	derisible	destine	devious	diagram	diazotize	difficile
denudate	derision	destiny	devisal	diagraph	dibasic	difficult
denude	derisive	destitute	devise	dial	dibber	diffident
deny	derisory	destroy	devisee	dialect	dibble	diffract
deodand	derive	desuetude	devitrify	dialectal	dicast	diffuse
deodar	derm	desultory	devoid	dialectic	dicastic	diffusion
deodorant	derma	detach	devoir	dialist	dice	diffusive
deodorize	dermal	detail	devolve	diallage	dicentra	dig
deoxidize	dermatoid	detain	devote	diallist	dicerous	digamist
deoxidate	dermic	detect	devotee	dialog	dichasial	digamma
depart	dermis	detection	devotion	dialogic	dichasium	digamous
departure	dermoid	detective	devour	dialogism	dichlorid	digamy
depasture	derogate	detent	devout	dialogist	dichogamy	digastric
depend	derrick	detention	dew	dialogize	dichotomy	digenesis
dependant	derrid	detentive	dewan	dialogue	dichroic	digenetic

digest	dinar	dipteral	discord	dismast	dissident	divalent
digestant	dine	dipterous	discount	dismay	dissipate	divan
digestion	dineric	diptych	discourse	dismember	dissocial	dive
digestive	dinero	dire	discover	dismiss	dissolute	diverge
digit	dinette	direct	discovert	dismissal	dissolve	divergent
digital	ding	direction	discovery	dismount	dissonant	divers
digitalin	dingey	directive	discreate	disnature	disspread	diverse
digitalis	dinghy	directly	discredit	disobey	dissuade	diversify
digitate	dingle	directory	discreet	disoblige	distaff	diversion
digitoxin	dingo	directrix	discrete	disodium	distain	diversity
diglot	dingy	direful	discrown	disodic	distal	divert
dignify	dinner	dirge	discus	disorder	distance	divest
dignitary	dinoceras	dirigible	discuses	disorient	distant	divide
dignity	dinosaur	diriment	discuss	disown	distaste	dividend
digraph	dinothere	dirk	disdain	disparage	distemper	divine
digraphic	dint	dirndl	disease	disparate	distend	divinity
digress	diobol	dirt	disembed	disparity	distich	divinize
dihedral	diobolon	dirty	disenable	dispart	distil	divisibly
dike	diocesan	disable	disendow	dispatch	distinct	division
dilantin	diocese	disabuse	disengage	dispel	distingue	divisive
dilatant	diode	disaccord	disentail	dispense	distome	divisor
dilatancy	dioicous	disaffect	disentomb	dispeople	distort	divorce
dilatate	diopside	disaffirm	disesteem	dispermic	distract	divorcee
dilatator	dioptase	disagree	disfavor	dispermy	distrain	divulgate
dilate	diopter	disallow	disfigure	dispersal	distraint	divulge
dilater	dioptre	disannul	disforest	disperse	distrait	divulsion
dilation	dioptric	disanoint	disfrock	dispirit	distraite	divulsive
dilative	dioptrics	disappear	disgorge	displace	distress	dixit
dilator	dioptry	disarm	disgrace	displant	district	dizen
dilatory	diorama	disarray	disguise	display	distrust	dizzy
dilemma	dioramic	disaster	disgust	displease	disturb	do
diligence	diorite	disavow	dish	disport	distyle	doaty
diligent	dioritic	disavowal	dishful	disposal	disulfate	dobber
dill	dioryte	disband	dishcloth	dispose	disulfide	dobla
dillantin	diosmosis	disbar	dishclout	dispraise	disunion	doblon
dilly	dioxid	disbelief	dishelm	dispread	disunite	dobra
diluent	dioxide	disbosom	disherit	disprize	disusage	dobson
dilute	dip	disbranch	dishevel	disproof	disuse	docent
dilution	diphase	disburden	dishonest	disproval	disvalue	docile
diluvial	diphenyl	disburse	dishonor	disprove	disyoke	docility
diluvian	diphasic	disc	dishpan	disputant	ditch	dock
dim	diphthong	discal	dishwater	dispute	ditheism	dockage
dime	diplex	discalced	disinfect	disquiet	ditheist	docket
dimension	diploid	discant	disinfest	disrate	dither	doctoral
dimer	diploma	discard	disinhume	disregard	dithery	doctorate
dimerous	diplomacy	discase	disinter	disrelish	dithionic	doctrinal
dimerism	diplomat	discept	disject	disrepair	dithyramb	doctrine
dimeter	diplopia	discern	disjoin	disrepute	dittany	document
dimethyl	diplopic	discharge	disjoint	disrobe	ditto	dodder
dimetric	diplopy	disci	disjunct	disroot	dittos	dodge
dimidiate	diplosis	disciple	disk	disrupt	dittogram	doe
diminish	dipnoan	disclaim	dislike	diss	ditty	doeskin
dimissory	dipody	disclose	dislocate	disseat	diuresis	doff
dimity	dipole	discoid	dislodge	dissect	diuretic	dog
dimorphic	dipsades	discolor	disloyal	dissemble	diurnal	dogbane
dimple	dipsas	discomfit	dismal	dissent	diva	dogberry
din	dipsey	discommon	dismantle	dissever	divagate	dogbrier

doge
dogedom
dogeship
dogfish
dogfennel
dogfight
doggerel
doggerman
doggish
doggy
doggie
dogie
dogma
dogmas
dogmata
dogmatic
dogmatics
dogmatism
dogmatize
dogmatist
dogtail
dogwood
dogy
doily
doings
doit
dolce
doldrums
dole
doleful
dolerite
doleritic
dolesome
doll
dollar
dollish
dolman
dolmans
dolmen
dolomite
dolomitic
dolor
dolorous
dolose
dolphin
dolt
doltish
domain
domanial
dome
domesday
domestic
domical
domicil
domicile
dominance
dominancy

dominant
dominate
domine
domineer
dominical
dominie
dominion
dominium
domino
dominoes
dominos
donate
donation
donative
done
donee
donga
dongola
donjon
donkey
donna
donor
doodle
doom
doomsday
doomster
door
doorman
doornail
doorplate
doorpost
doorsill
doorstep
doorway
dooryard
dope
dopey
dor
dorine
doris
dormancy
dormant
dormer
dormice
dormie
dormitory
dormouse
dormy
dornick
dornock
dorp
dorsa
dorsad
dorsal
dorsum
dory
dosage

dose
dosimeter
dosimetry
dossal
dosser
dossier
dossil
dotage
dotant
dotard
dotation
dote
dotterel
dottel
dottle
dotty
double
doublet
doubloon
doubt
doubtful
doubtless
douceur
douche
dough
doughface
doughnut
doughty
douzeper
dove
dovecot
dovecote
dovekey
dovekie
dovetail
dowager
dowcet
dowdy
dowel
dower
dowerless
dowery
dowitcher
dowl
dowle
down
downcast
downcome
downfall
downhaul
downhill
downpour
downright
downstage
downtake
downthrow
downward

downwards
downy
dowry
dowse
doxology
doyen
doyley
doyly
doze
dozen
dozenth
dozy
drab
drabble
dracaena
drachm
drachma
drachmae
drachmas
draff
draffish
draffy
draft
draftee
draftsman
drafty
drag
draggle
draghound
draghunt
dragline
draglink
dragnet
dragoman
dragon
dragonet
dragonfly
dragoon
dragrope
dragsail
dragsheet
drain
drainage
drainpipe
drake
drakefly
dram
drama
dramatic
dramatics
dramatist
dramatize
dramshop
drank
drape
drapery
drastic

draughts
draw
drawback
drawbar
drawbore
drawee
drawl
drawn
drawplate
drawshave
drawtube
dray
drayage
dread
dreadful
dreadless
dream
dreamed
dreamt
dreamful
dreamland
dreamless
dreamy
drear
dreary
dredge
dreggish
dreggy
dregs
drench
dress
dressy
drib
dribble
dribblet
driblet
drift
driftage
driftwood
drifty
drill
drink
drip
dripstone
drive
driveway
drivebolt
drivel
driven
drizzle
drizzly
drogue
droitural
droll
drollery
drolly
dromedary

dromoi
dromon
dromond
dromos
drone
drongo
dronism
drool
droop
droopy
drop
dropforge
dropkick
dropleaf
droplet
droplight
dropsical
dropsied
dropsy
dropwort
droshky
drosky
dross
drought
droughty
drouth
drouthy
drove
drovework
drow
drown
drowse
drowsy
drub
drudge
drudgery
drugget
druggist
drugstore
druid
druidess
druidic
druidical
druidism
druidry
drum
drumbeat
drumfire
drumfish
drumhead
drumlin
drumstick
drunk
drunkard
drunken
drupe
drupel

drupelet
drupeole
druse
drused
drusy
dry
dryad
dryadic
dryclean
drydock
dryfoot
drynurse
drypoint
dryrot
drysalt
drywash
duad
dual
dualism
dualist
dualistic
dub
dubh
dubiety
dubiosity
dubious
dubitate
ducal
ducat
duchess
duchy
duck
duckbill
duckling
duckmeat
duckmole
duckpin
duckweed
duct
ductile
ductility
dude
dudeen
dudgeon
due
duel
duelist
duellist
duenna
duet
duff
duffel
duffer
duffle
dug
dugong
dui

34

duiker
duikerbok
duke
dukedom
dulce
dulcet
dulciana
dulcify
dulcimer
dulcinea
dulia
dull
dullard
dullish
dully
dulosis
dulotic
dulse
duly
dumb
dumbbell
dumbfound
dummy
dump
dumpish
dumpling
dumpy
dun
dunce
dune
dunfish
dung
dungaree
dungeon
dunghill
dunk
dunlin
dunnage
dunnite
duo
duodecimo
duodenal
duodenary
duodenum
duograph
duolog
duologue
duotone
duotype
dupe
dupery
duple
duplex
duplexity
duplicate
duplicity
dura

durable
duramen
durance
duration
duresse
durian
during
durion
durmast
durr
durra
durst
durum
dusk
duskish
dusky
dust
dustless
dustman
dustpan
duststorm
dusty
dutchman
duteous
dutiful
duty
duumvir
duumviral
duumviri
duumvirs
duvetine
duvetyn
duvetyne
dwarf
dwarfish
dwell
dwelt
dyad
dyadic
dyarchy
dye
dyestuff
dyeweed
dyewood
dying
dyke
dynameter
dynamic
dynamical
dynamics
dynamism
dynamist
dynamite
dynamo
dynamotor
dynast
dynastic

dynasty
dyne
dynograph
dyscrasia
dyscrasic
dysemia
dysentery
dysgenic
dysgenics
dyspepsia
dyspeptic
dysphagia
dysphagic
dysphasia
dysphonia
dysphonic
dysphoria
dysphotic
dyspnea
dyspneal
dyspneic
dyspnoea
dystaxi
dystrophy
dysuria
dysuric
dziggetai

E

each
eager
eagre
eagle
eaglet
eaglewood
ear
earache
eardrop
eardrum
earl
earldom
earlock
early
earmark
earn
earnest
earphone
earring
earshot
earstone
earth
earthen
earthling
earthnut
earthstar
earthward

earthwork
earthworm
earthy
earwax
earwig
ease
easel
east
eastbound
easterly
eastern
easting
eastward
eastwards
easy
eatage
eau
eaux
eave
eavedrop
eaves
eavesdrip
eavesdrop
ebb
ebon
ebonite
ebonize
ebony
ebullient
eburnated
eburnean
eburnian
ecad
ecarte
eccentric
ecclesia
ecclesiae
ecdemic
ecdysis
ecdyses
ecesis
echard
echelon
echidna
echidnae
echinal
echinate
echinoid
echinus
echini
echo
echoes
echoic
echoism
echolalia
eclampsia
eclat

eclectic
eclipse
eclipsis
ecliptic
eclogite
eclog
eclogue
eclosion
ecmnesia
ecology
ecologic
ecologist
economic
economics
economist
economize
economy
ecraseur
ecru
ecstasize
ecstasy
ecstatic
ectoblast
ectoderm
ectoenzym
ectogenic
ectomere
ectomeric
ectopia
ectopic
ectoplasm
ectosarc
ectrogeny
ectropium
ectropion
ectypal
ectype
ecumenic
eczema
edacious
edacity
edaphic
eddoes
eddy
edelweiss
edema
edemata
edematous
edematose
edentate
edge
edgeways
edgewise
edgy
edh
edible
edibility

edict
edictal
edifice
edificial
edify
edile
edileship
edilian
edilic
edit
edition
editorial
educable
educate
education
educative
educatory
educe
educt
eduction
eductive
eel
eelgrass
eelpot
eelpout
eelworm
eely
eery
eerie
effable
efface
effacive
effect
effective
effectual
effendi
efferrent
effete
efficacy
efficient
effigy
efflation
effluence
effluency
effluent
effluvium
efflux
effluxion
effluvial
effort
effulge
effulgent
effuse
effusion
effusive
eft
egad

egest
egesta
egestion
egestive
egg
eggnog
eggplant
eggshell
egis
eglantine
ego
egoism
egoist
egoistic
egotism
egotist
egregious
egress
egret
egression
eh
eider
eidetic
eidograph
eidola
eidolon
eight
eighteen
eightfold
eighth
eightieth
eighty
eikon
einkorn
either
ejaculate
eject
ejection
ejective
ejido
eke
ekka
elaborate
elain
eland
elaphine
elapse
elastic
elastin
elastomer
elate
elaterid
elaterin
elaterite
elaterium
elation
elbow

elder	ellipsis	embolden	emotion	encage	endoblast	engine
eldership	elliptic	emboli	emotional	encamp	endocarp	engineer
eldest	ellwand	embolism	emotive	encase	endocrine	enginery
elect	elm	embolus	emotivity	encaustic	endocyte	engird
election	elmy	emborder	empale	encave	endocytic	engirt
elective	elocution	embosom	empanel	enceinte	endoderm	engirdle
electoral	eloin	emboss	empathy	encenia	endogamic	englacial
electress	eloign	embow	empennage	encephala	endogamy	engorge
electric	elongate	embowel	emperor	enchain	endogen	engraft
electrine	elope	embrace	empery	enchant	endogeny	engrail
electrize	eloquence	embracery	emphases	enchase	endolymph	engrain
electrode	eloquent	embranch	emphasis	enchoric	endometry	engram
electron	else	embrasure	emphasize	enchorial	endomixis	engrave
electrum	elsewhere	embrittle	emphatic	enchyma	endomorph	engross
electuary	elucidate	embrocate	emphysema	encipher	endopathy	engulf
elegance	elude	embroider	empire	encircle	endophyte	enhance
elegancy	elusion	embroil	empiric	enclasp	endoplasm	enigma
elegant	elusive	embrown	empirical	enclave	endoreic	enigmatic
elegiac	elusory	embryal	emplastic	enclavure	endorse	enisle
elegiacal	elute	embryo	employ	enclitic	endoscope	enjoin
elegiast	elutriate	embryon	employe	enclose	endoscopy	enjoy
elegist	elvan	embryonal	employee	enclosure	endosmose	enkindle
elegit	elver	embryonic	emporia	encode	endosperm	enlace
elegize	elves	embryos	emporium	encomia	endospore	enlarge
elegy	elvish	embusque	emporiums	encomiast	endostea	enlighten
element	elytra	emeer	empower	encomium	endosteum	enlink
elemental	elytroid	emend	empress	encomiums	endotoxic	enlist
elemi	elytron	emendate	empty	encompass	endotoxin	enliven
elench	elytrum	emerald	empurple	encore	endow	enmesh
elenchi	em	emerge	empyema	encounter	endplate	enmity
elenchic	emaciate	emergence	empyreal	encourage	endue	ennead
elenchus	emanant	emergency	empyrean	encrimson	endurance	enneagon
eleolite	emanate	emergent	empyreuma	encrinite	endure	ennoble
eleoplast	emanation	emeritus	emu	encroach	endwise	ennui
elephant	emanative	emersed	emulate	encrust	enema	enologist
elevate	embalm	emersion	emulation	encumber	enemas	enology
elevation	embank	emery	emulative	encyclic	enemata	enormity
elevator	embar	emesis	emulgent	encyst	enemy	enormous
eleven	embargo	emetic	emulous	end	energesis	enough
eleventh	embargoes	emetine	emulsify	endamage	energetic	enounce
elf	embark	emeu	emulsion	endameba	energid	enplane
elfchild	embarrass	emeute	emulsive	endanger	energize	enquire
elfin	embassage	emew	emunctory	endbrain	energumen	enquiry
elfish	embassy	emigrant	emyd	endbrush	energy	enrage
elicit	embathe	emigrate	emyde	endear	enervate	enrapt
elide	embattle	eminence	en	endeavor	enface	enrapture
eligible	embay	eminency	enable	endecagon	enfeeble	enravish
eliminate	embed	eminent	enact	endemial	enfeoff	enrich
elinguid	embellish	emir	enactive	endemic	enfetter	enring
elision	ember	emirate	enactory	endemical	enfilade	enrobe
elite	embezzle	emissary	enalid	endemism	enfold	enrol
elixir	embitter	emission	enallage	endermic	enforce	enroll
elk	emblaze	emissive	enamel	endermism	enframe	enroot
elkhound	emblazon	emmenagog	enamelist	endive	engage	ens
ell	emblem	emmenin	enamor	endless	engarland	entia
ellipse	emblemize	emollient	enate	endlong	engender	ensconce
ellipses	embody	emolument	enation	endmost	engild	ensemble

enshrine
enshroud
ensiform
ensign
ensigncy
ensilage
ensile
ensky
enslave
ensnare
ensoul
ensphere
ensue
ensure
entail
entangle
entasia
entasis
entastic
entelechy
entellus
entente
enter
enteric
enteritis
entera
enteron
entertain
enthalpy
enthetic
enthral
enthrall
enthrone
enthymeme
entice
entire
entirety
entitle
entity
entoblast
entoderm
entomb
entophyte
entopic
entoptic
entoptics
entosarc
entotic
entourage
entrails
entrain
entrammel
entrance
entrant
entrap
entreat
entreaty

entree
entremets
entrench
entrepot
entresol
entropy
entruck
entrust
entry
entryman
entryway
entwine
entwist
enucleate
enumerate
enunciate
enure
enuresis
envelop
envelope
envenom
envious
environ
environs
envisage
envision
envoi
envoy
envy
enwind
enwomb
enwrap
enwreathe
enzootic
enzym
enzymatic
enzyme
eoclimax
eohippus
eolian
eolipile
eolith
eolithic
eolopile
eon
eonian
eonism
eosere
eosin
eosine
eosinic
epact
eparch
eparchial
eparchy
epaulet
epaulette

epauliere
epee
epeeist
ependyma
ependymal
epergne
epha
ephah
epharmone
epharmony
ephebic
ephebi
epheboi
ephebos
ephebus
ephedrin
ephedrine
ephemera
ephemerae
ephemeral
ephemeras
ephemerid
ephemeris
ephemeron
ephod
ephor
ephori
epi
epiblast
epibolic
epibolism
epiboly
epic
epicalyx
epicarp
epicedium
epicene
epicenism
epicenter
epicentral
epicentrum
epicotyl
epicritic
epicure
epicurean
epicurism
epicycle
epidemic
epiderm
epidermal
epidermis
epidote
epidotic
epifocal
epigamic
epigeal
epigean

epigene
epigenous
epigeous
epigram
epigraph
epigraphy
epigynous
epigyny
epilepsia
epilepsy
epileptic
epilog
epilogic
epilogize
epilogue
epinastic
epinasty
epineuria
epinosic
epinosis
epiphysis
epiphyte
epiphytic
epirogeny
episcopal
episcope
episode
episodal
episodial
episodic
episperm
epispore
epistasis
epistatic
epistaxis
epistle
epistoler
epistolic
epistyle
epitaph
epitaphic
epitasis
epithet
epithetic
epitheton
epitome
epitomic
epitomist
epitomize
epitrite
epizeuxis
epizoon
epizootic
epizooty
epoch
epochal
epode

eponym
eponymic
eponymist
eponymous
eponymy
epopee
epopoeia
epopt
epoptic
epos
epsilon
equable
equably
equal
equalize
equate
equation
equator
equerry
equery
eques
equilenin
equine
equinox
equip
equipage
equipoise
equisetum
equitably
equitant
equites
equity
equivocal
equivoke
equivoque
era
eradiate
eradiation
eradicate
erase
erasion
erasure
erbium
erect
erectile
erection
erective
erector
erectores
erelong
eremic
eremite
eremitic
eremitish
erenow
erepsin
ereptase

ereptic
erethism
erg
ergo
ergograph
ergometer
ergon
ergophile
ergot
ergotism
erigeron
eringo
eriometer
eristic
erlking
ermine
ermined
erode
erodent
erogenic
erogenous
erose
erosion
erosive
erotic
erotical
eroticism
erotics
err
errancy
errand
errant
errantry
errata
erratic
erratical
erratum
errhine
erroneous
error
ers
ersatz
eruct
eructate
erudite
erudition
eruginous
erupt
eruption
eruptive
eryngo
erythema
erythemic
erythrean
erythrene
erythrism
erythrite

erythrol
escalade
escalate
escallop
escalop
escapade
escape
escapist
escarp
eschalot
eschar
escheat
eschew
escopate
escopet
escopeta
escopette
escort
escrol
escroll
escrow
escuage
escudo
esculent
eserine
eskar
esker
esne
esophagal
esophagus
esoteric
espalier
esparto
especial
espionage
esplanade
espontoon
espousal
espouse
esprit
espy
esquire
ess
essay
essayist
essence
essential
essoin
essoign
essonite
establish
estacade
estacado
estafet
estafette
estate
esteem

ester	ethologic	euphoria	eversive	excitant	exigence	expend
esterase	ethos	euphoric	evert	excite	exigency	expense
esterify	ethyl	euphotic	evertile	exclaim	exigent	expensive
esthesia	ethylate	euphrasy	every	exclave	exigible	expert
esthesis	ethylene	euphroe	everybody	exclude	exiguous	expiable
esthete	ethylic	euphuism	everyday	exclusion	exiguity	expiate
esthetic	etiolate	euphuist	everyone	exclusive	exile	expiation
esthetics	etiology	euphuize	evict	excoriate	exilic	expiatory
estimable	etiologist	euplastic	eviction	excrement	exist	expire
estimably	etiquette	eupnea	evidence	excreta	existence	explain
estimate	etna	eupnoea	evident	excretal	existent	explant
estival	etoile	eureka	evil	excrete	exit	expletive
estivate	etude	eurhythmy	evince	excretion	exocardia	expletory
estoile	etui	euripi	evincive	excretive	exocarp	explicate
estop	etwee	euripus	evocation	excretory	exoderm	explicit
estoppage	etyma	eurithmy	evocative	exculpate	exodic	explode
estoppel	etymology	europium	evoe	excurrent	exodontia	explodent
estrange	etymon	euryon	evohe	excursion	exodus	exploit
estray	etymons	eurythmic	evoke	excursive	exogamic	explore
estriol	eucain	eurythmy	evolute	excursus	exogamy	explosion
estrogen	eucaine	eusol	evolution	excuse	exogen	explosive
estrone	eucalypt	eutaxic	evolve	execrable	exonerate	exponent
estrus	eucalypti	eutaxy	evolvent	execrate	exopathic	exponible
estuarial	eucharis	eutectic	evulsion	executant	exorable	export
estuarian	euchre	eutectoid	evzone	execute	exorcise	exposal
estuarine	euclase	euthenics	ewe	execution	exorcize	expose
estuary	eudaemon	euthenist	ewer	executive	exorcism	expositor
esurient	eudemon	euxenite	exact	executrix	exorcist	exposure
esurience	eudemonia	evacuant	exaction	executory	exordia	expound
esuriency	eudemonic	evacuate	exalt	exedra	exordium	express
eta	eugenic	evacuee	examen	exedrae	exordial	expulsion
etagere	eugenical	evade	examinant	exegesis	exoreic	expunge
etamine	eugenics	evaginate	examine	exegeses	exosmose	expurgate
etape	eugenist	evaluate	examinee	exegete	exosmosis	exquisite
etch	eugenol	evanesce	example	exegetic	exosmotic	exscind
eternal	eulogia	evangel	exanimate	exegetist	exosmic	exsect
eternity	eulogist	evanish	exanthema	exegetics	exospore	exsert
eternize	eulogious	evaporate	exarch	exemplar	exostosis	exsection
etesian	eulogize	evasion	exarchate	exemplary	exostoses	exsertile
eth	eulogy	evasive	excaudate	exemplify	exoteric	exsertion
ethane	eulogism	eve	excavate	exempt	exotic	exsiccate
ethanol	eulogium	evection	exceed	exemption	exoticism	exsiccant
ether	eunuch	even	excel	exequatur	exotoxic	exstrophy
ethereal	eunuchoid	evenfall	excellent	exequy	exotoxin	extant
etherify	euonymus	evensong	excelsior	exercise	expand	extend
etherize	eupatrid	event	excentric	exergue	expanse	extensile
ethic	eupepsia	eventful	except	exert	expansile	extension
ethical	eupepsy	eventide	exception	exertion	expansion	extensity
ethicize	eupeptic	eventless	exceptive	exertive	expansive	extensive
ethics	euphemism	eventual	excerpt	exesion	expatiate	extensor
ethnarch	euphemist	eventuate	excess	exfoliate	expect	extent
ethnarchy	euphemize	ever	excessive	exhalant	expectant	extenuate
ethnic	euphonic	everglade	exchange	exhale	expedient	exterior
ethnical	euphonium	evergreen	exchequer	exhaust	expedite	extern
ethnogeny	euphonize	evermore	excipient	exhibit	expel	external
ethnology	euphony	eversible	excise	exhort	expellant	extinct
ethology	euphorbia	eversion	excision	exhume	expellent	extirpate

extol
extort
extortion
extortive
extra
extract
extradite
extrados
extravert
extreme
extremism
extremist
extremity
extricate
extrinsic
extrorsal
extrorse
extrovert
extrude
extrusion
extrusive
exuberant
exuberate
exudate
exudation
exudative
exude
exult
exultance
exultancy
exultant
exuviae
exuvial
exuviate
eyas
eye
eyeball
eyebar
eyebeam
eyebolt
eyebright
eyebrow
eyecup
eyeglass
eyeground
eyehole
eyeing
eyelash
eyeless
eyelet
eyeleteer
eyelid
eyepiece
eyeserver
eyeshot
eyesight
eyesome

eyesore
eyesplice
eyespot
eyestalk
eyestone
eyestrain
eyestring
eyetooth
eyewash
eyewater
eyewinker
eying
eyrie
eyry

F

fa
fabaceous
fable
fabliau
fabliaux
fabric
fabricate
fabulist
fabulize
fabulous
face
faceplate
facet
facette
facetiae
facetious
facial
faciend
facies
facile
facility
facsimile
fact
factice
faction
factional
factious
factitive
factor
factorage
factorial
factorize
factory
factotum
factual
facula
faculae
faculty
fad
faddist
faddle

fade
fadeless
fag
fagaceous
fagot
faggot
fahlband
faience
fail
faille
failure
fain
fainaigue
faineance
faineancy
faineant
faint
faintish
fair
fairground
fairish
fairway
fairy
fairyhood
fairyism
fairyland
faith
faithful
faithless
fake
fakeer
fakir
falcate
falcated
falcation
falchion
falciform
falcon
falconet
falconry
falcula
falderal
faldstool
fall
fallacia
fallacy
fallal
fallalery
fallen
fallfish
fallow
false
falsehood
falsetto
falsework
falsify
falsity

faltboat
falter
fame
familial
familiar
family
famine
famish
famous
fan
fanatic
fanciful
fanciless
fancy
fancywork
fandango
fane
fanfare
fanfarade
fang
fangled
fanion
fanlight
fano
fanon
fantail
fantasia
fantasm
fantasmal
fantasmic
fantast
fantastic
fantasy
fantom
fanum
fanwort
far
farad
faraday
faradaic
faradic
faradism
faradize
farce
farceur
farcial
farcical
farcy
fare
farewell
farina
farinose
farm
farmhand
farmhouse
farmstead
farmyard

faro
farrago
farrier
farriery
farrow
fasces
fascia
fasciae
fascial
fasciate
fascicle
fascinate
fascine
fascism
fascist
fashion
fast
fasten
feast
fat
fatal
fatalism
fatalist
fatality
fatback
fate
fateful
fathead
father
fathom
fatidic
fatidical
fatigable
fatigue
fatling
fatten
fattish
fatty
fatuity
fatuitous
fatuoid
fatuous
faubourg
faucal
fauces
faucet
faucial
faugh
fault
faultless
faulty
faun
fauna
faunae
faunal
faunas
faveolate
favor

favorite
favose
favus
fay
fayalite
faze
fazenda
fealdike
fealty
fear
fearful
fearless
fearsome
feasance
feasible
feasor
feasibly
feast
feastful
feat
feather
feathery
feature
feaze
febricity
febricula
febrific
febrifuge
febrile
feces
fecial
feckless
fecula
feculence
feculency
feculent
fecund
fecundate
fecundity
fed
federacy
federal
federate
fedora
fee
feeble
feeblish
feed
feedback
feedbag
feel
feet
feetless
feign
feignedly
feint
feist

feldspar
feldspath
felicific
felicity
felid
feline
felinity
fell
fellah
fellaheen
felloe
fellow
felly
felon
felonious
felonry
felony
felsite
felsitic
felspar
felstone
felt
felting
felucca
female
feme
feminacy
femineity
feminine
feminish
feminism
feminist
feminity
feminize
femora
femoral
femur
fen
fence
fenceless
fencible
fend
fenestra
fenestrae
fenestral
fenestrate
fennec
fennel
fennish
fenny
fenugreek
feod
feodal
feoff
feoffee
feracious
feracity
feral

feretory
ferial
ferine
ferity
ferment
fern
fernery
fernlike
fernwort
ferny
ferocious
ferocity
ferrate
ferret
ferrety
ferriage
ferric
ferrite
ferrotype
ferrous
ferrule
ferry
ferryboat
ferryman
fertile
fertility
fertilize
ferula
ferulae
ferule
fervent
fervency
fervid
fervidity
fervor
fescue
fess
fesse
fesswise
fessewise
festal
fester
festival
festive
festivity
festoon
festoony
fetal
fetation
fetch
fete
feterita
fetial
fetich
feticide
feticidal
fetid

fetish
fetichism
fetishism
fetishist
fetlock
fetor
fetter
fettle
fetus
fetuses
feu
feuar
feud
feudal
feudalism
feudalist
feudality
feudalize
feudary
feudatory
feudist
fever
feverbush
fevered
feverfew
feverish
feverous
feverroot
feverweed
feverwort
few
fey
fez
fezzed
fiacre
fiance
fiancee
fiasco
fiat
fib
fiber
fibre
fibriform
fibril
fibrilla
fibrillae
fibrillar
fibrin
fibrinous
fibroid
fibroin
fibroma
fibromata
fibrosis
fibrous
fibula
fibulae

fibular
fice
fichu
fickle
fico
fictile
fiction
fictional
fictive
fid
fiddle
fidelity
fidge
fidget
fidgety
fiducial
fiduciary
fie
fief
field
fieldfare
fieldsman
fieldwork
fiend
fiendish
fierce
fiery
fiesta
fife
fifteen
fifteenth
fifth
fiftieth
fifty.
fig
fight
figment
figuline
figural
figurant
figurante
figurate
figure
figurine
figwort
fike
filagree
filament
filar
filaria
filarial
filarian
filature
filbert
filch
file
filefish

filet
filial
filiate
filiation
filibeg
filicide
filicidal
filicoid
filiform
filigree
fillagree
fillet
fillip
fillister
filly
film
filmy
filose
filter
filth
filthy
filtrable
filtrate
fimbriate
fin
finagle
final
finale
finalist
finality
finance
financial
financier
finback
finch
find
findings
fine
finery
finesse
finetop
finfish
fingent
finger
finial
finic
finical
finikin
finis
finises
finish
finite
finitude
finnicky
finny
fiord
fipple

fique
fir
fire
firearm
fireback
fireball
firebird
fireboard
firebox
firebrand
firebrat
firebreak
firebrick
firedamp
firedog
firedrake
firefang
firefly
firefoam
fireguard
firehouse
fireirons
fireless
firelock
fireman
firenew
firepan
firepink
fireplace
fireplug
firepower
fireproof
fireroom
fireside
firestone
firetrap
firewall
firewater
fireweed
firewood
fireworks
fireworm
firkin
firlot
firm
firmament
firman
firmaun
firn
firry
first
firstly
fiscal
fishbolt
fishbone
fisher
fisherman

fishery
fishgig
fishgrass
fishmeal
fishnet
fishpot
fishpound
fishskin
fishspear
fishway
fishwife
fishy
fissate
fissile
fissility
fission
fissiped
fissure
fist
fistic
fisticuff
fistula
fistular
fistulous
fistulate
fistwise
fit
fitch
fitchet
fitchew
fitchole
fitful
fiumara
fiumaras
fiumare
five
fivefold
fivepence
fivepenny
fiver
fix
fixate
fixation
fixative
fixity
fixture
fizgig
fizz
fizzle
fizzy
fjord
flabby
flaccid
flag
flagella
flagellum
flageolet

flaggy
flagman
flagon
flagpole
flagrance
flagrancy
flagrant
flagship
flagstaff
flagstone
flail
flair
flak
flake
flakship
flaky
flam
flambeau
flambeaux
flame
flamen
flamenco
flamingo
flamingos
flammable
flamy
flan
flanch
flange
flank
flannel
flannelet
flanque
flap
flapjack
flare
flash
flashy
flask
flasket
flat
flatboat
flatfish
flatfoot
flatten
flatter
flattery
flattish
flatulent
flatuous
flatus
flatware
flatways
flatwise
flatwork
flatworm
flaunt

flaunty	flickery	flow	flyblow	foliose	footstalk	foregone
flautist	flied	flowage	flyblown	folium	footstall	foregut
flavin	flight	flower	flyboat	folk	footstep	forehand
flavism	flighty	flowerage	flyframe	folkfree	footstock	forehead
flavone	flimsies	floweret	flyleaf	folkland	footstone	foreign
flavor	flimsy	flowery	flynet	folklore	footstool	foreigner
flavorous	flinch	flown	flypaper	folkmoot	footstove	forejudge
flavous	flinder	flubdub	flyspeck	folkmote	footway	foreknow
flaw	fling	fluctuant	flystone	folkright	footwear	foreknew
flawless	flint	fluctuate	flytrap	folkways	footwork	foreknown
flawy	flinty	flue	flyweight	follicle	foozle	forelaid
flax	flip	fluent	flywheel	follow	fop	forelady
flaxen	flippant	fluey	flys	folly	fopling	foreland
flaxseed	flippancy	fluency	foal	foment	foppery	forelay
flaxwort	flipper	fluff	foam	fomes	foppish	foreleg
flaxy	flirt	fluffy	foamless	fomites	for	forelock
flay	flirty	fluid	foamy	fond	fora	foreman
flea	flit	fluidal	fob	fondant	forage	foremast
fleabane	flitch	fluidic	focal	fondle	foramen	foremost
fleam	float	fluidity	focalize	fondue	foramina	forename
fleawort	floaty	fluidram	foci	font	foray	forenenst
fleck	floatage	fluke	focus	fontal	forb	forenoon
fleckless	floccule	flukey	focuses	fontanel	forbad	forensic
flecky	flocculi	fluky	fodder	food	forbade	forepart
flection	flocculus	flume	foe	foodstuff	forbear	forepast
fled	floccus	fluminous	foeman	fool	forbid	forepeak
fledge	flock	flummery	foetal	foolery	forbidden	foreran
fledgling	floe	flung	foetation	foolhardy	forbore	forerank
fledgy	flog	flunkey	foetus	foolish	forborne	forereach
flee	flood	flunky	fog	foolproof	force	forerun
fleece	floodgate	fluor	fogey	foolscap	forceful	foresaid
fleecy	floorage	fluoresce	fogbow	foot	forcemeat	foresail
fleer	flooring	fluoric	fogfruit	footage	forceps	foresaw
fleet	flop	fluorid	foggage	football	ford	foresee
flench	floppy	fluoride	foggy	footboard	fordless	foreseen
flense	flora	fluorin	foghorn	footboy	fordid	foreseer
flesh	floral	fluorine	fogie	footcloth	fordo	foresheet
fleshpot	florence	fluorite	fogram	footfall	fordoing	foreshore
fleshy	floret	fluorosis	fogy	footgear	fordone	foreshow
fletch	floriated	fluorspar	fogyish	footguard	fore	foreshew
fletcher	florid	flurry	fogyism	foothill	forearm	foreside
fleured	floridity	flush	foh	foothold	forebear	foresight
fleury	florin	fluster	foible	footle	forebode	foreskin
flew	florist	flustrate	foil	footless	forebrace	forest
flewed	floss	flute	foilsman	footling	forebrain	forested
flews	flossy	fluted	foist	footlog	forecast	forestage
flex	flotage	fluting	fold	footloose	forecited	forestall
flexile	flotation	flutist	foldboat	footman	foreclose	forestay
flexion	flotilla	flutter	folderol	footmark	foredate	forester
flexional	flotsam	fluttery	folia	footnote	foredeck	forestral
flexor	flotsan	fluty	foliage	footpace	foredo	forestry
flexuose	flotson	fluvial	foliaged	footpad	foredoom	foretaste
flexuous	flounce	fluviatic	foliar	footpath	forefeel	foretell
flexural	flounder	flux	foliate	footprint	forefelt	forethink
flexure	flour	fluxation	foliation	footrest	forefend	foretime
fliaum	flourish	fluxion	foliature	footrope	forefoot	foretoken
flick	floury	fluxional	folio	foots	forefront	foretold
flicker	flout	fly	foliolate	footsore	forego	foretop

forever
forewarn
forewent
forewoman
foreword
foreyard
forfeit
forficate
forgather
forgave
forge
forgery
forget
forgetful
forgetive
forgive
forgo
forgone
forgot
forgotten
forjudge
fork
forked
forky
forlorn
form
formal
formalism
formalist
formality
formalize
formally
format
formate
formation
formative
former
formic
formicant
formicary
formicate
formless
formula
formulae
formulary
formulate
formulism
formulize
formyl
fornicate
forsake
forsaken
forsook
forsooth
forspeak
forspent
forswear
forswore

forsworn
forsythia
fort
fortalice
forte
fortes
forth
forthwith
fortieth
fortify
fortis
fortitude
fortress
fortuity
fortunate
fortune
forty
forum
forward
forwent
forworn
foss
fossa
fossae
fosse
fossick
fossil
fossilist
fossilize
fossorial
foster
fosterage
fostress
fouadin
fought
foul
foulard
foumart
foulimart
found
foundery
foundling
foundry
fount
fountain
four
fourfold
fourpence
fourscore
foursome
fourteen
fourth
foveate
foveola
foveolae
foveolate
foveole
foveolet

fowl
fox
foxbane
foxberry
foxfire
foxfish
foxglove
foxhole
foxhound
foxhunt
foxskin
foxtail
foxtrot
foxwood
foxy
foyer
fracas
fraction
fractious
fractural
fracture
fragile
fragility
fragment
fragrance
fragrancy
fragrant
frail
frailty
fraiter
fraitor
frambesia
frame
framework
franc
franchise
francolin
frangible
frank
franklin
frantic
frap
fraternal
fraud
fraudful
fraudless
fraught
fray
frazil
frazzle
freak
freakish
freaky
freckle
freckly
free
freeboard
freeboot

freebooty
freedman
freedom
freehand
freehold
freeman
freesia
freeze
freight
freighter
frenetic
frenum
frena
frenzied
frenzy
frequence
frequency
frequent
fresco
frescoes
frescoist
frescos
fresh
freshen
freshet
freshman
fresno
fret
fretful
fretty
fretwork
friable
friar
friarbird
friary
fribble
fricassee
fricative
friction
friend
frieze
frigate
fright
frighten
frightful
frigid
frigidity
frijol
frijole
frijoles
frill
frilly
fringe
fringy
fripper
frippery
frisette
friseur

frisk
frisky
frit
fritt
fritter
frivolity
frivolous
frizette
friz
frizz
frizzle
fro
frock
froe
frog
frogbit
frogfish
froggery
froggy
frolic
frolicky
from
fromenty
frond
fronded
front
frontage
frontal
frontier
frontless
frontlet
fronton
frore
frost
frostbite
frostfish
frostweed
frostwork
frostwort
frosty
froth
frother
frothy
frounce
frouzy
frow
froward
frown
frowzled
frowzy
froze
frozen
fructify
fructose
fructuous
frugal
frugality
frugally

fruit
fruitage
fruiter
fruitful
fruition
fruitless
fruity
frumenty
frump
frumpish
frumpy
frusta
frustrate
frustule
frustum
frustums
fruticose
fry
fuadin
fub
fubsy
fuchsia
fuchsin
fuchsine
fucoid
fucoidal
fucous
fucus
fucuses
fuddle
fuder
fudge
fuel
fugacious
fugacity
fugio
fugitive
fugle
fugleman
fugue
fulcra
fulcrum
fulfil
fulfill
fulgency
fulgent
fulgid
fulgurate
fulgurite
fulgurous
fulham
full
fullam
fullery
fully
fulmar
fulminant
fulminate

fulmine
fulminic
fulminous
fulsome
fulvous
fumaric
fumarole
fumatoria
fumatory
fumble
fume
fumet
fumette
fumigant
fumigate
fumitory
fumulus
fumy
fun
function
fund
fundament
funeral
funereal
funest
fungal
fungi
fungible
fungicide
fungoid
fungous
fungus
funguses
fungiform
funicle
funicular
funiculus
funnel
funny
fur
furan
furane
furbelow
furbish
furcal
furcate
furcraea
furcula
furculum
furfur
furfural
furfuran
furfures
furfurol
furibund
furious
furl
furlong

furlough
furmenty
furmety
furmity
furnace
furnish
furniture
furor
furore
furrier
furriery
furrow
furry
further
furthest
furtive
furuncle
fury
furze
furzy
fusain
fuscous
fuse
fusee
fusel
fuselage
fusifórm
fusil
fusilade
fusile
fusillade
fusion
fusionism
fusionist
fuss
fussy
fust
fustian
fustic
fustigate
fusty
futhorc
futhork
futile
futility
futtock
futural
future
futurism
futurity
fuze
fuzee
fuzil
fuzz
fuzzy
fyke
fylfot

G

gab
gabardine
gabble
gabbro
gabbroid
gabel
gabelle
gabelled
gaberdine
gabion
gabionade
gable
gad
gadabout
gadbee
gadfly
gadid
gadoid
gadroon
gadsman
gadwall
gaff
gaffer
gaffle
gag
gage
gaggle
gagman
gahnite
gaiety
gaily
gain
gainful
gainless
gainly
gainsaid
gainsay
gairish
gait
gaited
gala
galactic
galactose
galangal
galantine
galax
galaxy
galbanum
gale
galea
galeae
galeate
galeated
galeiform
galena

galenite
galenical
galingale
galiot
galipea
galipot
gall
gallant
gallantry
gallberry
galleass
galleon
gallery
galley
gallfly
galliard
gallic
gallinazo
gallinule
galliot
gallipot
gallium
galliwasp
gallnut
gallon
gallonage
galloon
gallop
gallopade
gallows
gallowses
gallstone
gallus
galop
galopade
galore
galosh
galoshe
galvanic
galvanism
galvanist
galvanize
galyak
gam
gamb
gambade
gambado
gambadoes
gambados
gambit
gamble
gamboge
gambol
gambrel
game
gamesome
gamester

gamete
gametic
gamic
gamin
gaming
gamma
gammacism
gammadia
gammadion
gammation
gammon
gamomania
gamp
gamut
gamy
ganef
gang
ganglia
gangliate
ganglion
ganglioid
gangplank
gangrene
gangster
gangue
gangway
ganister
gannet
gannister
ganof
ganoid
gantlet
gantline
gantlope
gantry
gap
gape
gapeseed
gapeworm
gappy
gapy
gar
garage
garb
garbage
garbel
garble
garboard
gardant
garden
gardenia
garderobe
garfish
garganey
garget
gargle
gargoyle

gargoyled
garibaldi
garish
garishly
garland
garlic
garlicky
garment
garner
garnet
garnish
garnishee
garniture
garote
garotte
garpike
garret
garreteer
garrison
garrote
garrotte
garruline
garrulity
garrulous
garter
gas
gascon
gasconade
gaselier
gaseous
gases
gash
gasifier
gasiform
gasify
gasket
gaskin
gasking
gasman
gasogene
gasolene
gasolier
gasoline
gasometer
gasometry
gasp
gassing
gassy
gastrin
gastritic
gastritis
gastropod
gastrula
gastrulae
gastrular
gat
gate

gateage
gatehouse
gateman
gatepost
gateway
gather
gating
gauche
gaucherie
gaud
gaudery
gaudy
gauffer
gauge
gaunt
gauntlet
gauntree
gauntry
gaur
gauss
gauze
gauzy
gave
gavel
gavelkind
gavial
gavot
gavotte
gawk
gawky
gay
gayety
gaywings
gaze
gazebo
gazeboes
gazebos
gazehound
gazelle
gazette
gazetteer
gear
gearcase
gearshift
gearwheel
geck
gecko
geckoes
geckos
gee
geepound
geese
gel
gelatin
gelatine
gelation
geld

gelding
gelid
gelidity
gelsemine
gelsemium
gem
gemel
geminate
gemmate
gemmation
gemmeous
gemmology
gemmule
gemmy
gemot
gemote
gemsbok
gender
gene
genealogy
genera
generable
general
generalcy
generalty
generate
generic
generical
generous
geneses
genesis
genet
genetic
genetical
genetics
genette
geneva
geniality
genic
genie
genii
genion
genital
genitival
genitive
genitor
geniture
genius
geniuses
genocide
genom
genome
genotype
genotypic
genro
gens
genteel

gentes
gentian
gentile
gentilism
gentility
gentle
gentleman
gentry
genuflect
genuine
genus
geobion
geobotany
geode
geodesic
geodesist
geodesy
geodetic
geodic
geognosy
geography
geoid
geologer
geologic
geologist
geologize
geology
geomancer
geomancy
geomantic
geometer
geometric
geometrid
geometry
geophagy
geophyte
geoponic
geoponics
georgette
georgic
georgical
geostatic
geotaxis
geotropic
geranial
geranium
gerbil
gerbille
gerent
gerenuk
gerfalcon
gerkin
germ
german
germander
germane
germanium

germicide
germinant
germinate
gerontal
gerund
gerundial
gerundive
gesso
gest
gestate
gestation
gestatory
geste
gestic
gestical
gesture
get
gettable
geyser
geyserite
ghastly
gherkin
ghetti
ghetto
ghettos
ghost
ghostlike
ghoul
giant
giantess
giantism
giaour
gib
gibber
gibberish
gibbet
gibbon
gibbosity
gibbous
gibbose
gibe
giblet
gibus
gid
giddy
gift
gifted
gig
gigantean
gigantic
gigantism
giggle
gigolo
gigolos
gigot
gilbert
gild

gildhall
gildry
gill
gilsonite
gilt
gilthead
gimbals
gimcrack
gimel
gimlet
gimp
gin
gingal
gingall
gingeley
gingeli
ginger
gingery
gingival
ginglymi
ginglymus
ginseng
gip
gipon
gipsify
gipsy
gipsyish
gipsyism
giraffe
girandole
girasol
girasole
gird
girderage
girdle
girl
girlhood
girlish
giro
girosol
girt
girth
gisement
gist
gitano
gitanos
gittern
gittith
giunta
give
gizzard
glabella
glabellae
glabrate
glabrous
glace
glacial

glaciate
glacier
glacis
glad
gladden
glade
gladiate
gladiator
gladiola
gladiole
gladioli
gladiolus
gladsome
glair
glaire
glaireous
glairy
glamor
glamour
glamorous
glance
gland
glandered
glanders
glandular
glandule
glandes
glans
glare
glary
glass
glassful
glassine
glassman
glassware
glasswool
glasswork
glasswort
glassy
glaucedo
glaucoma
glaucous
glaze
glazy
glaziery
gleam
gleamy
glean
glebe
gled
glede
glee
gleeful
gleesome
gleet
gleety
glen

glenoid
gliadin
glib
glide
glimmer
glimpse
glint
glioma
gliomata
gliosa
glissade
glissandi
glissando
glisten
glister
glitter
glittery
gloam
gloaming
gloat
global
globate
globated
globe
globefish
globin
globoid
globose
globosity
globous
globular
globule
globulin
globulous
glomerate
glomerule
glonoin
glonoine
gloom
glooming
gloomy
gloria
glorify
gloriole
glorious
glory
gloss
glossa
glossae
glossal
glossary
glossator
glossitic
glossitis
glossy
glost
glottal

glottic
glottides
glottis
glove
glow
glower
glowfly
glowworm
gloxinia
gloze
glucinium
glucinum
glucose
glucosic
glucoside
gluey
glum
glume
glut
glutamic
glutamine
gluteal
glutelin
gluten
glutenous
glutei
gluteus
glutinous
glutton
gluttony
glyceric
glycerid
glyceride
glycerin
glycerine
glycerol
glyceryl
glycin
glycine
glycocoll
glycogen
glycol
glycoside
glyph
glyphic
glyptic
glyptics
gnar
gnarl
gnarly
gnarr
gnash
gnat
gnathic
gnathion
gnathonic
gnaw

gneiss
gneissic
gneissoid
gnome
gnomic
gnomical
gnomish
gnomology
gnomon
gnomonic
gnomonics
gnosis
gnostic
gnostical
gnu
go
goa
goad
goadsman
goal
goalie
goanna
goat
goatbeard
goatee
goatfish
goatherd
goatish
goatlike
goatsrue
gob
goban
gobang
gobbe
gobbet
gobble
gobies
goblet
goblin
gobo
gobstick
goby
gocart
god
godchild
goddess
godfather
godhead
godhood
godless
godlike
godling
godly
godmother
godown
godparent
godroon

godrooned	goodish	gown	granite	gravitate	gridiron	grogram
godsend	goods	gownman	granitic	gravity	grief	grogshop
godship	goody	gownsman	granitoid	gravure	grievance	groin
godson	googly	gownsmen	granivore	gravy	grieve	grommet
godwit	googol	graal	grannie	gray	grievous	gromwell
goethite	gooney	grab	grannies	grayback	griff	groom
goffer	goop	grabble	granny	graybeard	griffe	groomsman
goggle	gooral	graben	grant	grayfish	griffin	groove
goglet	goosander	grace	grantee	grayish	griffon	grope
goiter	goose	graceful	grantor	graylag	grifter	grosbeak
goitre	gooses	graceless	granular	grayling	grig	grosgrain
goitrous	goosefoot	gracile	granulate	graywacke	grigri	gross
gold	gooseherd	gracility	granule	graze	grill	grot
goldbrick	gooseneck	gracious	granulite	grazier	grillage	grotesque
goldbug	goosy	grackle	granulose	grease	grille	grotto
golden	goosey	gradate	granulous	greasy	grillroom	grottoes
goldeneye	gopher	gradation	grape	great	grilse	grottos
goldenrod	goral	gradatory	grapery	greatcoat	grilses	grouch
goldfinch	gore	grade	grapeshot	greaten	grim	grouchy
goldfinny	gorge	gradient	grapevine	greaves	grimace	ground
goldfish	gorgeous	gradin	graph	grebe	grimalkin	groundage
goldsmith	gorgerin	gradine	graphic	greed	grime	groundnut
goldstick	gorget	gradual	graphical	greedy	grimy	groundsel
goldstone	gorgon	graduale	graphics	greegree	grin	group
golf	gorgonean	graduate	graphite	green	grind	grouse
golgotha	gorgonian	gradus	graphitic	greenback	grindelia	grout
goliard	gorgoneia	graft	graplin	greenbelt	grindery	grouty
goliardic	gorgoneum	graftage	grapline	greenery	grindle	grove
golliwog	gorgonize	grail	grapnel	greenfly	gringo	grovel
golliwogg	gorhen	grain	grapple	greengage	gringos	grow
gombroon	gorilla	graine	grapy	greenhead	grip	growl
gomphosis	gormand	grainy	grasp	greenhorn	gripe	grown
gonad	gorse	gram	grass	greening	gripy	growth
gonadal	gorsy	grama	grassland	greenish	grippe	grub
gonadial	gory	gramma	grassplot	greenlet	grippy	grubby
gonadic	gosh	gramary	grasstree	greenling	gripsack	grubstake
gondola	goshawk	gramarye	grassy	greenroom	grisaille	grudge
gondolier	gosling	grammarye	grate	greensand	griseous	gruel
gone	gospel	grammar	grateful	greenth	grisette	gruesome
goneness	gossamer	grammatic	gratify	greenwood	grisly	gruff
gonfalon	gossamery	gramme	gratinate	greet	grison	gruffish
gonfanon	gossip	grampus	gratis	gregarine	grist	gruffy
gong	gossipry	granary	gratitude	grego	gristle	grum
gonia	gossipy	grand	gratuity	greige	gristmill	grumble
gonidia	got	grandam	gratulant	greisen	grit	grume
gonidial	gothic	grandame	gratulate	gremial	gritty	grummet
gonidium	gotten	grandaunt	graul	gremlin	grivet	grumose
gonion	gouache	grandee	graupel	grenade	grizzle	grumous
gonium	gouge	grandeur	gravamen	grenadier	grizzly	grumpy
gonocci	goulash	grandiose	gravamina	grenadine	groan	grunion
gonof	goumier	grandma	grave	grew	groat	grunt
gonoph	gourd	grandmama	gravel	grewsome	groats	gryllid
gonophore	gourmand	grandsir	graven	greyhound	grocer	guacharo
gonorrhea	gourmet	grandsire	graves	gribble	grocery	guaiac
gony	gout	grandson	graveyard	grid	grog	guaiacol
good	gouty	grange	gravid	griddle	groggery	guaiacum
goodbye	govern	graniform	gravidity	gride	groggy	guan
	governess					

guanaco	gula	gusty	habit	hairbird	halt	hanse
guanase	gulae	gut	habitancy	hairbrush	halting	hansel
guanidin	gulash	gutta	habitant	haircloth	halter	hansom
guanidine	gulch	guttae	habitat	haircut	halteres	hanuman
guanin	gulden	guttate	habitual	hairline	halve	hap
guanine	gules	guttated	habituate	hairpin	halves	haphazard
guano	gulf	gutte	habitude	hairseal	halyard	hapless
guanos	gulfweed	guttee	habitue	hairshirt	ham	haplite
guarantee	gulfy	gutty	habu	hairspace	hamadryad	haplitic
guarantor	gull	guttery	hachure	hairworm	hamburg	haploid
guaranty	gullet	guttural	hacienda	hairy	hamburger	haploidic
guard	gullies	guy	hack	haj	hame	haplosis
guardian	gully	guzzle	hackberry	haje	hamlet	haply
guardrail	gulp	gybe	hackbut	haji	hammer	happen
guardroom	gum	gymbals	hackee	hajj	hammertoe	happy
guardsman	gumboil	gymnasium	hackery	hajji	hammock	haptere
guava	gumdrop	gymnast	hackle	hake	hammy	haptera
guayule	gumma	gymnastic	hackly	hakeem	hamper	hapteron
gudgeon	gummata	gynander	hackman	hakem	hamster	harangue
guenon	gummatous	gynandry	hackney	hakim	hamstring	harass
guerdon	gummosis	gynarchic	hacksaw	halachist	hamulate	harbinger
guernsey	gummous	gynarchy	had	halation	hamuli	harbor
guerrilla	gummy	gyne	haddock	halbard	hamulus	harborage
guess	gumshoe	gynecea	hade	halberd	hanaper	hard
guesswork	gumwood	gyneceum	hadj	halbert	hance	harden
guest	gun	gynics	hadjee	halcyon	hand	hardhack
guff	gunboat	gynobase	hadji	hale	handbag	hardhead
guffaw	guncotton	gynobasic	hafiz	haler	handball	hardihood
guha	gunfire	gynoecium	hafnium	half	handbill	hardly
guidance	gunflint	gynophore	haft	halfback	handbook	hardpan
guide	gunlock	gypsum	hag	halfbeak	handcuff	hards
guidebook	gunman	gypseous	hagadic	halfcrown	handed	hardshell
guidepost	gunnel	gyral	hagberry	halfpenny	handfast	hardship
guiderope	gunnery	gyrant	hagbush	halibut	handful	hardtack
guideway	gunny	gyrate	hagbut	halic	handgrip	hardware
guidon	gunpaper	gyration	hagdel	halid	handicap	hardwood
guild	gunpowder	gyratory	hagden	halide	handiwork	hardy
guilder	gunroom	gyre	hagdon	halidom	handle	hare
guildhall	gunrunner	gyrfalcon	hagfish	halite	handlebar	harebell
guildship	gunshot	gyro	haggadic	halitosis	handless	harelip
guildsman	gunsmith	gyron	haggadist	hall	handmaid	harem
guile	gunstock	gyroplane	haggard	halliard	handsel	haricot
guileful	gunwale	gyroscope	haggish	hallmark	handset	hark
guileless	guppy	gyrostat	haggle	hallo	handsome	harkee
guillemot	gurge	gyri	hagiarchy	halloa	handspike	harken
guilloche	gurgle	gyrus	hagiology	halloo	handwork	harl
guillotine	gurglet	gyve	haglet	hallow	handy	harlequin
guilt	gurnard		haglin	halluces	hang	harlot
guiltless	gurnet	**H**	hagseed	hallux	hangar	harlotry
guilty	gush	ha	hah	hallway	hangbird	harm
guimpe	gushy	haaf	haik	halm	hangdog	harmful
guinea	gusset	haak	hail	halma	hangfire	harmless
guipure	gust	habanera	haily	halo	hangman	harmonic
guise	gustation	habenda	hailstone	halobios	hangnail	harmonica
guitar	gustative	habendum	hailstorm	halogen	hangwire	harmonics
guitguit	gustatory	habergeon	hair	haloid	hank	harmonist
guja	gusto	habile	hairless	halophyte	hanker	harmonium

harmonize	haunch	headmost	hebetate	helicon	hemipter	herby
harmony	haunched	headphone	hebetic	heliogram	hemistich	herculean
harmotome	haunt	headpiece	hebetude	heliology	hemitrope	herd
harness	haustella	headpin	hecatomb	heliostat	hemlock	herdic
harp	haustoria	headrace	heckle	heliotype	hemoid	herdgrass
harpings	hautboy	headrest	hectare	heliotypy	hemolysin	herdman
harpins	hauteur	headright	hectic	helium	hemolysis	herdsman
harpist	have	headsail	hectical	helix	hemolytic	here
harpoon	havelock	headset	hectogram	helixes	hemophile	hereabout
harpy	haven	headship	hector	hell	hemostat	hereafter
harquebus	haverel	headsman	heddle	hellbroth	hemp	hereat
harridan	haversack	headspin	hedge	hellcat	hempen	hereby
harrow	haversine	headstall	hedgy	helldiver	hempseed	heredity
harrowing	havoc	headstock	hedgehog	hellebore	hempy	herein
harry	havocked	headstone	hedgehop	heller	hemstitch	hereinto
harsh	havocking	headwater	hedgerow	hellfire	hen	hereof
harshen	havrel	headway	hedonic	hellhound	henbane	hereon
harslet	haw	headwork	hedonics	hellion	henbit	heresy
hart	hawfinch	heady	hedonism	hellish	hence	heretic
hartal	hawk	heal	hedonist	hellkite	henchman	heretical
hartbeest	hawkbill	heald	heed	hello	hencoop	hereto
hartshorn	hawkweed	health	heedful	helm	hendiadys	hereunto
haruspex	hawse	healthful	heedless	helmet	henequen	hereupon
haruspicy	hawthorn	healthy	heel	helmeted	henequin	herewith
harvest	hay	heap	heelpiece	helminth	henhussy	heriot
has	haycock	hear	heelpost	helmsman	henna	heritable
hash	hayfork	heard	heeltap	helophyte	hennery	heritably
hasheesh	hayloft	hearken	heft	helotism	henpeck	heritage
hashish	haymaker	hearsay	hegemony	helotry	henroost	heritor
haslet	haymow	hearse	hegemonic	help	henry	heritrix
haslock	hayrack	heart	hegira	helpful	hepar	herl
hasp	hayrick	heartache	hegumen	helpless	heparin	herma
hassock	hayseed	heartbeat	hegumenos	helpmate	hepatic	hermae
hast	haystack	heartburn	hegumene	helpmeet	hepatica	hermes
hastate	hayward	hearted	hegumeny	helve	hepaticae	hermetic
haste	hazard	hearten	heifer	hem	hepatical	hermit
hasten	hazardous	heartfree	heigh	hemal	hepaticas	hermitage
hasty	haze	hearth	height	hematal	hepatitis	hermitic
hat	hazel	heartless	heighten	hematein	heptad	hern
hatband	hazelly	heartseed	heinous	hematic	heptaglot	hernia
hatbox	hazelnut	heartsick	heir	hematin	heptagon	hernial
hatch	hazy	heartsore	heiress	hematinic	heptane	hernshaw
hatchway	he	heartsome	heirless	hematite	heptarchy	hero
hatchel	head	heartwood	heirloom	hematitic	heptode	heroic
hatchery	headache	heartworm	heirdom	hematoid	her	heroical
hatchet	headachy	hearty	heirship	hematoma	herald	heroin
hate	headband	heat	hejira	hematose	heraldic	heroine
hateful	headboard	heath	hektare	hematosis	heraldry	heroism
hath	headdress	heathen	hektogram	hematozoa	herb	heron
hatred	headfirst	heathenry	helcosis	hematuria	herbage	heronbill
hatteria	headgear	heather	helcotic	hemelytra	herbal	heronry
hauberk	headland	heathery	heliac	hemialgia	herbalist	herpes
haughty	headless	heathy	heliacal	hemic	herbaria	herpetic
haul	headlight	heaume	heliast	hemicrany	herbarium	herpetism
haulage	headline	heave	helical	hemicycle	herbary	herring
haulm	headliner	heaven	helices	hemihedra	herbicide	herse
haulmy	headlock	heavy	helicline	hemin	herbist	herself
haulyard	headlong	hebdomad	helicoid	hemiplegy	herbivore	hesitance

hesitancy	hiddenite	hircine	hod	holt	honeycomb	hornbook
hesitant	hide	hire	hodiernal	holy	honeydew	hornless
hesitate	hidebound	hireling	hodograph	holystone	honeymoon	hornet
hesp	hideous	hirsute	hodometer	holytide	honeypot	hornpipe
hessian	hidrosis	hirudin	hodoscope	homage	hong	hornstone
hessite	hidrotic	hirudo	hoe	home	honk	horntail
hessonite	hie	hirundine	hoecake	homeless	honor	hornworm
het	hielaman	his	hog	homelike	honoraria	hornwort
hetaera	hiemal	hispid	hogan	homemaker	honorary,	horny
hetaira	hierarch	hispidity	hogback	homeopath	honorific	horologe
hetairai	hierarchy	hiss	hogchain	homerule	hoo	horologer
hetaerism	hieratic	hist	hogfish	homesick	hooch	horologic
hetairism	hieratica	histamine	hoggish	homespun	hoochinoo	horology
heterodox	hierodule	histidine	hognose	homestake	hood	horoscope
heteronym	hierogram	histioid	hognut	homestead	hoodlum	horoscopy
heterosis	hierology	histoid	hogscore	homeward	hoodman	horrent
hetman	higgle	histogeny	hogshead	homework	hoodoo	horrible
hetmans	high	histogram	hogsucker	homicidal	hoodwink	horrid
heuristic	highball	histology	hogtight	homicide	hoof	horrific
hew	highboy	histon	hogwallow	homilist	hoofprint	horrify
hewn	highland	histone	hogwash	homily	hook	horror
hexabasic	highlight	historian	hogweed	hominal	hooka	horse
hexachord	highroad	historic	hoicks	hominy	hookah	horseback
hexad	hight	historied	hoiden	hommock	hookworm	horseboat
hexadic	highway	historify	hoigh	hommocky	hooky	horseboot
hexagon	hike	history	hoist	homo	hooligan	horsebot
hexagonal	hila	hit	holard	homocercy	hoop	horseboy
hexagram	hilarious	hitch	holcodont	homodyne	hoople	horsefish
hexahedra	hilarity	hither	hold	homogamic	hoopoe	horsefly
hexameral	hill	hitherto	holdback	homogamy	hoopoo	horsefoot
hexameter	hillman	hive	holdfast	homogen	hooray	horsehair
hexane	hillo	ho	holdover	homogene	hoot	horsehead
hexapod	hilloa	hoa	hole	homogeny	hootch	horseless
hexapody	hillock	hoactzin	holey	homogony	hooves	horseman
hexarchy	hillocky	hoar	holibut	homograde	hooy	horsemint
hexastich	hillside	hoard	holiday	homograph	hop	horseplay
hexastyle	hilltop	hoarfrost	holiness	homolog	hopcalite	horsepond
hexone	hilly	hoarhound	holla	homologue	hope	horserake
hexosan	hilt	hoarse	holland	homologic	hopeful	horseshoe
hexose	hilum	hoarsen	hollo	homology	hopeless	horsetail
hexyl	hilus	hoary	holloa	homonym	hopesick	horseweed
hey	him	hoatzin	hollocain	homonyme	hoplite	horsewhip
heyday	himself	hoazin	hollow	homonymic	hopple	horst
hiaqua	hind	hoax	holly	homonymy	hopscotch	horste
hiatus	hindbrain	hob	hollyhock	homophone	horal	horsey
hiatuses	hinder	hobble	holm	homophony	horarious	horsy
hibernal	hindgut	hobby	holmia	homoplasy	horary	hortative
hibernate	hindmost	hobgoblin	holmic	homopolar	horde	hortatory
hibiscus	hindrance	hobnail	holmium	homospory	hordein	hosanna
hiccough	hindsight	hobnob	holocain	homostyly	hordenine	hose
hiccup	hinge	hobo	holocaine	homotaxis	horehound	hosier
hickey	hinny	hoboes	holocaust	homotaxic	horizon	hosiery
hickory	hint	hobos	holograph	homy	hormonal	hospice
hickup	hip	hoboism	holophote	hone	hormone	hospital
hid	hipparch	hock	holophyte	honest	hormonic	hospitia
hidalga	hippiatry	hockey	holotype	honesty	horn	hospitium
hidalgo	hippocras	hockshop	holozoic	honewort	hornbeam	hospodar
hidden	hippus	hocus	holster	honey	hornbill	host

hostage	hub	humpy	hydrangea	hymnodist	hyssop	identical
hostel	hubble	humus	hydrant	hymnody	hysteria	identify
hosteler	hubbly	hunch	hydranth	hymnology	hysteric	identity
hosteller	hubbub	hunchback	hydrate	hyoid	hysteroid	ideograph
hostelry	huck	hundred	hydration	hyoscine	hyther	ideogram
hostess	huckaback	hundredth	hydraulic	hypallage		ideologic
hostile	huckabuck	hung	hydrazine	hyperacid	**I**	ideology
hostility	huckle	hunger	hydrazoic	hyperbola		ideomotor
hostler	huckster	hungry	hydric	hyperbole	iamb	ideophone
hostlery	huddle	hunkerish	hydrid	hyperemia	iambi	ides
hot	hue	hunkerism	hydride	hyperemic	iambic	idioblast
hotbed	huff	hunks	hydriodic	hyperpnea	iambus	idiocrasy
hotbox	huffish	hunt	hydrocele	hypethral	iatric	idiocy
hotchpot	huffy	huntress	hydrogen	hypha	iatrical	idiograph
hotel	hug	huntsman	hydroid	hyphae	ibex	idiom
hotfoot	huge	hurdle	hydrology	hyphal	ibis	idiomatic
hothead	hula	hurds	hydromel	hypheme	iboga	idiopathy
hothouse	hulk	hurl	hydropath	hyphemia	ice	idioplasm
hotpot	hulking	hurra	hydropic	hyphaemia	iceberg	idiot
hotpress	hulky	hurrah	hydrops	hyphen	iceblink	idiotic
hotspur	hull	hurricane	hydropsia	hyphenate	iceboat	idiotical
houdah	hullo	hurry	hydropsy	hyphenize	icebone	idiotism
hound	hum	hurt	hydrosere	hypnic	icebox	idle
hour	human	hurtful	hydrosol	hypnoidal	icefall	idly
hourglass	humane	hurtle	hydrosoma	hypnology	icehouse	idocrase
houri	humanism	hurtless	hydrosome	hypnoses	iceman	idol
hourly	humanist	husband	hydrostat	hypnosis	icequake	idolater
house	humanity	husbandry	hydrous	hypnotic	ichneumon	idolatry
housecarl	humanize	hush	hydroxide	hypnotism	ichnite	idolism
houseful	humankind	husk	hydroxy	hypnotist	ichnolite	idolize
household	humble	husky	hydroxyl	hypnotize	ichorous	idoneous
houseleek	humbly	hussar	hyena	hypoblast	ichthyic	idyl
houseline	humblebee	hussy	hyetal	hypocaust	ichthyoid	idylist
housemaid	humbug	husting	hyetology	hypocotyl	icicle	idyll
houseroom	humdrum	hustle	hygiene	hypocrisy	icily	idyllist
housetop	humeral	hut	hygienic	hypocrite	icon	idyllic
houseware	humeri	hutch	hygienics	hypoderm	icones	idyllical
housewife	humerus	huzza	hygeist	hypoderma	iconic	if
housework	humic	huzzah	hygieist	hypogea	iconical	igloo
houslin	humid	huzzay	hygienist	hypogeal	iconology	iglu
hove	humidify	hyacinth	hyla	hypogene	icons	ignatia
hovel	humidity	hyaline	hylic	hypogeous	icteric	igneous
hover	humidor	hyalite	hylicism	hypogeum	icterical	ignescent
now	humiliate	hyalogen	hylicist	hypogyny	icterus	ignify
howbeit	humility	hyaloid	hylism	hypomania	ictus	ignite
howdah	hummock	hybrid	hylozoic	hyponasty	ictuses	ignition
howe	hummocky	hybridism	hylozoism	hypophyge	icy	ignoble
howel	humor	hybridity	hylozoist	hypoploid	id	ignominy
however	humoral	hybridize	hymen	hyposcope	idea	ignoramus
howitzer	humorism	hybridous	hymeneal	hypostyle	ideal	ignorance
howl	humorist	hydathode	hymenean	hypotaxis	idealism	ignorant
howsoever	humorous	hydatid	hymenia	hypothec	idealist	ignore
hoy	humorsome	hydra	hymenium	hypotonic	ideality	iguana
hoyden	humous	hydrae	hymeniums	hypsophyl	idealize	iguanodon
huanaco	hump	hydras	hymn	hyracoid	ideate	ileac
huarache	humpback	hydracid	hymnal	hyrax	ideation	ileitis
huaracho	humph	hydragog	hymnist	hyson	ideatum	ileostomy
					idem	

ileum	immanent	impeccant	impress	incense	incur	indium
ilex	immature	impedance	imprest	incentive	incurable	indocile
iliac	immediacy	impede	imprimis	incept	incurious	indole
ilia	immediate	impedient	imprint	inception	incurrent	indolence
ilium	immense	impel	imprison	inceptive	incursion	indolency
ill	immensity	impellent	improbity	incertain	incursive	indolent
illation	immerge	impend	impromptu	incessant	incurvate	indoor
illative	immerse	impendent	improper	incest	incurve	indorse
illegal	immersion	impennate	improve	inch	incudal	indorsee
illegible	immesh	imperator	improvise	inchmeal	incudes	indow
illiberal	immew	imperfect	imprudent	inchoate	incus	indoxyl
illicit	immigrant	imperial	impudence	inchworm	incuse	indraft
illinium	immigrate	imperil	impudency	incidence	indaba	indraught
illiquid	imminence	imperious	impudent	incident	indagate	indrawn
illocal	imminency	imperia	impugn	incipient	indamin	indri
illogic	imminent	imperium	impulse	incise	indamine	induce
illogical	immingle	impetigo	impulsion	incision	indebted	inducible
illume	immission	impetrate	impulsive	incisive	indecency	induct
illumine	immit	impetuous	impunity	incisory	indecent	inductee
illusion	immix	impetus	impure	incisor	indecorous	inductile
illusive	immixture	imphee	impurity	incisure	indeed	induction
illusory	immobile	impi	impurple	incitant	indelible	inductive
illy	immodest	impiety	impute	incite	indemnify	indue
ilmenite	immodesty	imping	in	incivility	indemnitor	indulge
image	immolate	impinge	inability	incivism	indemnity	indulgent
imagery	immoral	impious	inaction	inclasp	indene	induline
imaginal	immortal	impish	inactive	inclement	indent	indult
imaginary	immotile	implant	inaffable	incline	indention	indulto
imagine	immovable	implead	inaidable	inclose	indenture	indurate
imagist	immune	impledge	inamorata	inclosure	indevout	indusia
imagism	immunity	implement	inamorato	include	index	indusial
imago	immunize	impletion	inane	inclusion	indexes	indusium
imagoes	immure	implicate	inanimate	inclusive	indexical	industry
imam	immusical	implicit	inanition	incogent	indicant	indwell
imamate	immutable	implode	inanity	incognita	indicate	inearth
imaret	imp	implore	inapt	incognito	indices	inebriant
imbalance	impact	implosion	inarable	income	indicia	inebriate
imbalm	impaction	implosive	inarch	incomer	indicium	inebriety
imbecile	impair	impluvia	inarm	incommode	indict	inebrious
imbibe	impala	impluvium	inasmuch	incompact	indictee	inedible
imbricate	impale	imply	inaudible	incorrect	indiction	inedited
imbroglio	impanate	impolicy	inaugural	incorrupt	indigen	ineffable
imbrue	impanel	impolite	inbeing	increase	indigenal	inelastic
imbrute	impar	impolitic	inboard	increate	indigence	inelegant
imbue	imparity	imporous	inborn	incremate	indigene	inequable
imid	impark	import	inbound	increment	indigency	inept
imidazole	impart	important	inbreathe	incretion	indigent	inequity
imide	impartial	importune	inbred	incrust	indignant	inerrable
imidogen	impasse	impose	inbreed	incubate	indignity	inerrancy
imine	impassive	impost	inburst	incubi	indigo	inerrant
imitable	impaste	impostor	inby	incubus	indigoid	inert
imitate	impatiens	imposture	incage	incubuses	indigotin	inertia
imitation	impatient	impotence	incapable	inculcate	indirect	inerudite
imitative	impavid	impotency	incarnant	inculpate	indiscreet	inexact
immanacle	impawn	impotent	incarnate	incult	indiscrete	inexpert
immanence	impeach	impound	incase	incumbent	indispose	infamize
immanency	impearl	imprecate	incaution	incumber	indite	infamous

infamy
infancy
infant
infanta
infante
infantile
infantine
infantry
infarct
infatuate
infect
infection
infective
infecund
infelt
infeoff
infer
inference
inferior
infernal
inferno
infertile
infest
infidel
infield
infilter
infinite
infinity
infirm
infirmary
infirmity
infit
infix
infixion
inflame
inflate
inflation
inflect
inflexion
inflexed
inflict
inflow
influence
influent
influenza
influx
infold
inform
informal
informant
infract
infringe
infuriate
infuscate
infuse
infusion
infusive

ingather
ingenious
ingenuity
ingenuous
ingest
ingesta
ingestion
ingestive
inglenook
ingoing
ingot
ingraft
ingrain
ingress
ingrow
ingrown
ingrowth
inguinal
ingulf
inhabit
inhalant
inhale
inhalent
inhaul
inhere
inherence
inherency
inherent
inherit
inhesion
inhibit
inhuman
inhumane
inhume
inimical
inia
inion
iniquity
initial
initiate
inject
injection
injure
injurious
injury
injustice
ink
inkberry
inkhorn
inkle
inkling
inkstand
inkwell
inkwood
inky
inlace
inlaid

inland
inlander
inlaw
inlawry
inlay
inlet
inly
inmate
inmesh
inmost
inn
innate
inner
innermost
innervate
innerve
innholder
inning
innkeeper
innocence
innocency
innocent
innocuous
innovate
innoxious
innuendo
innuendos
inoculate
inoculum
inodorous
inorganic
inositol
inosite
inotropic
inoxidize
inpatient
inphase
input
inquest
inquiet
inquiline
inquinate
inquire
inquiry
inro
inroad
inrush
insane
insanity
insatiate
insatiety
inscribe
insect
insectean
insectary
insection
insecure

insensate
insert
insertion
inset
insheathe
inshore
inshrine
inside
insider
insidious
insight
insigne
insignia
insincere
insinuate
insipid
insipient
insist
insistent
insnare
insocial
insolate
insole
insolence
insolent
insoluble
insolvent
insomnia
insomniac
insomuch
insoul
inspan
inspect
insphere
inspire
inspirit
instable
install
instance
instancy
instant
instanter
instar
instate
instead
instep
instigate
instil
instill
instinct
institute
instroke
instruct
insula
insulae
insular
insulate

insulin
insulize
insult
insurance
insurant
insure
insurgent
inswathe
inswept
intact
intagli
intaglio
intaglios
intake
intarsia
integer
integral
integrand
integrant
integrate
integrity
intellect
intend
intendant
intendent
intense
intensify
intension
intensity
intensive
intent
intention
inter
interact
intercede
intercept
intercrop
interdict
interest
interface
interfere
interfold
interfuse
interim
interior
interject
interjoin
interknit
interknot
interlace
interlap
interlard
interlay
interleaf
interline
interlock
interlope

interlude
interment
intermit
intermix
intern
internal
interne
internee
internode
interplay
interpose
interpret
interrex
interrule
interrupt
intersect
intersex
interstice
interval
intervale
intervein
intervene
interview
interwind
interwork
interwove
intestacy
intestate
intestine
inthral
inthrone
intima
intimacy
intimae
intimal
intimate
intine
intitle
intitule
into
intomb
intonate
intone
intrados
intrant
intrench
intrepid
intricacy
intricate
intrigant
intrigue
intrinsic
introduce
introit
introject
intromit
introrse

introvert
intrude
intrusion
intrusive
intrust
intubate
intuit
intuition
intuitive
intumesce
inturn
intwine
intwist
inuendo
inulase
inulin
inunction
inundant
inundate
inurbane
inure
inurn
inutile
inutility
invade
invalid
invariant
invasion
invasive
invected
invective
inveigh
inveigle
inveil
invent
invention
inventive
inventory
inverness
inverse
inversion
invert
invertase
invertin
invest
invidious
inviolacy
inviolate
invisible
invite
invoice
invoke
involucel
involucra
involucre
involute
involve

inwall
inward
inwards
inweave
inwind
inwove
inwoven
inwrap
inwreathe
inwrought
io
iodate
iodation
iodic
iodide
iodin
iodine
iodism
iodize
iodoform
iodol
iodimetry
iodometry
iodous
iolite
ion
ionic
ionize
ionone
iota
iotacism
ipecac
ipomea
ipomoea
iracund
irascible
irate
ire
ireful
irenic
irenical
irenics
irenist
iridic
iridium
iridotomy
irides
iris
irisated
irisation
irised
irisitis
iritic
iritis
irk
irksome
iron

ironbark
irone
ironic
ironside
ironsmith
ironstone
ironware
ironweed
ironwood
ironwork
ironworks
ironwort
irony
irradiant
irradiate
irregular
irrigate
irrigable
irriguous
irritable
irritant
irritancy
irritate
irruption
irruptive
is
isagoge
isagogic
isallobar
isandrous
isanomaly
isanthous
isatin
isatine
isatinic
ischaemia
ischemia
ischemic
ischia
ischiac
ischiatic
ischion
ischium
isinglass
island
isle
islesman
islet
ism
isobar
isobaric
ischeim
isochime
isochor
isochoric
isochore
isochron

isochrone
isoclinal
isocline
isoclinic
isocracy
isocrat
isocratic
isocyclic
isogamete
isogamy
isogenous
isogeny
isogon
isogonal
isogonic
isogram
isograph
isohel
isohydric
isohyet
isolate
isolog
isologue
isologous
isomer
isomeric
isomerism
isomerous
isometric
isometry
isomorph
isonomic
isonomy
isopathic
isopathy
isophane
isophene
isophotic
isophylly
isopleth
isopod
isopodan
isopolity
isopract
isoprene
isopropyl
isopyre
isosceles
isosmotic
isospore
isospory
isostasy
isostatic
isotheral
isothere
isotherm
isotonic

isotope
isotopic
isotopy
isotrope
isotropic
isotropy
issuance
issuant
issue
isthmian
isthmus
istle
italic
italicize
itch
itchy
item
itemize
iterable
iterance
iterant
iterate
iteration
iterative
itineracy
itinerant
itinerary
itinerate
its
itself
ivied
ivory
ivorybill
ivorytype
ivy
ivyberry
ixia
ixodiasis
ixtle
izzard

J

jab
jabber
jabot
jacal
jacales
jacamar
jacana
jacaranda
jacinth
jack
jackal
jackall
jackass
jackboots
jackbox

jackdaw
jacket
jackey
jackie
jackknife
jackleg
jacko
jackplane
jackpot
jackscrew
jackshaft
jackstay
jackstone
jackstraw
jacobus
jaconet
jactation
jaculate
jade
jadish
jadite
jady
jaeger
jag
jaggary
jaggery
jaghery
jagra
jaggy
jagouar
jaguar
jail
jailbird
jakes
jalap
jalapic
jalapin
jalousie
jam
jamb
jambe
jambeau
jambeaux
jangle
janitor
janizary
janty
japan
jape
japery
japonica
japonism
jar
jarabe
jarfly
jargon
jargonel

jargonize
jargoon
jarina
jarl
jarosite
jasmine
jaspe
jasper
jasperite
jasperize
jaspidean
jaundice
jaunt
jauntily
jaunty
javelin
jaw
jay
jayhawker
jaywalk
jazerant
jazz
jazzy
jealous
jealousy
jean
jebel
jee
jeep
jeepable
jeer
jehad
jejuna
jejune
jejunum
jellify
jelly
jellyfish
jelutong
jemmy
jennet
jenny
jeofail
jeofaile
jeopard
jeopardy
jequerity
jequirity
jerboa
jereed
jeremiad
jerid
jerk
jerky
jerkin
jerkwater
jerreed

jerrid
jerry
jersey
jess
jessamine
jessant
jessed
jest
jet
jetsam
jettison
jetton
jetty
jewel
jewelry
jewelweed
jewfish
jib
jibe
jig
jigget
jiggle
jigsaw
jihad
jill
jilt
jimmy
jingal
jingall
jingko
jingle
jinglet
jinn
jinnee
jinni
jinny
jinriksha
jinx
jipijapa
jirky
jitter
jitterbug
jive
job
jobbery
jobe
jockey
jockeyism
jocko
jockstrap
jocose
jocosity
jocular
jocund
jocundity
jodhpurs
jog

joggle	jug	juvenilia	kathartic	kerosine	kin	knapweed
join	jugal	juxtapose	kathode	kersey	kinase	knar
joinder	jugate	**K**	kation	kestrel	kind	knave
joinery	juggle		katydid	ketch	kindle	knavery
joint	jugglery	ka	kauri	ketchup	kindred	knavish
jointress	jugular	kaas	kaury	ketene	kinematic	knead
jointure	jugulate	kab	kava	ketone	kinescope	knee
jointweed	juice	kabab	kavass	ketonic	kinetic	kneecap
jointworm	juiceless	kabala	kayak	ketosis	kinetics	kneehole
joist	juicy	kabar	kazoo	kettle	king	kneel
joke	jujitsu	kabbala	keck	kevel	kingbird	kneepan
jole	juju	kadi	keckle	kex	kingbolt	kneepiece
jollify	jujube	kaffir	kedge	key	kingcraft	knell
jollity	jujutsu	kaftan	keef	keyboard	kingdom	knelt
jolly	julep	kago	keel	keyhole	kingfish	knew
jolt	julienne	kaiak	keelhaul	keynote	kinglet	knickers
johnnycake	jumble	**kain**	keelson	keystone	kingpalm	knife
jonquil	jumbo	kainite	keen	keyway	kingpin	knight
jonquille	jump	kaiser	keep	khaki	kingpost	knightage
jordanon	jumpy	kakapo	keepsake	khalif	kingship	knit
joram	junco	kaki	keeshond	khamsean	kingtruss	knives
jorum	juncoes	kale	**keeve**	khamsin	kingwood	knob
joseph	junction	kalends	kef	khan	kink	knobby
jostle	juncture	kali	kefir	khanate	kinky	knobstick
jot	jungle	kalian	keg	khirkah	kinkajou	knock
jougs	jungly	kalif	keir	kibblings	kino	knockdown
joule	junior	kalium	keitloa	**kibe**	kinogum	knockout
jounce	juniority	kalmia	keloid	kiblah	kinsfolk	knoll
journal	juniper	kalong	kelp	kick	kinship	knop
journey	junk	kalsomine	kelter	kickshaw	kinsman	knosp
joust	junket	kalyptra	kench	kickshaws	kiosk	knot
jovial	junkman	kamala	kennel	kid	kip	knotgrass
joviality	junta	kame	keno	kidnap	kipper	knothole
jovialty	jupon	kampong	kenosis	kidney	kipskin	knotty
jovialize	jura	kana	kenotic	kidskin	kirmess	knotweed
jowl	jural	kangaroo	kentledge	kief	kirtle	knout
jowled	jurant	kaolin	kephalin	kier	kish	know
jowler	jurat	kaoline	kephir	kieserite	kismet	knowledge
joy	juratory	kaolinite	kepi	kilderkin	kiss	known
joyful	juridic	kaph	kept	kilim	kist	knubbly
joyless	juridical	kapok	ker	kill	kistvaen	knuckle
joyous	jurist	karabiner	keramic	killdee	kit	knur
juba	juristic	karakul	keramics	killdeer	kitchen	knurl
jubate	juror	karat	keratin	killifish	kite	knurly
jube	jury	karma	keratitis	killkid	kith	kob
jubilance	juryman	karroo	keratoid	killock	kithara	koba
jubilancy	jus	karyomere	keratose	kiln	kitten	kobold
jubilant	jussive	karyosome	kerb	kilocycle	kittenish	koel
jubilate	just	karyotin	kerbstone	kilogram	kittiwake	kohemp
jubile	justice	karyotype	kerchief	kiloliter	kittool	kohl
jubilee	justiciar	kas	kerf	kilolitre	kittul	kohlrabi
judge	justicier	kasher	kermes	kilometer	kitty	kola
judgeship	justify	katabasis	kermess	kilometre	klepht	kolanut
judicable	justle	katabatic	kermis	kilowatt	knack	kolinsky
judicator	jut	katabolic	kern	kilt	knag	komondor
judicial	jute	katalysis	kerne	kilter	knaggy	koodoo
judiciary	jutty	katalytic	kernel	kimono	knap	kopeck
judicious	juvenile	katharsis	kerosene	kimonos	knapsack	kopek

koph
kor
koruna
kos
kosher
koumiss
koumys
kousso
kowtow
kraal
kraft
krait
kraken
kremlin
kreutzer
kreuzer
krimmer
krona
krone
kronen
kroner
kronor
kroon
krubi
krubut
kruller
kryolite
krypton
kudu
kumiss
kumquat
kunzite
kurbash
kusso
kurrajong
kuvasz
kyanite
kyanize
kylix
kymograph
kyphosis
kyphotic

L

la
labara
labarum
label
labella
labellum
labia
labial
labialism
labialize
labiate
labile
lability
labium

labor
laborious
labret
labroid
laburnum
labyrinth
lac
laccate
laccolith
laccolite
lace
lacerate
lacertian
lacewing
lacewood
laches
lachrymal
laciniate
laciniose
lack
lackaday
lackey
lacmus
laconic
laconical
laconism
lacquer
lacrimal
lacrimary
lacrimose
lacrosse
lactam
lactary
lactase
lactate
lactation
lacteal
lactean
lacteous
lactic
lactone
lactonic
lactose
lacuna
lacunae
lacunal
lacunar
lacunary
lacune
lacunose
lacustral
lacy
lad
ladanum
ladder
laddie
lade
laden

ladino
ladle
ladrone
ladronism
lady
ladybird
ladybug
ladykin
ladylike
ladylove
ladypalm
ladyship
lag
lagan
lager
laggard
lagnappe
lagniappe
lagoon
lagune
laic
laical
laid
lain
lair
laity
lake
laker
lakh
laky
lallation
lama
lamasery
lamb
lambaste
lambdoid
lambency
lambent
lambert
lambie
lambish
lambkill
lambkin
lamblike
lamboys
lambskin
lame
lamellate
lamella
lamellar
lamelloid
lemellose
lament
lamia
lamina
laminar
laminaria
laminary

laminate
laminal
laminable
laminitis
laminose
laminous
lamp
lampad
lampas
lampblack
lampers
lampereel
lampion
lampoon
lampreel
lamprey
lanary
lanate
lanated
lance
lancelet
lanceolar
lancet
lanceted
lancewood
lanciers
land
landau
landaulet
lande
landfall
landgrave
landlady
landless
landloper
landlord
landman
landmark
landowner
landscape
landside
landslide
landslip
landsman
landward
landwards
lane
langrage
langrel
langridge
language
languet
languette
languid
languidly
languish
languor
laniard

laniary
lanital
lank
lanky
lanner
lanneret
lanolin
lanoline
lanose
lansdowne
lant
lantana
lantern
lanthanum
lanugo
lanyappe
lanyard
lap
lapboard
lapel
lapful
lapidary
lapidate
lapides
lapidific
lapidify
lapillus
lapis
lappet
lapsation
lapse
lapstone
lapstrake
lapstreak
lapwing
larboard
larcener
larcenist
larcenous
larceny
larch
lard
lardacein
larder
lardon
lardoon
lardy
large
largess
largesse
larghetto
largo
lariat
larine
larithmic
larithmics
lark
larksome

larkspur
larrigan
larrikin
larva
larval
larvate
laryngal
laryngeal
laryngean
larynges
larynx
larynxes
lascar
lash
lass
lassitude
lasso
last
lat
latania
latch
latchet
latchkey
late
lated
lateen
latency
latent
lateral
laterite
latescent
latex
lath
lathe
lathery
lathwork
lathy
latices
laticlave
latish
latitude
latria
latrine
latten
latter
lattice
laud
laudanum
laudation
laudative
laudatory
laugh
laughter
launce
launch
launder
laundress
laundry

laura
laureate
laurel
lava
lavabo
lavage
lavalier
lavaliere
lavation
lavatory
lave
lavender
lavish
lavolt
lavolta
lavolto
law
lawful
lawgiver
lawing
lawless
lawmaker
lawmaking
lawn
lawnmower
lawny
lawsone
lawsuit
lawyer
lax
laxation
laxative
laxity
lay
layerage
layette
layman
laywoman
lazar
lazaret
lazarette
lazarlike
lazarly
laze
lazulite
lazy
lazybones
leach
leachy
lead
leadsman
leadwort
leady
leaf
leafage
leafless
leaflet
leafstalk

leafy	legato	leperous	levity	lick	limb	linguae
league	legator	lepidote	levulin	licorice	limbate	lingual
leak	legend	leporid	levulose	lictor	limber	linguist
leakage	legendary	leporide	levy	lid	limbic	lingulate
lean	leger	leporine	levyist	lidless	limbless	lingy
leant	leges	leprose	lewisite	lidded	limbo	liniment
leap	leggy	leprosy	lex	lie	limbus	linin
leapfrog	leghorn	leprous	lexical	lief	lime	link
leapt	legible	lepta	lexicon	liege	limekiln	linkage
lear	legion	leptome	li	liegeman	limelight	linkboy
learn	legionary	lepton	liability	lien	limen	linkwork
learnt	legislate	leptotene	liable	lientery	limerick	linn
lease	legist	lesion	liana	lierne	limestone	linnet
leash	legless	less	lianae	lieu	limetree	linoleic
least	legume	lessee	liaison	life	limewater	linoleum
leather	legumin	lessen	liar	lifeboat	liminal	linsang
leathern	lehr	lesser	libation	lifebuoy	limit	linseed
leave	lehua	lesson	libeccio	lifeful	limitary	linstock
leaven	lei	lessor	libel	lifeguard	limn	lint
leavy	leister	lest	libelist	lifeless	limnetic	lintel
leben	leisure	let	libellist	lifelike	limnology	linter
lecher	leitmotif	lethal	libelant	lifelong	limonene	lintwhite
lecherous	leitmotiv	lethargic	libellant	lifetime	limonite	liny
lechery	lemma	lethargy	libelee	lifework	limonitic	lion
lecithin	lemmata	letter	libellee	lift	limosis	lioness
lectern	lemming	lettuce	libellula	ligament	limousine	lionet
lection	lemnisci	leu	libellous	ligan	limp	lionheart
lector	lemniscus	leucin	libelous	ligate	limpet	lionize
lectual	lemon	leucine	liber	ligation	limpid	lip
lecture	lemonade	leucite	liberal	ligature	limpidity	liparoid
led	lempira	leucocyte	liberate	ligeance	limpkin	lipase
ledge	lemur	leucosin	libertine	light	limpsy	lipid
ledger	lemures	leud	liberty	lighten	limuloid	lipide
ledgy	lemurine	leudes	libido	lightface	limulus	lipocaic
lee	lemuroid	leuds	libidinal	lightning	limy	lipoid
leeangle	lend	leukaemia	libra	lightsome	linage	lipolysis
leeboard	lene	leukemia	librarian	lightwood	linalool	lipolytic
leech	lenetic	leukemic	library	lignaloes	linchpin	lipoma
leek	length	leukocyte	librate	ligneous	linden	lipotropy
leer	lengthen	leukoma	libration	ligniform	line	lippen
leery	lengthy	lev	libratory	lignify	lineage	lipstick
leesome	lenience	leva	libretist	lignin	lineal	liquate
leet	leniency	levant	libretti	lignite	lineament	liquation
leeward	lenient	levanter	libretto	lignose	linear	liqueur
leeway	lenitive	levantine	librettos	ligroin	lineate	liquid
left	lenity	levator	libriform	ligroine	lineation	liquidate
leg	lens	levatores	lice	ligula	lineman	liquify
legacy	lent	levators	licence	ligulate	linen	liquidity
legal	lenten	levee	licencee	ligule	lineolate	liquity
legalism	lenticel	level	license	ligure	liney	liquor
legalist	lentigo	lever	licensee	like	ling	liquorice
legality	lentil	leverage	lichee	liken	linga	lira
legalize	lentoid	leveret	lichen	likewise	lingam	lire
legantine	lentor	leviable	lichenin	lilac	linger	liripipe
legate	lenvoy	leviathan	lichenose	lilt	lingerie	liripoop
legatine	leonine	levigate	lichenous	lily	lingo	lisle
legatee	leopard	levirate	lichgate	lilywort	lingoes	lisp
legation	leper	levitate	licit	limacine	lingua	lissom

lissome	liverish	lock	loll	lory	lucency	lunation
list	liverleaf	lockage	lollipop	losable	lucent	lunch
listel	liverwort	locket	lollypop	lose	lucernal	luncheon
listen	livery	lockfast	loment	losel	lucern	lune
listless	liveryman	lockjaw	lomentum	loss	lucerne	lunet
lit	livestock	lockram	lone	lot	lucid	lunette
litas	livid	locksman	lonesome	lote	lucidity	lung
litai	lividity	locksmith	long	loth	lucifee	lunge
litu	livre	loco	longan	lotion	lucifer	lungfish
litany	lixivial	locoweed	longboat	loto	luciferin	lungi
litchi	lixiviate	locomotor	longbow	lottery	luciform	lungee
liter	lixivium	locular	longcloth	lotto	lucivee	lungworm
literal	lizard	loculate	longeron	lotus	luck	lungwort
literary	llama	loculi	longevity	loud	luckless	lunitidal
literate	llano	loculus	longevous	louden	lucky	lunkhead
literati	lo	locus	longhand	lough	lucrative	lunula
literatim	loach	locust	longhead	louis	lucre	lunular
literator	load	locution	longhorn	lounge	lucubrate	lunulate
literatus	loadstar	locutory	longicorn	loup	lucule	lunule
litharge	loadstone	lode	longish	loupe	luculent	luny
lithe	loaf	lodestar	longitude	lour	ludicrous	lupin
lithaemia	loam	lodestone	longshore	loury	lues	lupine
lithemia	loamy	lodge	longsome	louse	luetic	lupulin
lithemic	loan	lodgement	longspur	lousewort	luff	lupus
lithesome	loasis	lodgment	longwise	lousy	luffa	lurch
lithia	loath	loess	loo	lout	lug	lurdan
lithiasis	loathe	loft	loof	loutish	luggage	lurdane
lithic	loathful	lofty	loofah	louver	lugsail	lure
lithium	loathsome	log	look	lovage	lugworm	lurid
lithoid	loaves	logaoedic	loom	love	lukewarm	lurk
lithoidal	lob	logarithm	loon	lovebird	lull	luscious
lithology	lobar	logbook	loony	loveknot	lullaby	lush
lithopone	lobate	loge	loop	loveless	lumachel	lust
lithotint	lobation	logan	loophole	lovelock	lumbago	lustful
lithotomy	lobby	loggan	loopy	lovelorn	lumbar	lustral
lithy	lobbyism	loggia	loose	lovesick	lumber	lustrate
litigable	lobbyist	logia	loosen	lovesome	lumberman	lustre
litigant	lobe	logic	loot	lovevine	lumberyard	lustrous
litigate	lobelia	logical	looves	low	lumbrical	lustrum
litigious	lobeline	logician	lop	lowermost	lumen	lusty
litmus	loblolly	logion	lope	lowery	lumina	lûtantist
litoral	lobscouse	logistic	loppy	lowland	luminance	lute
litotes	lobster	logistics	loquat	lowly	luminary	lutenist
litre	lobule	logogram	loran	lown	luminesce	lutist
litter	lobular	logograph	lord	loxodromy	luminous	lutation
littery	lobulate	logogriph	lordling	loyal	lummox	luteal
little	lobworm	logomachy	lordoma	loyalism	lump	lutecium
littoral	local	logopathy	lordosis	loyalist	lumpfish	lutein
liturgic	locale	logothete	lordotic	loyalty	lumpish	luteolin
liturgist	localism	logotype	lordship	lozenge	lumpy	luteous
liturgy	locality	logotypy	lore	lozenger	luna	luxate
livable	localize	logway	lorgnette	lubber	lunacy	luxmeter
live	locate	logwood	lorica	lubricant	lunar	luxuriant
liveable	location	logwork	loricae	lubricate	lunarian	luxuriate
livelong	locative	loiasis	loricate	lubricity	lunary	luxurious
liven	lochia	loin	lorikeet	lubricous	lunate	luxury
liver	lochial	loincloth	loris	lucarne	lunatic	lyceum
liveried	loci	loiter	lornlorry	luce	lunatical	lychnis

lycopod	mackinaw	magnesia	major	maltha	manganous	manta
lyddite	mackle	magnesian	majordomo	maltose	mange	manteau
lye	macle	magnesic	majority	maltreat	mangel	manteaus
lymph	macrame	magnesite	majuscule	maltster	manger	manteaux
lymphatic	macrocosm	magnesium	make	malty	mangle	mantel
lymphoid	macrocyst	magnet	makebate	malvasia	mango	mantelet
lyncean	macrodome	magnetic	makepeace	malvasian	mangoes	mantes
lynch	macrogamy	magnetics	makeshift	malvoisie	mangos	mantic
lynx	macron	magnetism	malaceous	mama	mangonel	mantilla
lyophilic	macropia	magnetite	malachite	mamba	mangrove	mantis
lyophobic	macropsia	magnetize	malacoid	mamma	mangy	mantises
lyotropic	macrural	magneto	maladroit	mameluke	manhandle	mantissa
lyrate	macruran	magnetron	malady	mamey	manhole	mantle
lyre	macruroid	magnific	malaise	mammae	manhood	mantlet
lyrebird	macrurous	magnifico	malamute	mammal	mania	mantua
lyric	mactation	magnify	malanders	mammary	maniac	manual
lyrical	macula	magnitude	malapert	mammate	maniacal	manubria
lyricism	maculae	magnolia	malar	mammilla	manic	manubrial
lyriform	maculate	magnum	malaria	mammillae	manicure	manubrium
lyrism	macule	magot	malarial	mammitis	manifest	manumit
lyrist	mad	magpie	malarian	mammology	manifesto	manure
lyse	madam	maguey	malarious	mammon	manifold	manus
lysigenic	madcap	maharaja	malate	mammonish	manihot	manward
lysimeter	madden	maharajah	malax	mammonism	manikin	manwards
lysin	maddish	maharanee	malaxate	mammonist	manila	manwise
lysine	made	maharani	male	mammonite	manioc	many
lysis	madman	mahatma	malefic	mammoth	maniple	manyplies
lyssa	madwoman	mahlstick	maleic	mammy	manipular	manzanita
lyssae	madras	mahogany	malformed	man	manito	map
lytta	madrepore	mahout	malic	manacle	manitou	maple
	madrigal	maid	malice	manage	manitu	maquis
M	madrona	maiden	malicious	manakin	mankind	mar
ma	madrono	maidhood	malign	manatee	manlike	marabou
macaber	madstone	maieutic	malignant	mancipium	manna	marabout
macabre	maduro	maieutics	malignity	manciple	mannequin	maranta
macaco	madwort	maigre	maline	mancus	manner	marasca
macadam	maelstrom	maihem	malines	mandamus	mannered	marasmic
macaque	maenad	mail	malinger	mandarin	mannerism	marasmus
macaroni	maenadic	mailbag	malison	mandatary	mannerist	maraud
macaronic	maestro	mailbox	mall	mandate	mannikin	maravedi
macaroon	maffick	mailman	mallard	mandatory	mannish	marble
macaw	magazine	maim	malleable	mandelic	mannitol	marbelize
maccabaw	mage	main	malleate	mandible	mannite	marbly
maccaboy	magenta	mainland	mallei	mandola	mannitic	marc
maccaroni	maggot	mainmast	mallein	mandolin	mannose	marcasite
macchia	maggoty	mainor	malleine	mandrake	manoeuver	marcato
maccoboy	magic	mainour	mallemuck	mandrel	manoeuvre	marcel
mace	magical	mainsail	malleolar	mandril	manometer	march
macerate	magician	mainsheet	malleolus	mandrill	manor	marchland
machete	magilp	mainstay	mallet	manducate	manorial	marchpane
machinal	magilph	maintain	malleus	mane	manpower	mare
machinate	magistery	maintop	mallow	manege	manrope	margaric
machine	magistral	maiolica	malm	maneuver	mansard	margarin
machinery	magma	maiosis	malmsey	manful	manse	margarine
machinist	magmata	maize	malodor	manganate	mansion	margay
machree	magmatic	majestic	malonic	manganese	manswear	margent
macintosh	magnaflux	majesty	malt	manganic	manswore	margin
mackerel	magnate	majolica	maltase	manganite	mansworn	marginal

marginate	martyrize	matey	mayhap	medicate	mellow	menstruum
margrave	martyry	math	mayhappen	medicinal	melodeon	mensural
marigold	marvel	matico	mayhem	medicine	melodia	mensurate
marimba	marvelous	matin	mayor	medieval	melodic	mental
marimeter	marzipan	matinal	mayoral	mediocre	melodics	mentality
marina	mascara	matinee	mayoralty	meditate	melodious	menthane
marinade	mascle	matrass	maypop	medium	melodize	menthene
marinate	mascot	matriarch	maze	medjidie	melodist	menthol
marine	masculine	matrices	mazourka	medlar	melodrama	mention
mariner	mash	matricide	mazurka	medley	melody	mentor
marital	mashie	matrimony	mazy	medula	melomania	mentum
maritime	mashy	matrix	me	medulae	melon	menu
marjoram	mask	matron	mead	medular	melonite	mephitic
mark	masochism	matronal	meadow	medulary	melt	mephitis
market	masochist	matronage	meager	medulated	meltage	mephitism
markka	mason	matronize	meagre	medusoid	melton	mercaptan
marksman	masonry	matte	meal	meech	meltwater	mercapto
marl	masque	matter	mealtime	meed	member	mercenary
marlin	mass	mattin	mealworm	meek	membrane	mercer
marline	massacre	mattock	mean	meet	memento	mercerize
marlite	massage	mattoid	meander	megalith	mementoes	mercery
marly	massagist	mattrass	meandrous	megaphone	mementos	merchant
marmalade	masse	mattress	meant	megapod	memo	merciful
marmoreal	masseter	maturate	meantime	megascope	memoir	merciless
marmorean	massicot	mature	meanwhile	megaspore	memoirist	mercurial
marmoset	massif	maturity	measle	megass	memorable	mercuric
marmot	massive	matutinal	measled	megasse	memorably	mercurous
maroon	massy	matzoon	measles	megathere	memoranda	mercury
marplot	mast	matzoth	measly	megatherm	memorial	mercy
marque	mastaba	maukin	measure	megilp	memorize	mere
marquee	mastabah	maul	meat	megrim	memory	merely
marquess	master	maulstick	meatless	meiosis	men	merganser
marquetry	masterdom	maunder	meatus	meiotic	menace	merge
marquis	masterful	maundy	meatuses	mel	menacme	mergence
marquise	mastery	mausolean	meaty	melamine	menad	meridian
marram	masthead	mausoleum	mechanic	melanemia	menadic	meringue
marriage	mastic	mauve	mechanism	melanemic	menage	merino
marron	masticate	mauvein	mechanist	melanian	menagerie	meristem
marrow	mastiff	mauveine	mechanize	melanic	menarche	meristic
marrowfat	mastitis	mavis	medal	melanin	mend	merit
marry	mastodon	mavournin	medalist	melanism	mendable	merl
marseille	mastoid	maw	medallic	melanite	mendacity	merle
marsh	masurium	mawkish	medallion	melanoid	mendicant	merlin
marshal	mat	maxilla	medallist	melanoma	mendicity	merlon
marshalcy	matador	maxillae	meddle	melanosis	menhaden	mermaid
marshy	match	maxillary	media	melanotic	menhir	mermaiden
marsupial	matchless	maxim	mediacy	melanous	menial	merman
marsupium	matchlock	maxima	mediaeval	melaphyre	meningeal	meroblast
martello	matchmark	maximal	medial	meld	meninges	merozoite
marten	matchwood	maximite	median	melee	meninx	merriment
martial	mate	maximize	mediate	melic	meniscus	ꜰmerry
martin	mateless	maximum	mediative	melilot	menology	mesa
martinet	matelote	maxixe	mediatory	melinite	menopause	mescal
martingal	matelotte	maxwell	mediation	meliorate	mensa	mescaline
martlet	material	may	mediatize	meliorism	mensal	mesdames
martonite	materiel	maybe	medic	meliorist	menses	mesentery
martyr	maternal	mayfly	medicable	meliority	menstrua	mesh
martyrdom	maternity	maybug	medical	mellite	menstrual	meshwork

meshy	metazoan	miaow	midship	millenary	minimal	miser
mesial	metazoic	miasm	midships	milleped	minimize	miserere
mesian	metazoon	miasma	midst	millepede	minimum	misery
mesmeric	mete	miasmal	midstream	millepora	minimus	misfeasor
mesmerism	meteor	miasmas	midsummer	millepore	minion	misfire
mesmerize	meteoric	miasmata	midway	millerite	minister	misfit
mesualty	meteorite	miasmatic	midweek	millet	ministry	misgive
mesnality	meteroid	miasmic	midwife	millhand	minium	misguide
mesne	meter	miaul	midwifery	milliard	miniver	mishap
mesoblast	meterage	mib	midwinter	milliary	mink	misinform
mesocarp	metestrum	micaceous	midyears	millier	minnow	mislay
mesoderm	metestrus	mice	mien	milligram	minor	mislead
mesologic	methane	micell	miggle	milline	minority	mislike
mesology	methanol	micella	might	milliner	minster	mismanage
meson	metheglin	micellae	mighty	millinery	minstrel	mismarry
mesophyl	method	micellar	mignon	million	mint	misnomer
mesophyll	methodic	micelle	mignonne	millionth	mintage	misogamy
mesophyte	methodism	micra	migraine	milliped	minuend	misogyny
mesoplast	methodist	micraner	migrant	millipede	minuet	misology
mesotron	methodize	micrify	migrate	millpond	minus	misoneism
mesquit	methyl	microbe	migration	millrace	minuscule	misoneist
mesquite	methylal	microbial	migratory	millrun	minute	mispickel
mess	methylate	microbian	mikado	millstone	minuteman	misplay
message	methylene	microbic	mikron	millwheel	minutia	misplead
messaline	methylic	microbion	mil	milo	minutiae	misprint
messenger	metochy	microcosm	miladi	milord	minx	misprison
messuage	metonym	microcyte	milady	milreis	miocardia	misrule
messy	metonymic	microdont	milage	milt	miosis	miss
mestee	metonymy	microfilm	milch	milter	miotic	missal
mesteso	metralgia	microgram	mild	mime	miquelet	missay
mestino	metre	microgyne	milden	mimesis	mir	misshape
mestiza	metric	micrology	mildew	mimetic	miracle	misshapen
mestizo	metrical	micron	mildewy	mimetical	mirador	missile
met	metrician	micropia	mile	mimic	mirage	mission
metabolic	metricize	micropsia	mileage	mimical	mire	missional
metaboly	metrics	microptic	milestone	mimicry	mirk	missive
metage	metrify	micropyle	milfoil	mimosa	mirmillon	misspeak
metal	metrist	microsome	miliaria	mina	mirror	misstep
metalist	metritic	microtome	miliary	minae	mirth	missy
metalize	metritis	microtomy	militancy	minah	mirthful	mist
metallic	metrology	micrurgic	militant	minaceous	mirthless	mistake
metalline	metronome	micrurgy	military	minacity	miry	mistaken
metallist	metronym	micturate	militate	minaret	mirza	mistletoe
metalloid	mettle	mid	militia	minas	misbecome	mistook
metalwork	mettled	midbrain	milium	minatory	misbrand	mistral
metamer	mew	midday	milk	mince	miscall	mistress
metameral	mezcaline	midden	milkfish	mincemeat	miscarry	mistrial
metamere	mezereon	middle	milkmaid	mind	mischance	mistrust
metameric	mezerum	middleman	milkman	mindful	mischief	misty
metameron	mezquite	midge	milksop	mindless	miscible	misusage
metamery	mezuzah	midget	milkvetch	mine	miscolor	misuse
metaphase	mezuzoth	midgut	milkweed	mineral	miscreant	mite
metaphor	mezza	midland	milkwort	mingle	miscue	miter
metaplasm	mezzo	midmost	milky	miniature	misdeed	miterwort
metapod	mezzotint	midnight	mill	minify	misdid	mitigable
metapode	mho	midnoon	millboard	minikin	misdo	mitigant
metasome	mi	midrib	millcake	minim	misdone	mitigate
metaxylem	miaou	midriff	milldam	minima	mise	mitosis

mitotic	mofette	monandry	monograph	moonshine	morgen	mothy
mitral	moffette	monarch	monogyny	moonshiny	morgue	motif
mitre	mogul	monarchal	monoicous	moonstone	moribund	motile
mitrewort	mohair	monarchic	monolater	moonwort	morion	motility
mitsvah	mohur	monarchy	monolatry	moony	morn	motion
mitt	moidore	monas	monolayer	moor	morning	motional
mitten	moiety	monastery	monolith	moorage	morocco	motivate
mittimus	moil	monastic	monolog	moorcock	moron	motive
mity	moist	monatomic	monologic	moorfowl	moronic	motivity
mitzvah	moisten	monaxial	monologue	moorhen	moronism	motley
mitzvoth	moisture	monazite	monology	moorland	moronity	motmot
mix	mojarra	monecian	monomania	moorwort	morose	motor
mixture	mol	monecious	monomial	moory	morosity.	motorboat
mizen	mola	monetary	monoplane	moose	morpheme	motorbus
mizzen	molae	monetize	monopode	moosebird	morphia	motorcar
mizzle	molal	money	monopodia	moosecall	morphic	motorist
mizzly	molality	moneys	monopoly	moosewood	morphine	motorium
mneme	molar	moneywort	monorail	moot	morphosis	motorize
mnemonic	molarity	monger	monosome	mop	morphotic	motorman
moa	molasses	mongolism	monostich	mope	morrice	motorship
moan	mold	mongoose	monostome	mopish	morrion	mottle
moat	moldboard	mongrel	monotint	mopoke	morris	motto
mob	moldwarp	monism	monotone	moppet	morrow	moue
mobbish	moldy	monist	monotony	moquette	morsel	moujik
mobile	mole	monistic	monotreme	mora	mort	moulage
mobility	molecular	monition	monotropic	morae	morte	mould
mobilize	molecule	monitive	monotypic	moraceous	mortal	moulin
mobocracy	molehill	monitor	monoxide	morainal	mortality	mouline
mobocrat	moleskin	monitory	monsignor	moraine	mortar	moulinet
moccasin	molest	monitress	monsoon	morainic	mortgage	moult
mocha	molewarp	monk	monster	moral	mortice	mound
mock	mollah	monkery	monstrous	morale	mortician	mount
mockery	mollient	monkey	montage	moralism	mortify	mountain
modal	mollify	monkeyish	montane	moralist	mortise	mourn
modality	molluscan	monkhood	montanic	morality	mortmain	mournful
mode	molluscum	monkish	monte	moralize	morula	mouse
model	mollusk	monkshood	monteith	morass	morulae	mousebane
moderate	moloch	monoacid	montero	moratoria	morular	mousebird
modern	molt	monobasic	month	moratory	mosaic	mousetail
modernism	molten	monochord	monument	moray	mosaicist	mousse
modernist	moly	monocle	monzonite	morbid	moscatel	moustache
modernity	molybdate	monocled	moo	morbidity	moschate	mousey
modernize	molybdic	monocline	mood	morbific	moschatel	mousy
modest	molybdous	monocot	moody	morbilli	mosque	mouth
modesty	moment	monocracy	moolah	mordacity	mosquital	mouthful
modica	momenta	monocular	mooley	mordancy	mosquito	mouthy
modicum	momental	monocycle	moon	mordant	moss	move
modify	momentary	monocyte	moonbeam	mordent	mossback	mow
modillion	momentous	monodic	moonblind	mordente	mossboard	mown
modiolus	momentum	monodical	mooncalf	more	mossy	moxa
modish	monachal	monodist	moonfish	moreen	most	mozetta
modiste	monachism	monodrama	moonglade	morel	mot	much
modular	monacid	monody	moonish	morelle	mote	mucic
modulate	monad	monogamic	moonlight	morello	motet	mucid
module	monadic	monogamy	moonlit	moreover	motetto	mucilage
moduli	monadical	monogenic	moonrise	mores	moth	mucin
modulus	monadism	monogeny	moonseed	morganite	mother	mucinous
moellon	monadnock	monogram	moonset	morgantic	mothery	muck

muckrake
muckworm
mucky
mucoid
mucosa
mucosal
mucose
mucosity
mucous
mucro
mucronate
mucrones
mucus
mud
mudcap
mudcat
muddle
muddy
mudfish
mudguard
mudpot
mudpuppy
mudsill
mudstone
mueddin
muezzin
muff
muffin
muffineer
muffle
mufti
mug
muggar
muggur
muggins
muggy
mugwort
mugwump
mujik
mulatto
mulberry
mulch
mulct
mule
muleteer
muley
mulish
mull
mulla
mullah
mullen
mullein
mullet
mulley
mullion
mullock
mullocky
mulse

multifid
multifoil
multifold
multiform
multipara
multiped
multipede
multiple
multiplet
multiplex
multiply
multitude
multure
mum
mumble
mumm
mummery
mummiform
mummify
mummy
mump
mumpish
mumps
munch
mundane
mungo
mungoose
municipal
muniment
munition
munity
munnion
muraena
mural
murder
murderess
murderous
mure
murex
murexes
murexide
muriate
muriatic
muricate
murices
muriform
murine
murk
murky
murmur
murmurous
murr
murrain
murre
murrelet
murrey
murrhine
murrine

musaceous
musca
muscae
muscadine
muscarine
muscat
muscadel
muscatel
muscavada
muscid
muscle
muscoid
muscovade
muscovado
muscovite
muscovy
muscular
muse
museful
musette
museum
mush
mushroom
mushy
music
musical
musicale
musician
musk
muskeg
musket
musketeer
musketry
muskit
muskmelon
muskrat
muskroot
musky
muslin
musquash
musquito
muss
mussel
mussy
must
mustache
mustachio
mustang
mustard
mustee
musteline
muster
musty
mutable
mutably
mutant
mutate
mutation

mutative
mute
mutic
muticate
muticous
mutilate
mutineer
mutinous
mutiny
mutter
mutton
mutual
mutualism
mutuality
mutualize
mutule
muzhik
muzjik
muzzle
my
myalgia
myalgic
myasis
mycelium
mycele
mycelial
mycelian
myceliod
mycetoma
mycologic
mycology
mycosis
mycotic
mydriasis
mydriatic
myelin
myeline
myeloid
myiasis
mylonite
myna
mynah
myogenic
myogenous
myogram
myograph
myography
myoid
myologic
myologist
myology
myoma
myomata
myomatous
myopathia
myopathic
myopathy
myope

myopia
myopic
myopy
myops
myosin
myosis
myosote
myosotis
myotic
myriad
myriagram
myriapod
myrica
myrmidon
myrobalan
myrrh
myrrhin
myrrhine
myrtle
myself
mystae
mystagog
mystagogy
mystery
mystic
mystical
mysticism
mystify
myth
mythic
mythical
mythicize
mythology
mythopeic
myxedema
myxedemic
myxoderma
myxoma
myxomata

N

nab
nabob
nacelle
nacre
nacreous
nadir
naevoid
naevus
nag
nagana
naiad
naiant
naif
nail
nainsook
naive
naivete

naked
namable
namaycush
name
nameless
namesake
nankeen
nankin
naos
nap
nape
napery
naphtha
naphthene
naphthol
naphtol
napiform
napkin
napless
napoleon
nappy
naprapath
narceia
narcein
narceine
narcism
narcissus
narcoma
narcose
narcosis
narcotic
narcotism
narcotize
nard
nardine
nares
naris
narghile
nargile
nargileh
narrate
narration
narrative
naratory
narrow
narthex
narwal
narwhal
narwhale
nasal
nasality
nasalize
nascence
nascency
nascent
naseberry
nasial
nasion

nasology
nasoscope
nastic
nasty
natal
natality
natant
natation
natatory
nates
nation
national
native
nativism
nativist
nativity
natrium
natrolite
natron
natural
nature
naught
naughty
naumachia
naumachy
nauplius
nausea
nauseate
nauseous
nautch
nautic
nautical
nautili
nautilus
naval
nave
navel
navelseed
navelwort
navicert
navicular
navigate
navvy
navy
neap
near
nearby
neat
neb
nebula
nebulae
nebular
nebulize
nebulose
nebulous
necessary
necessity
neck

neckband	neon	neuralist	nickelic	ninny	nodule	noontime
neckcloth	neophyte	neuration	nickelous	ninon	nodulose	noose
necklace	neoplasm	neuraxis	nickernut	ninth	nodulous	nopal
neckwear	neoplasty	neuraxon	nickname	niobium	nodus	nor
neckyoke	neostyle	neuremia	nicol	nip	noematic	noraghe
necremia	neoteric	neuremic	nicotin	nipa	noes	noria
necrology	neoterism	neuric	nicotine	nipple	noesis	norm
necropsy	neoterist	neurilema	nicotinic	nippy	noetic	normal
necrose	neotype	neurine	nictate	nirvana	nog	normalcy
necrosis	nep	neuritic	nictation	nisi	noggin	normality
necrotic	nepenthe	neuritis	nictitate	nit	noil	normalize
necrotomy	nepenthes	neurocele	nide	nite	noise	north
nectar	nepenthic	neurocyte	nidi	niter	noiseless	northeast
nectareal	neper	neuroid	nidify	nitid	noisome	northern
nectarean	nephelite	neurology	nidus	niton	noisy	northland
nectarial	nephew	neuroma	niece	nitrate	noma	northward
nectarine	nephology	neuromata	nielli	nitre	nomad	northwest
nectary	nephric	neuron	niello	nitric	nomadic	nose
nee	nephridia	neurone	niggard	nitrid	nomadical	noseband
need	nephrism	neuronic	niggle	nitride	nomadism	nosebleed
needfire	nephrite	neuropath	nigh	nitrify	nomarch	nosedive
needful	nephritic	neurosal	night	nitrile	nomarchy	nosegay
needle	nephritis	neuroses	nightbird	nitrite	nombril	nosepiece
needleful	nephroid	neurosis	nightcap	nitrogen	nome	nosology
needless	nephrosis	neurotic	nightfall	nitrolic	nominal	nostalgia
needy	nephrotic	neurotomy	nightgown	nitrosyl	nominate	nostalgic
nefarious	nepotic	neuter	nighthawk	nitrous	nominee	nostoc
negate	nepotism	neutral	nightjar	nitty	nomism	nostology
negation	nepotist	neutron	nightlong	nival	nomistic	nostril
negative	neptunium	never	nightmare	niveous	nomogram	nostrum
negatory	nereis	nevermore	nightrobe	nix	nomograph	not
neglect	neritic	nevi	nighttide	nixie	nomology	notarial
negligee	neroli	nevoid	nighttime	nizam	nomos	notarize
negligent	nervate	nevus	nigrify	nizamate	nonage	notary
negotiant	nervation	new	nigritude	no	nonagon	notation
negotiate	nervature	newcomer	nigrosine	nobble	nonane	notch
negus	nerval	newel	nihil	nobiliary	nonce	note
neigh	nerve	newish	nihilism	nobility	nonconcur	notebook
neighbor	nerveless	newmarket	nihilist	noble	nonduty	nothing
neither	nerviduct	news	nihility	nobleman	none	notice
nekton	nervine	newsboy	nil	nobody	nonentity	notify
nelson	nervosity	newsman	nilgai	nock	nones	notion
nelumbo	nervous	newspaper	nilgau	noctiluca	nonesuch	notional
nematode	nervule	newsprint	nilghai	noctuid	nonfeasor	notochord
nemertean	nervure	newsreel	nilghau	noctule	nonillion	notoriety
nemertian	nervy	newt	nill	noctuoid	nonpareil	notorious
nemertine	nescience	next	nimble	nocturnal	nonplus	notornis
nemesis	nescient	nexus	nimbus	nocturne	nonrigid	nougat
nemoral	ness	niacin	nimbuses	nocuous	nonsense	nought
nemorose	nest	nib	nimbi	nod	nonskid	noumenal
neodymium	nestle	nibble	nimiety	nodal	nonstop	noumenon
neogeic	net	niblick	nimious	noddy	nonsuit	noun
neogenic	netground	niccolite	nine	node	nonuple	nounal
neolith	nether	nice	ninefold	nodical	noodle	nourish
neologism	nettle	nicety	ninepin	nodose	nook	nous
neologist	neural	niche	nineteen	nodosity	noon	nova
neology	neuralgia	nick	ninetieth	nodous	noonday	novae
neomorph	neuralgic	nickel	ninety	nodular	noontide	novas

novation
novel
novelist
novelize
novelty
novena
novenary
novennial
novercal
novice
noviciate
novitiate
now
nowadays
noway
noways
nowhere
nowheres
nowhither
nowise
noxal
noxious
nozle
nozzle
nth
nuance
nub
nubia
nubile
nubility
nubilose
nubilous
nucellar
nucelli
nucellus
nucha
nuchae
nuchal
nucleal
nuclear
nuclease
nucleate
nucleic
nuclein
nuclei
nucleolar
nucleolus
nucleus
nude
nudge
nudism
nudist
nudity
nugatory
nugget
nuggety
nuisance
null

nullify
nullipara
nullipore
nullity
numb
number
numbskull
numen
numerable
numeral
numerary
numerate
numerical
numerous
numina
nummular
nummulite
numskull
nun
nunbird
nuncio
nuncius
nunnation
nunnery
nunnish
nuptial
nuragh
nuraghe
nurl
nurse
nurseling
nursemaid
nursery
nursling
nurture
nut
nutant
nutation
nutgall
nuthatch
nutlet
nutmeg
nutria
nutrient
nutriment
nutrition
nutritive
nutshell
nutty
nuzzle
nyanza
nyctalopy
nycterine
nylghi
nylghau
nymph
nympha
nymphae

nymphalid
nymphal
nymphean
nymphic
nymphical
nystagmic
nystagmus

O

oaf
oafish
oak
oaken
oakum
oar
oarfish
oarlock
oarsman
oary
oasis
oast
oat
oatcake
oaten
oatgrass
oath
oatmeal
obbligato
obcordate
obduracy
obdurate
obe
obeah
obedience
obedient
obeisance
obeisant
obeliscal
obelisk
obelize
obelus
oberek
obertas
obese
obesity
obey
obfuscate
obi
obit
obituary
object
objectify
objection
objective
objurgate
oblate
oblation
oblatory

obligate
oblige
obligee
oblique
obliquity
oblivion
oblivious
oblong
obloquy
obnoxious
oboe
oboist
obol
oboli
obolus
obovate
obovoid
obscene
obscenity
obscure
obscurity
obsecrate
obsequy
observant
observe
obsess
obsession
obsidian
obsolete
obstacle
obstetric
obstinacy
obstinate
obstruct
obstruent
obtain
obtect
obtest
obtrude
obtrusion
obtund
obtundent
obturate
obtuse
obverse
obversion
obvert
obviate
obviation
obvious
obvolute
ocarina
occasion
occident
occipital
occiput
occlude
occludent

occult
occultism
occultist
occupancy
occupant
occupy
occur
occurrent
ocean
oceanad
oceanic
ocellate
ocellar
ocelli
ocellus
ocelot
ocher
ocherous
ochery
ochre
ochreous
ochlocrat
ochone
ochroid
ocotillo
ocrea
ocreae
ocreate
octachord
octad
octadic
octagon
octagonal
octahedra
octameter
octan
octane
octangle
octant
octantal
octarchy
octaval
octave
octavo
octavos
octennial
octet
octette
octillion
octonary
octopi
octopodes
octopus
octopuses
octoroon
octuple
octuply
octyl

ocular
oculist
od
odalisk
odalisque
odd
oddity
oddment
odds
ode
odea
odeon
odeum
odic
odious
odium
odograph
odometer
odometry
odonatous
odontoid
odor
odorless
odorous
odyl
odyle
oedema
oenology
oenomel
oersted
oestrin
oestrum
oestrus
of
off
offal
offcast
offence
offend
offense
offensive
offer
offertory
office
official
officiant
officiary
officiate
officinal
officious
offing
offish
offprint
offset
offshoot
offshore
offside
oft

often
ofttimes
ogam
ogdoad
ogee
ogham
ogival
ogive
ogle
ogre
ogreish
ogrish
ogress
oh
ohm
ohmage
ohmic
ohmmeter
oii
oil
oilbird
oilcake
oilcloth
oilskin
oilstone
oilwell
oily
oinology
oinomel
ointment
oka
okapi
okay
oke
okra
old
oldish
oldster
oldstyle
oldwife
oleander
oleaster
oleate
olecranal
olecranon
olefiant
olefin
oleic
olein
oleograph
oleoresin
olfactie
olfaction
olfactory
olfacty
olibanum
oligarch
oligarchy

olio	ontologic	ophite	orange	orichalc	oscitant	otiose
olivary	ontology	ophitic	orangeade	orichalch	oscula	otiosity
olive	onus	opthalmy	orangery	oriel	osculant	otitis
olivine	onward	opiate	orate	orient	oscular	otocyst
olla	onyx	opine	oration	oriental	osculate	otolith
olykoek	oocyte	opinion	oratorio	orientate	oscule	otologist
omasa	oogamy	opium	oratory	orifice	osculum	otology
omasum	oogenesis	opiumism	oratress	oriflamme	ose	otoscope
omber	oogenetic	opodeldoc	orb	origan	osier	ottar
ombre	oogeny	opossum	orbicular	origin	osmic	otter
omega	oogone	oppidan	orbit	original	osmious	otto
omelet	oogonia	oppilant	orbital	originate	osmium	ottoman
omelette	oogonium	oppilate	orby	orinasal	osmose	ouabain
omen	oolite	opponency	orc	oriole	osmosis	ouch
omenta	oologic	opponent	orchard	orle	osmotic	ought
omental	oological	opportune	orcheitis	orlop	osmund	ounce
omentum	oologist	opposable	orchestra	ormer	osnaburg	our
omer	oology	oppose	orchid	ormolu	osphresia	ourebi
omicron	oolong	opposite	orchil	ornament	osphresis	ours
omikron	oomiak	oppress	orchis	ornate	osphretic	ourself
ominous	oomycete	oppugn	orchitic	ornis	osprey	ousel
omissible	oophore	oppugnant	orchitis	ornithic	ossa	oust
omission	oophoric	opsonic	orcinol	ornithine	ossature	out
omissive	oophyte	opsonify	ordain	ornithoid	ossein	outbid
omit	oophytic	opsonin	ordeal	orogenic	osseous	outboard
ommatidia	oosperm	opsonize	order	orogeny	ossicle	outbound
omnibus	oosphere	opt	ordinal	orography	ossicular	outbrave
omnific	oospore	optative	ordinance	oroide	ossific	outbreak
omophagia	oosporic	optic	ordinant	orologist	ossifrage	outbreed
omophagic	oosporous	optical	ordinary	orology	ossify	outburst
omphalos	ootheca	optician	ordinate	orometer	ossuary	outcast
on	oothecae	optics	ordnance	orometric	osteal	outclass
onager	oothecal	optime	ordure	orotund	osteitis	outcome
onagri	ooze	optimism	ore	orphan	ostensive	outcrop
onanism	oozy	optimist	oread	orphanage	ostensory	outcross
onanist	opacity	optimize	orectic	orphrey	osteoid	outcry
onanistic	opah	optimum	orective	orpiment	osteology	outcurve
once	opal	optima	oreide	orpine	osteoma	outdo
oncology	opalesce	option	orexis	orrery	osteomata	outdoor
ondogram	opalesque	optional	orfray	orrhology	osteopath	outer
ondograph	opaline	optometer	organ	orris	osteotome	outface
ondometer	opaque	optometry	organdie	orseille	ostiary	outfall
one	ope	optotype	organdy	ort	ostinato	outfield
onerous	open	opulence	organic	orthodox	ostiolar	outfit
oneself	opera	opulency	organical	orthodoxy	ostiole	outflow
onestep	operable	opulent	organism	orthoepic	ostler	outfoot
onion	operand	opuntia	organist	orthoepy	ostosis	outgo
onionskin	operate	opus	organize	orthogamy	ostracism	outgone
onlooker	operatic	opuscule	organon	orthopter	ostracize	outgrow
only	operation	oquassa	organzine	orthoptic	ostrich	outgrowth
onomastic	operative	or	orgasm	ortolan	otalgia	outguard
onomatopy	opercele	ora	orgastic	oryx	otalgic	outgush
onrush	opercule	orach	orgeat	os	otalgy	outhaul
onset	operetta	orache	orgiac	osar	otarian	outhouse
onslaught	operose	oracle	orgiastic	oscillate	otary	outing
onto	ophidian	oracular	orgic	oscine	other	outland
ontogenic	ophidism	oral	orgy	oscitance	otherwise	outlast
ontogeny	ophiology	orang	oribi	oscitancy	otic	outlaw

outlawry	ovarial	overmight	oviferous	oxyntic	pagan	palladous
outlay	ovarian	overmuch	oviform	oxyphyte	paganism	pallah
outleap	ovaritis	overpart	ovine	oxysalt	paganize	pallet
outlet	ovarium	overpass	ovipara	oxytocic	page	pallette
outlier	ovary	overpay	oviparous	oxytocin	pagent	pallia
outline	ovate	overplay	oviposit	oxytone	pagentry	palliasse
outlive	ovation	overplus	ovisac	oyer	paginal	palliate
outlook	ovational	overpower	ovoid	oyes	paginate	pallid
outlying	oven	overprint	ovoidal	oyez	pagod	pallium
outmoded	ovenbird	overprize	ovoli	oyster	pagoda	pallor
outmost	over	overproof	ovolo	oysterman	pagurian	palm
outplay	overact	overrate	ovotestis	ozaena	pagurid	palmar
outpoint	overage	overreach	ovulate	ozaenic	pah	palmate
outpost	overalls	override	ovulation	ozena	pahlavi	palmation
outpour	overbear	overrule	ovular	ozenic	pahoehoe	palmette
output ·	overbid	overrun	ovulary	ozocerite	paid	palmetto
outrage	overbite	oversea	ovule	ozonation	paidology	palmettos
outrance	overblow	overseas	ovum	ozone	pail	palmiped
outrange	overblown	oversee	owe	ozonic	pailful	palmist
outre	overboard	oversell	owl	ozonide	paillasse	palmistry
outreach	overbuild	overset	owlet	ozonize	paillette	palmitate
outride	overbuilt	oversew	owlish	ozonous	pain	palmitic
outrigger	overcast	overshade	own		painful	palmitin
outright	overcheck	overshine	ownerless	**P**	painless	palmy
outroot	overcloud	overshoe	ownership	pa	paint	palmyra
outrun	overcoat	overshoot	ox	pabular	pair	palnut
outsell	overcome	oversight	oxalate	pabulum	pais	palomino
outsentry	overcrop	oversize	oxalic	pac	pajamas	palp
outsert	overdo	overskirt	oxalis	paca	paktong	palpable
outset	overdose	oversleep	oxazin	pace	palace	palpably
outshine	overdraft	oversoul	oxazine	pacemaker	paladin	palpate
outshoot	overdraw	overspend	oxbow	pacha	palankeen	palpation
outside	overdue	overstate	oxen	pachalic	palanquin	palpebra
outsight	overdye	overstay	oxeye	pachisi	palatal	palpebrae
outsize	overfall	overstep	oxidase	pachyderm	palate	palpebral
outskirt	overflow	overt	oxidasic	pacific	palatial	palpi
outsole	overglaze	overtake	oxidate	pacifical	palatine	palpitate
outspan	overgrow	overthrow	oxidation	pacifism	palaver	palpus
outspeak	overhand	overtime	oxidative	pacifist	palay	palsgrave
outspent	overhang	overtone	oxid	pacify	pale	palsy
outspoken	overhaul	overtop	oxide	pack	palish	palter
outspread	overhead	overtrade	oxidize	package	palea	paltry
outstand	overhear	overtrick	oxim	packet	paleae	paludal
outstrip	overhours	overtrump	oxime	packsack	paleface	paludism
outstroke	overissue	overture	oxlip	packwax	paleocene	paly
outtell	overjoy	overturn	oxpecker	pact	paleolith	pam
outturn	overlade	overwatch	oxtail	pad	paleology	pampas
outward	overland	overwear	oxyacid	paddle	palestra	pampean
outwards	overlap	overweary	oxygen	paddock	palet	pamper
outwash	overlay	overween	oxygenate	paddy	paletot	pamphlet
outwear	overleap	overweigh	oxygenic	padlock	palette	pan
outweigh	overlie	overwhelm	oxygenize	padre	palfrey	panacea
outwit	overlive	overwind	oxygenous	padrone	palikar	panacean
outwork	overlook	overword	oxygon	padronism	palinode	panache
ouzel	overlord	overwork	oxygonal	paduasoy	palisade	panada
'ova	overly	overwrite	oxymel	paean	pall	pancake
oval	overman	ovibos	oxymora	paederast	palladic	pancratic
ovaria	overmatch	oviduct	oxymoron	paeon	palladium	pancreas

panda	papaya	parameter	parkee	partook	patchwork	pauperism
pandanus	paper	paramount	parkway	partridge	patchy	pauperize
pandect	papery	paramour	parlance	party	pate	pause
pandemic	papilla	parang	parlay	parure	patella	pavan
pander	papillae	paranoia	parley	parura	patellae	pavane
panderage	papillary	paranoea	parlor	parvenu	patellar	pave
panderess	papilloma	paranoic	parlous	parvis	patellate	pavilion
panderism	papillon	paranoeac	parochial	parvolin	paten	pavior
pandoor	papillose	paranoid	parodic	parvoline	patency	paviour
pandour	papillous	paranymph	parodical	pas	patent	pavonine
pandowdy	papist	parapet	parodist	pasch	patentee	paw
pandurate	papistic	paraph	parody	pascha	patera	pawl
pandy	papistry	paraplegy	paroecism	paschal	paterae	pawn
pane	papoose	parasang	parol	pascual	paternal	pawnage
panegyric	pappi	parasceve	parole	pasha	paternity	pawnee
panel	pappoose	parasite	paronym	pashalic	path	pawnshop
panelwork	pappus	parasitic	paronymic	pashalik	pathetic	pawpaw
pang	pappose	paratroop	paroquet	pasquil	pathless	pax
pangamic	pappous	paravane	paroral	pasquin	pathogen	paxwax
pangamous	pappy	parboil	parotic	pass	pathogene	pay
pangamy	paprica	parbuckle	parotid	passage	pathogeny	payee
pangen	paprika	parcel	parotitic	passant	pathology	paymaster
pangolin	papula	parcenary	parotitis	passbook	pathos	paynim
panhandle	papulae	parcener	parotoid	passenger	pathway	payroll
panic	papule	parch	paroxysm	passerine	patience	pea
panicky	papyri	parcheesi	parquet	passible	patient	peabird
panicle	papyrus	parchesi	parquetry	passim	patina	peace
panmixia	par	parchisi	parquette	passion	patine	peaceful
pannier	para	parchment	parr	passional	patio	peach
pannikin	parablast	parcimony	parrakeet	passive	patois	peachy
panocha	parable	pardon	parramata	passivity	patriarch	peacock
panoche	parabola	pare	parrel	passkey	patrician	peacocky
panoply	parabole	parecious	parricide	passover	patricide	peafowl
panoptic	parabolic	paregoric	parroquet	passport	patrimony	peag
panorama	parachor	parent	parrot	passus	patriot	peahen
pansophic	parachute	parentage	parry	passuses	patriotic	peajacket
pansophy	paraclete	parental	parse	password	patristic	peak
pansy	parade	paresis	parsec	paste	patrol	peal
pant	paradigm	paretic	parsimony	pastel	patrolman	pean
pantalets	paradise	pareu	parsley	pastern	patron	peanut
pantaloon	parados	parfait	parsnip	pastiche	patronage	pear
pantheism	paradox	parfleche	parson	pastil	patronal	pearl
pantheist	paraffin	parflesh	parsonic	pastille	patroness	pearlite
pantheon	paraffine	parget	parsonage	pastime	patronize	pearmain
panther	paragoge	pargo	part	pastor	patronym	peasant
pantile	paragogic	parhelic	partake	pastorage	patroon	peasantry
pantoffle	paragon	parhelion	parterre	pastoral	patten	peascod
pantofle	paragraph	parhelium	partial	pastorate	patter	peasecod
pantology	parakeet	pariah	partible	pastorium	pattern	pease
pantomime	paralalia	paries	particle	pastrami	patty	peat
pantry	parallax	parietes	partisan	pastry	patulous	peatman
panzer	parallel	parietal	partite	pasturage	paucity	peaty
pap	paralogic	parillin	partition	pasture	pauldron	peavy
papa	paralysis	paris	partitive	pasty	paulin	peavey
papacy	paralytic	parish	partizan	pat	paulownia	pebble
papain	paralyze	parity	partlet	patagium	paunch	pebbly
papal	paramatta	park	partly	patch	paunchy	pecan
papaw	paramecia	parka	partner	patchhead	pauper	peccable

peccancy
peccant
peccary
peck
pectase
pectate
pecten
pectinate
pectic
pectin
pectines
pectize
pectoral
peculate
peculiar
peculium
pedagog
pedagogue
pedagogic
pedagogy
pedal
pedalier
pedant
pedantic
pedantry
pedate
pedatifid
peddle
peddlery
pederast
pederasty
pedes
pedestal
pediatric
pedicel
pedicle
pedicellar
pedicular
pedicure
pediform
pedigree
pedigreed
pediment
pedipalp
pedlar
pedler
pedograph
pedology
pedometer
pedrail
pedro
peduncle
pee
peek
peel
peen
peep
peephole

peepshow
peepul
peer
peerage
peeress
peerless
peeve
peevish
peewee
peg
pegmatite
pekan
pekin
pekoe
pelage
pelagian
pelagic
pelerine
pelf
pelican
pelisse
pelite
pelitic
pellagra
pellagrin
pellet
pellicle
pellitory
pellmell
pellucid
peloria
pelorism
peloriate
peloric
pelorus
pelota
pelt
peltast
peltate
peltry
pelvic
pelvis
pemican
pemmican
pemphigus
pemphix
pen
penal
penalize
penalty
penance
pence
pencel
penchant
pencil
pend
pendant
pendency

pendent
pendragon
pendulous
pendulum
peneplain
peneplane
penes
penetrant
penetrate
pengo
pengos
penguin
penholder
penial
penile
peninsula
penis
penitence
penitent
penknife
penman
penna
pennae
pennant
pennate
penniless
pennon
pennoncel
penny
pennywort
penology
penoncel
penpoint
pensil
pensile
pensility
pension
pensive
penstemon
penstock
pent
pentacle
pentagon
pentagram
pentalpha
pentane
pentarchy
penthouse
pentose
penuchle
penuckle
penult
penultima
penumbra
penumbrae
penumbral
penumbras
penurious

penury
peon
peonage
peony
people
pepla
peplos
peplum
peplus
pepo
peponida
pepper
pepperbox
pepperpot
peppery
pepsin
pepsine
pepsinate
peptic
peptide
peptize
peptone
peptonic
peptonize
peracid
perborate
perboric
percale
percaline
perceive
percent
percept
perch
perchance
percoid
percolate
percuss
perdition
perdu
perdue
perdure
peregrin
peregrine
pereirine
perennate
perennial
perfect
perfecto
perfervid
perfidy
perforate
perforce
perform
perfume
perfumery
perfuse
perfusion
perfusive

pergola
perhaps
peri
perianth
periblem
pericarp
pericline
pericycle
periderm
peridia
peridial
peridium
peridot
peridotic
perigeal
perigean
perigee
perigonia
perigyny
peril
perilous
perimeter
perimetry
perimorph
perinaeum
perineal
perineum
period
periodate
periodic
periodid
periodide
periotic
periphery
peripter
periptery
perisarc
periscope
perish
perisperm
peristoma
peristome
peristyle
periwig
periwinkle
perjure
perjury
perk
perky
perlite
permanent
permeable
permeably
permeance
permeant
permeate
permit
permute

peroneal
perorate
peroxid
peroxide
perpend
perpent
perpetual
perplex
perplexity
perron
perry
persalt
perse
persecute
persevere
persicary
persienne
persimmon
persist
person
persona
personae
personage
personal
personate
personify
personnel
perspire
persuade
pert
pertain
pertinent
perture
pertusis
pertussal
peruke
perusal
peruse
pervade
pervasion
pervasive
perverse
pervert
pervious
pes
pesade
pesky
pessary
pessimism
pessimist
pest
pesthole
pesthouse
pestilent
pestle
pet
petal
petaline

petalism
petalodic
petalody
petaloid
petalous
petard
petasos
petasus
petcock
petechia
petechiae
petechial
peter
petersham
petiolar
petiolate
petiole
petit
petite
petition
petitory
petrel
petrify
petroleum
petrolic
petrology
petronel
petrosal
petrous
petticoat
pettish
pettitoes
petty
petulance
petulancy
petulant
petunia
pew
pewage
pewee
pewit
pewter
pewterer
peyote
peyotl
pfennig
pfennige
pfennigs
phaenogam
phaeton
phagedena
phagocyte
phalange
phalangal
phalangeal
phalangean
phalanger
phalanges

phalanx	phlegmy	phototypy	pickaxe	pilar	piney	pipy
phalanxes	phloem	phrasal	pickerel	pilaster	pinfish	piquant
phalarope	phlogosed	phrase	picket	pilau	pinfold	pique
phalin	phlogosis	phratric	pickle	pilaff	ping	piquet
phallic	phlogotic	phratry	picklock	pilaw	pingrass	piracy
phallical	phlorizin	phreatic	picknick	pilchard	pinguid	piranha
phalism	phlox	phrenetic	pickthank	pilcher	pinhead	pirate
phallist	phlyctena	phrenic	pickup	pilcherd	pinhole	piratic
phallus	phobia	phrenitis	picnic	pile	pinion	piratical
phaneric	phobic	phrenosin	picolin	pileate	pinite	piraya
phanic	phoca	phthalein	picoline	piles	pinitol	pirouette
phantasm	phocae	phthalic	picot	pileum	pink	piscary
phantom	phocine	phthalin	picotee	pileus	pinkeye	piscina
pharisaic	phocoid	phthisic	picquet	pilewort	pinkie	piscinae
pharmacal	phoebe	phthisis	picrate	pilfer	pinkish	piscinal
pharmacy	phoebean	phycology	picric	pilgarlic	pinkroot	piscine
pharos	phoenix	phylae	picrite	pilgrim	pinky	pish
pharynx	phonate	phyle	picrol	pili	pinna	pisiform
pharynges	phonation	phyletic	pictorial	pill	pinnae	pismire
phase	phoneme	phylic	picture	pillage	pinnal	pisolite
phasic	phonemics	phyllium	piddle	pillar	pinnace	pisolitic
phasin	phonetic	phyllode	piddock	pillbox	pinnacle	pistache
phasine	phonetics	phyllody	pidgin	pillion	pinnate	pistachio
phasis	phonetist	phylloid	pie	pilloby	pinnation	pistareen
phat	phonic	phyllome	piebald	pillow	pinniped	pistil
pheasant	phonics	phyllopod	piece	pilose	pinnula	pistol
phellogen	phonodeik	phylum	piecemeal	pilosity	pinnular	pistole
phenacite	phonogram	physic	piecework	pilot	pinnulate	pistoleer
phenazin	phonolite	physical	piedmont	pilotage	pinnule	pistolier
phenazine	phonology	physician	pier	pilule	pinochle	piston
phenetol	phonotype	physics	pierce	pilular	pinocle	pit
phenetole	phonotypy	physique	pieridine	pimelosis	pinscher	pita
phenix	phoresis	phytin	pierrot	pimelotic	pint	pitch
phenol	phoresy	phytoid	piet	pimento	pintado	pitchfork
phenolate	phosgene	pi	pietism	pimola	pintados	pitchman
phenolic	phosphate	piacular	piety	pimp	pintail	pitchy
phenology	phosphene	piaffer	piffle	pimpernel	pintano	piteous
phenomena	phosphid	pianism	pig	pimple	pintle	pitfall
phenotype	phosphide	pianist	pigeon	pin	pinto	pith
phenyl	phosphin	piano	piggery	pinaceous	pinweed	pithless
phenylene	phosphine	piasaba	piggie	pinafore	pinwheel	pithy
phew	phosphite	piasava	piggin	pinang	pinworm	pitiful
phial	phosphor	piassaba	piggish	pinaster	piny	pitiless
philander	phot	piaster	piggy	pinball	pioneer	pitman
philately	photic	piastre	pigment	pincenez	pious	pitmans
philogyny	photics	piazza	pigmy	pincers	pip	piton
philolog	photocell	pibal	pignora	pinch	pipage	pittance
philologue	photogen	pica	pignus	pinchbar	pipal	pituitary
philology	photogene	pical	pignut	pinchbeck	pipe	pituitous
philomath	photomap	picador	pigpen	pinchbug	piperazin	pity
philomel	photon	picaroom	pigskin	pindling	piperine	pivot
philomela	photopia	piccolo	pigsty	pine	piperonal	pivotal
philopena	photopic	pice	pigtail	pineal	pipestone	pixilated
philter	photoplay	piceous	pigweed	pineapple	pipet	pixy
philtre	photostat	pichurim	pika	pinedrops	pipette	placable
phlebitic	phototaxy	pick	pike	pinene	pipit	placably
phlebitis	phototube	pickaroon	pikeman	pinery	pipkin	placard
phlegm	phototype	pickax	pikestaff	pinesap	pippin	placate

placation	plastic	pledget	plumage	podagra	polite	polypous
placatory	plastid	plena	plumate	podagral	politic	polypus
placative	plastomer	plenary	plumb	podesta	political	polysperm
place	plastral	plenism	plumbago	podgy	politician	polytopic
placebo	plastrom	plenist	plumbagos	podia	politico	polytypic
placeman	plastrum	plenitude	plumbeous	podiatry	politics	polyuria
placenta	plat	plenteous	plumbery	podium	polity	polyuric
placentae	platan	plentiful	plumbic	podsol	polka	polyzoic
placental	platane	plenty	plumbism	podurid	poll	pomace
placentas	plate	plenum	plumbous	podzol	pollack	pomaceous
placid	plateau	plenums	plumbum	podzolic	pollard	pomade
placidity	plateaus	pleonasm	plume	poem	pollen	pomander
plack	plateaux	pleopod	plumelet	poenology	pollenate	pome
placket	plateful	plerom	plumiped	poesy	pollex	pomelo
placoid	platelet	plerome	plumipede	poet	pollices	pomelos
plagal	platen	plesser	plummet	poetess	pollical	pommel
plagiary	platform	plessor	plummy	poetaster	pollinate	pomology
plague	platina	plethora	plumose	poetic	pollinia	pomp
plaguy	platinic	plethoric	plumosity	poetical	pollinium	pompadour
plaice	platinize	pleura	plump	poetics	polliwog	pompano
plaid	platinoid	pleurae	plummule	poetize	pollock	pompanos
plain	platinous	pleural	plumy	poetry	pollute	pompon
plainsman	platinum	pleurisy	plunder	pogonia	pollution	pompous
plaint	platitude	pleuritic	plunge	pogonip	polo	pomposity
plaintiff	platoon	pleuron	plunk	pogrom	poloist	poncho
plaintive	platypus	pleuston	plural	pogy	polonaise	ponchos
plait	plaudit	plexiform	pluralism	poh	polonium	pond
plan	plausible	plexor	pluralist	poignant	poltroon	ponder
planar	plausive	plexus	plurality	poinciana	polyandry	ponderous
planarian	play	plexuses	pluralize	point	polyarchy	pondlily
planch	playa	pliable	plus	pointless	polybasic	pondweed
planche	playback	pliancy	plush	poise	polydemic	pone
planchet	playbill	pliant	plushy	poison	polygala	ponent
plane	playboy	plica	plutarchy	poisonous	polygamy	pongee
planet	playday	plicae	plutocrat	poitrel	polygenic	poniard
planetary	playful	plicate	plutonic	poke	polyglot	pontianak
planetoid	playgoer	plication	plutonium	pokeberry	polygon	pontifex
plangency	playhouse	plicature	pluvial	pokerface	polygonal	pontiff
plangent	playmate	plight	pluviose	pokerish	polygonum	pontific
planiform	plaything	plinth	pluvious	pokeweed	polygony	pontil
planish	playtime	plod	ply	pokeroot	polygraph	ponton
plank	plaza	plop	plywood	pokey	polygyny	pontonier
plankton	plea	plosion	pneuma	poky	polyhedra	pontoon
plant	pleach	plosive	pneumatic	polacca	polymer	pony
plantain	plead	plot	pneumonia	polacre	polymeric	pood
plantar	pleasance	plough	pneumonic	polar	polymorph	poodle
planula	pleasant	ploughman	poaceous	polarity	polyose	pooh
planulae	please	plover	poach	polarize	polyp	poohpooh
planular	pleasure	plow	poachy	pole	polypary	pool
planulate	pleat	plowboy	pochard	polecat	polyphase	poon
plaque	pleb	plowman	pock	polemic	polyphemus	poop
plash	plebian	plowshare	pocket	polemical	polyphonic	pooquaw
plashy	plebs	plowstaff	pockety	polemics	polyphony	poor
plasma	plectron	ploy	pockmark	polestar	polypi	poorhouse
plasmatic	plectra	pluck	pocky	police	polypidom	pop
plasmic	plectrum	plucky	pocosin	policeman	polyploid	popcorn
plastein	pledge	plug	pocoson	policy	polypod	pope
plaster	pledgee	plum	pod	polish	polypody	popedom

popery	pose	pother	prandial	pregnable	pressmark	primp
popgun	posit	pothole	prank	pregnancy	presspahn	primrose
popinjay	position	pothook	prankish	pregnant	pressure	prince
popish	positive	pothouse	prase	prejudge	presswork	princekin
poplar	positron	pothunter	prate	prejudice	prester	princess
poplin	posologic	potion	pratique	prelacy	prestige	princesse
popliteal	posology	potlatch	prattle	prelate	presto	principal
poplitic	posse	potlead	pravity	prelatic	presume	principia
popover	possess	potpie	prawn	prelatism	pretence	principle
poppet	posset	potpourri	praxis	prelatist	pretend	prink
popple	possible	potshard	pray	prelature	pretense	print
poppy	possibly	potsherd	praya	prelect	preterit	printery
poppyhead	possum	potstone	prayer	prelude	preterite	printless
populace	possumhaw	pott	prayerful	preludial	pretermit	prior
popular	post	pottage	preach	prelusion	pretext	priorate
populate	postage	pottery	preadamic	prelusive	pretor	priorship
populous	postal	pottinger	preagonal	prelusory	pretorian	prioress
porbeagle	postcard	pottle	preamble	premature	prettify	priority
porcelain	postdate	potto	preaxial	premier	pretty	priory
porch	posterior	pottos	prebend	premise	pretzel	prise
porcine	posterity	pouch	prebendal	premium	prevail	prism
porcupine	postern	pouched	precancel	premolar	prevalent	prismatic
pore	postfix	pouchy	precative	premonish	prevent	prismoid
porgy	posthaste	poulaine	precatory	premorse	preverb	prison
porism	postil	poulard	precede	prenatal	prevernal	prissy
pork	postilion	poult	precedent	prenomen	preview	pristine
porky	postlude	poulterer	precent	prenotion	previous	privacy
porkwood	postman	poultice	precept	prentice	previse	private
poroscopy	postmark	poultry	precinct	preoccupy	prevision	privateer
porosity	postnatal	pounce	precious	preordain	prewar	privation
porous	postpone	pound	precipe	prepare	prey	privative
porphyrin	postulant	poundage	precipice	prepay	price	privet
porphyry	postulata	poundal	precis	prepense	priceless	privilege
porpoise	postulate	pour	precise	prepostor	pricelist	privity
porridge	posture	pourpoint	precisian	prepotent	prick	privy
porringer	postural	poussette	precision	prepuce	pricket	prize
port	posturist	pout	preclude	preputial	prickle	pro
portage	posturize	poverty	precocial	presage	pride	proa
portal	postwar	powder	preconize	presbyopia	prideful	probable
porte	posy	powdery	precursor	presbyopic	priest	probably
portee	pot	power	predacity	presbyter	priestess	probands
portend	potable	powerful	predate	prescient	priestly	probang
portent	potash	powerless	predatory	prescind	prig	probate
portfolio	potass	powter	predicant	prescribe	priggish	probation
porthole	potassium	powther	predicate	prescript	priggism	probative
portico	potassic	pox	predict	presence	prim	probatory
porticoes	potation	practical	predigest	present	primacy	probe
porticoed	potato	practice	preempt	presentee	primage	probity
porticos	potatory	practicum	preen	presentive	primal	problem
portiere	potbelly	practise	preexilic	preserve	primary	proboscis
portion	potboy	praenomen	preface	preside	primate	procaine
portly	poteen	praetor	prefatory	presidency	primatial	procarp
portrait	potence	pragmatic	prefect	president	primavera	procedure
portray	potency	prahu	prefer	presidial	prime	proceed
portrayal	potent	prairie	prefigure	presidium	primero	proceeds
portress	potentate	praise	prefix	press	primeval	process
porteress	potential	praline	prefixal	pressgang	primine	prochain
portulaca	potentize	prance	prefixion	pressman	primipara	prochein

proclaim
proclitic
proconsul
procreant
procreate
proctor
procubent
procuracy
procural
procure
procuress
prod
prodigal
prodigy
prodromal
prodrome
prodromi
prodromus
produce
product
proem
proemial
profane
profanity
profert
profess
professor
proffer
profile
profit
profiteer
profluent
profound
profuse
profusion
prog
progeny
progestin
prognosis
program
programme
progress
prohibit
project
prolactin
prolamin
prolamine
prolapse
prolapsus
prolate
proleg
prolepsis
proleptic
proletary
prolicide
prolific
prolix
prolixity

prolog
prologue
prologize
prolong
prolonge
prolusion
promenade
prominent
promise
promisee
promissory
promote
promotion
promotive
prompt
promulge
pronate
pronation
prone
prong
pronghorn
pronoun
pronounce
pronto
proof
prop
propagate
propane
propel
propene
propense
proper
property
prophase
prophecy
prophesy
prophet
prophetic
propionic
propolis
propone
proponent
proposal
propose
propositi
propound
propretor
propriety
proptosis
propyl
propyla
propylaea
propylene
propylite
propylon
prorate
proration
prorogue

prosaic
prosaical
prosaism
proscenia
proscribe
proscript
prose
prosect
prosecute
proselyte
proser
prosodist
prosodic
prosodiac
prosodial
prosody
prospect
prosper
prostate
prostatic
prostrate
prostyle
prosy
protamin
protamine
protasis
protean
protease
protect
protege
protegee
protein
proteose
protest
prothesis
prothetic
prothorax
protist
protistan
protistic
protocol
protogram
proton
protonema
protoneme
prototype
protoxide
protozoan
protozoic
protozoon
protract
protrude
protyl
protyle
proud
prove
proven
proverb

provide
provident
province
provision
proviso
provisory
provoke
provost
prow
prowess
prowl
proximate
proximity
proximo
proxy
prude
prudenee
prudent
prudery
prudish
pruinose
prune
prunella
prunelle
prunello
prurience
pruriency
prurient
prurigo
prussiate
prussie
pry
psalm
psalmist
psalmody
psalter
psaltery
psamite
psamitic
psellism
psephite
psephitic
pseudaxes
pseudaxis
pseudonym
pseudopod
pshaw
psilosis
psilotic
psoas
psora
psoric
psoriasis
psoriatic
psyche
psychic
psychical
psychics

psychopath
psychosis
psychotic
psyllium
ptarmigan
pteropod
pterygoid
ptisan
ptomain
ptomaine
ptosis
ptotic
ptyalin
ptyalism
puberty
pubes
pubescent
pubic
pubis
public
publican
publicist
publicity
publish
puccoon
puce
pucelle
puck
puckish
pucker
puckery
pudding
puddle
puddly
puddlebar
pudency
pudenda
pudendum
pudic
pudendal
pudgy
pueblo
pueblos
puerile
puerility
puff
puffball
puffery
puffin
puffy
pug
pugh
pugilism
pugilist
pugnacity
puisne
puissance
puissant

puke
pulay
pule
pulex
pulicene
pulkha
pull
pullback
pullet
pulley
pullulate
pulmonary
pulmonate
pulmonic
pulp
pulpless
pulpit
pulpiteer
pulpwood
pulpy
pulque
pulsate
pulsatile
pulsation
pulsative
pulsatory
pulse
pulseless
pulverize
pulvillus
pulvinar
pulvinate
puma
pumice
pummel
pump
pumpkin
pun
puna
punch
puncheon
punctate
punctilio
punctual
punctuate
puncture
pundit
pungence
pungency
pungent
punish
punitive
punitory
punk
punka
punkah
punkey
punkie

punky
punster
punt
punto
punty
puny
pup
pupa
pupae
pupal
pupate
pupation
pupil
pupilage
pupilary
puppet
puppy
puppyish
pur
purblind
purchase
pure
pureblood
purebred
puree
purfle
purgative
purgatory
purge
purify
purin
purine
purism
purist
puristic
purity
purl
purlieu
purlin
purline
purloin
purple
purplish
purport
purpose
purpura
purpure
purpuric
purr
purse
purser
purslane
pursuance
pursuant
pursue
pursuit
pursy
pursiness

purulent	pyorrheal	quack	quassin	quinine	rabboni	radium
purulence	pyosis	quackery	quassiin	quinnat	rabid	radius
purulency	pyralid	quackhood	quatorze	quinoid	rabic	radix
purvey	pyralidan	quackism	quaver	quinoidin	rabies	radices
purview	pyralidid	quad	quavery	quinolin	raca	radixes
pus	pyramid	quadrant	quay	quinone	raccoon	radon
push	pyramidal	quadrat	quayage	quinonoid	race	radula
pushball	pyramidic	quadrate	quean	quinsy	racetrack	radulae
pushcart	pyran	quadratic	queasy	quint	raceme	raff
puss	pyre	quadric	quebracho	quintal	racemic	raffia
pussley	pyrene	quadrifid	queen	quintan	racemism	raffinose
pussly	pyrenoid	quadriga	queenpost	quintet	racemize	raffish
pussy	pyrethrum	quadrigae	queer	quintette	racemoid	raffle
pussyfoot	pyretic	quadrille	quell	quintile	racemose	rafflesia
pustulant	pyrexia	quadrivia	quench	quintuple	racemous	raft
pustular	pyrexial	quadroon	quercetic	quip	raceway	rafter
pustulate	pyrexic	quadruped	quercetin	quippish	rachial	raftsman
pustule	pyridic	quadruple	quercine	quipster	rachides	rag
put	pyridine	quaere	querist	quipu	rachis	rage
putamen	pyriform	quaestor	querl	quire	rachises	ragee
putamina	pyrite	quaff	quern	quirk	rachitic	ragged
putative	pyrites	quag	querulous	quirky	rachitis	raggstone
putlog	pyritic	quagga	query	quirl	racial	raggy
putrify	pyritical	quaggy	quest	quirt	racialism	ragi
putrid	pyrogenic	quagmire	question	quish	racialist	raglan
putridity	pyrograph	quagmiry	quetzal	quisling	racism	ragman
putt	pyrology	quahaug	quetzales	quite	racist	ragout
puttee	pyrolysis	quahog	quezal	quittance	rack	ragpicker
puttier	pyrolitic	quail	queue	quiver	racket	ragstone
putty	pyromancy	quaint	quibble	quixotic	rackety	ragtime
puttyroot	pyromania	quake	quick	quixotism	racketeer	ragweed
puy	pyrometer	qualify	quicken	quiz	rackwork	ragwort
puzzle	pyrometry	quality	quicklime	quizzical	racon	raia
pyaemia	pyrone	qualm	quicksand	quod	raconteur	raid
pycnidia	pyrope	qualmish	quickset	quohog	racoon	rail
pycnidial	pyrophore	qualmy	quickstep	quoin	racquet	railbird
pycnidium	pyrosis	quamash	quid	quoit	racy	railhead
pye	pyrostat	quandary	quiddity	quondam	radar	railery
pyeletee	pyrotic	quandong	quiddle	quorum	raddle	railroad
pyeletis	pyrotoxin	quanta	quidnunc	quota	radial	railway
pyelogram	pyroxene	quantic	quiescent	quotation	radian	raiment
pyemia	pyroxenic	quantify	quiet	quote	radiance	rain
pyemic	pyroxylin	quantity	quietism	quoth	radiancy	rainband
pygidia	pyrrhic	quantum	quietist	quotidian	radiant	rainbow
pygidium	pyrrol	quarrel	quietude	quotient	radiate	raincoat
pygmaean	pyrrole	quarry	quietus		radiative	raindrop
pygmean	python	quart	quill	**R**	radiation	rainfall
pygmy	pythoness	quartan	quillai	rabat	radiator	rainproof
pyic	pythonic	quarte	quillaia	rabato	radiatory	rainstorm
pyin	pyuria	quarter	quillback	rabbet	radical	rainy
pyknic	pyx	quartern	quilt	rabbi	radicel	raise
pylon	pyxides	quartet	quinary	rabbin	radicle	raisin
pyloric	pyxidium	quartile	quinate	rabbinic	radii	raisonne
pylorus	pyxie	quarto	quince	rabbinism	radio	raj
pyogenic	pyxis	quartz	quincunx	rabbinist	radiode	raja
pyoid		quartzite	quinic	rabbit	radiogram	rajah
pyorrhea	**Q**	quash	quinidine	rabbitry	radiology	rake
pyorrhoea	qua	quassia	quinin	rabble	radish	rakehell

rakehelly	ransom	ratlin	reality	recital	redcap	refer
rakish	rant	ratline	realize	recite	redcoat	referral
rale	ranunculi	ratling	realm	reckless	redd	referee
ralliform	rap	ratoon	realtor	reckon	redden	reference
ralline	rapacious	ratsbane	realty	reclaim	reddenda	refill
rally	rapacity	rattan	ream	recline	reddendum	refine
ram	rape	ratten	reanimate	recluse	reddish	refinery
ramble	rapist	rattish	reap	reclusive	reddle	refit
rambutan	rapeseed	rattle	rear	reclusion	reddleman	reflate
ramee	raphe	rattlebox	rearhorse	recognize	redeem	reflect
ramekin	raphia	rattrap	rearm	recoil	redeliver	reflex
ramenta	raphide	ratty	rearmost	recollect	redemand	reflexive
ramentum	raphis	raucous	rearmouse	recommend	redevelop	refluence
ramequin	rapid	raucity	rearrange	recommit	redfin	refluency
ramet	rapidity	ravage	rearward	recompose	redhead	refluent
ramie	rapier	rave	rearwards	reconcile	redingote	reflux
ramiform	rapine	ravel	reason	recondite	redirect	reforest
ramify	rapparee	ravelin	reassure	reconsign	redolence	reform
ramilie	rappee	raven	rebat	reconvey	redolent	reformist
ramillie	rappel	ravenous	rebate	record	redolency	refract
rammish	rapport	ravin	rebato	recount	redouble	refractor
rammy	rapt	ravine	rebec	recoup	redoubt	refrain
ramose	raptorial	ravioli	rebeck	recourse	redound	refresh
ramous	rapture	ravish	rebel	recover	redowa	reft
ramp	rapturous	raw	rebeldom	recovery	redpoll	refuge
rampage	rare	rawhide	rebellion	recreant	redraft	refugee
rampancy	rarebit	rawish	rebill	recreate	redress	refulgent
rampant	rarefy	ray	rebirth	recrement	redroot	refund
rampart	rareripe	raya	reboant	recruit	redshank	refusal
rampion	rarity	rayah	reborn	recta	redskin	refuse
ramrod	rascal	raygrass	rebound	rectal	redstart	refutal
ramson	rascality	rayless	rebuff	rectangle	redtop	refute
ramtil	rase	rayon	rebuke	recti	reduce	regain
ramulose	rash	raze	rebus	rectify	reductase	regal
ramus	rasher	razee	rebut	rectitude	reduction	regale
rami	rasorial	razor	rebuttal	recto	reductive	regalia
rance	rasp	razorback	recall	rector	redundant	regality
ranch	raspberry	razorbill	recant	rectorate	redware	regard
ranche	raspy	razzia	recap	rectorial	redwing	regardant
rancheria	rasure	re	recapture	rectory	redwood	regardful
ranchero	rat	reach	recast	rectum	ree	regatta
ranchman	ratafee	react	recede	rectus	reed	regelate
rancho	ratafia	reactance	receipt	recumbent	reedling	regency
ranchos	ratal	reaction	receive	recur	reedmace	regent
rancid	ratan	reactivate	recension	recurrent	reedy	regicidal
rancidity	ratany	reactive	recent	recurvate	reef	regicide
rancor	rataplan	read	recency	recurve	reefy	regime
rancorous	ratch	readjust	recept	recusant	reek	regimen
rand	ratchet	readmit	receptacle	recusancy	reeky	regiment
randan	rate	ready	reception	recuse	reel	reginal
randem	ratel	reagent	receptive	red	reenforce	region
random	rather	real	receptor	redact	reenter	regional
rang	ratify	reales	recess	redaction	reentrant	register
range	ratio	reals	recession	redan	reentry	registrar
rangy	ration	realgar	recessive	redbird	reeve	registry
rank	rational	realism	recipe	redbreast	refection	reglet
rankle	rationale	realist	recipient	redbud	refective	regma
ransack	ratite	realistic	recision	redbug	refectory	regnal

regnant	relique	renitency	reproof	resist	retention	revere
regorge	relish	renitent	reproval	resistant	retentive	reverence
regrade	relocate	rennet	reprove	resistive	retiarii	reverend
regrate	relucent	rennin	reptant	resole	retiarius	reverent
regress	reluct	renounce	reptile	resoluble	retiary	reverie
regret	reluctant	renovate	reptilian	resolute	reticence	revers
regula	relume	renown	republic	resolve	reticency	reversal
regulae	relumine	renowned	republish	resolvent	reticent	reverse
regular	rely	rent	repudiate	resonance	reticle	reversion
regulate	remain	rental	repugnant	resonant	reticula	reverso
reguli	remainder	reopen	repulse	resonate	reticular	revert
reguline	reman	reorient	repulsion	resonator	reticule	revertive
regulus	remand	repair	repulsive	resorb	reticulum	revery
rehash	remanence	repand	repute	resorcin	retiform	revest
rehearsal	remanent	reparable	reputed	resort	retina	revet
rehearse	remark	reparably	request	resound	retinae	review
reheat	remarque	repartee	requiem	resource	retinas	reviewal
reify	remarry	repast	require	respect	retinal	revile
reign	remedial	repay	requisite	respell	retinene	revisal
reimburse	remedy	repeal	requital	respire	retinite	revise
rein	remember	repeat	requite	respite	retinitis	revision
reindeer	remex	repel	reredos	respond	retinol	revisit
reinforce	remiges	repellent	rerun	response	retinue	revisory
reins	remigial	repent	rescind	rest	retiracy	revival
reinstall	remind	repentant	rescript	rester	retire	revive
reinstate	remindful	repeople	rescue	restful	retort	revivify
reinsure	reminisce	repertory	research	restiform	retorsion	revocable
reinvest	remise	repetend	reseat	restive	retortion	revocably
reis	remiss	repine	resect	restless	retouch	revoice
reissue	remission	replace	resection	restock	retrace	revoke
reitbok	remit	repleader	reseda	restore	retract	revolt
reiterate	remittal	replenish	resell	restrain	retral	revolute
reject	remittent	replete	resemble	restraint	retread	revolve
rejection	remnant	repletion	resent	restrict	retreat	revolving
rejoice	remodel	replevin	resentful	result	retrench	revue
rejoin	remontant	replevy	reserve	resultant	retrieval	revulsion
rejoinder	remontoir	replica	reservist	resumable	retrieve	revulsive
relapse	remora	replicate	reservoir	resume	retroact	reward
relate	remorse	reply	reset	resupine	retrocede	rewind
relation	remote	report	resh	resurface	retroflex	rewire
relative	remotion	reposal	reship	resurge	retrorse	reword
relax	remount	repose	reside	resurgent	retrospect	rewrite
relay	removal	reposeful	residence	resurrect	retrousse	reynard
release	remove	reposit	residency	ret	retrovert	rhaphe
relegate	renal	repossess	resident	retable	return	rhapsodic
relent	renascent	repousse	residual	retail	retuse	rhapsody
relevance	rend	reprehend	residuary	retain	reunion	rhatany
relevancy	render	represent	residue	retake	reunite	rhea
relevant	rendition	repress	residuum	retaliate	revamp	rhein
reliance	renegade	reprieve	residuua	retard	reveal	rhematic
reliant	renegado	reprimand	resign	retardant	reveille	rhenium
relic	renege	reprint	resile	retch	revel	rheology
relict	renig	reprisal	resilient	rete	revelator	rheometer
relief	renew	reprise	resin	retia	revelry	rheoscope
relieve	renewal	reproach	resinate	retell	revenant	rheostat
religion	reniform	reprobate	resinoid	retem	revenge	rheotaxis
religious	renin	reprocess	resinous	retene	revenue	rheotron
reliquary	renitence	reproduce	resiny	retent	reverb	rheotrope

rhesus	ricer	ringshake	roborant	roofage	rotche	rubbery
rhetor	rich	ringworm	robot	roofless	rote	rubberize
rhetoric	richweed	rink	roburite	rooftree	rotenone	rubbish
rheum	ricin	rinse	robust	rook	rotifer	rubbishy
rheumatic	rick	riot	roc	rookery	rotiferal	rubble
rheumy	rickets	riotous	rocambole	rookie	rotiform	rubella
rhigolene	rickety	rip	rochet	rooky	rotl	rubellite
rhinal	ricochet	riparian	rock	room	rotograph	rubeola
rhinitis	rictal	riparious	rockaby	roomful	rotor	rubeolar
rhino	rictus	ripcord	rockabye	roommate	rotten	rubescent
rhinology	rid	ripe	rockaway	roomy	rotund	rubicund
rhizobium	riddance	ripen	rocket	roorback	rotunda	rubidium
rhizoid	ridden	ripost	rocketeer	roost	rotundity	rubigo
rhizoidal	riddle	riposte	rockfish	root	rouble	rubious
rhizoma	ride	ripple	rockrose	rootless	rouche	ruble
rhizome	rident	ripplet	rockweed	rootlet	roue	rubric
rhizopod	riderless	ripply	rockwork	rootstalk	rouge	rubrical
rhizotomy	ridge	ripsaw	rocky	rootstock	rough	rubricate
rhodamin	ridgy	rise	rococo	rooty	roughage	rubrician
rhodamine	ridicule	risible	rod	rope	roughen	ruby
rhodic	ridotto	risky	rodent	ropery	roughneck	rucervine
rhodium	rife	risque	rodential	ropewalk	rouleau	ruche
rhodolite	riffle	rissole	rodeo	ropy	roulette	ruching
rhodonite	rifle	risus	rodman	roque	round	ruck
rhodopsin	rifleman	rite	rodsman	roquet	roundel	rucksack
rhodora	rift	ritual	roe	rorqual	roundelay	ructation
rhomb	rig	ritualism	roebuck	rosaceous	roundhand	rudbeckia
rhombic	rigadoon	ritualist	roentgen	rosary	roundish	rudd
rhombical	right	rival	rogation	rose	roundlet	rudder
rhomboid	righteous	rivalry	rogatory	roseate	roundworm	ruddle
rhombus	rightful	rive	rogue	rosebay	roup	ruddleman
rhonchal	rightist	river	roguery	rosebud	roupy	ruddock
rhonchi	rigid	riven	roguish	rosefish	rouse	ruddy
rhonchial	rigidity	riverine	roil	rosemary	roust	rude
rhonchus	rigmarole	riverside	roily	roseola	rout	rudiment
rhubarb	rigor	riverweed	roister	rosette	route	rue
rhumb	rigorism	rivet	rokelay	rosewater	routine	rueful
rhumba	rigorist	rivulet	role	rosewood	routinism	rufescent
rhyme	rigorous	roach	roll	rosin	routinist	ruff
rhymeless	riley	road	rollick	rosiny	rove	ruffe
rhyolite	rill	roadbed	rollicky	rosinweed	rowan	ruffed
rhythm	rille	roadblock	rollway	rosolio	rowboat	ruffian
rhythmic	rillet	roadstead	rollypoly	roster	rowdy	ruffle
rhythmics	rim	roadster	romaine	rostra	rowdyish	rufous
rhythmist	rime	roadway	roman	rostral	rowdyism	rug
rial	rimester	roam	romance	rostrate	rowel	ruga
rialto	rimose	roan	romantic	rostrum	rowen	rugae
riant	rimosity	roar	romaunt	rostrums	rowlock	rugate
riata	rimous	roast	romp	rosy	royal	rugged
rib	rimple	rob	rompish	rot	royalism	rugose
ribald	rimy	robalo	rondeau	rota	royalist	rugosity
ribaldry	rind	roband	rondel	rotary	royalmast	rugous
riband	ring	robbin	rondelet	rotate	royalty	ruin
ribband	ringbone	robber	rondo	rotation	rub	ruinate
ribbon	ringent	robbery	rondure	rotative	rubace	ruination
ribwort	ringhals	robe	ronquil	rotatores	rubasse	ruinous
rice	ringlet	robin	rood	rotatory	rubato	rule
ricebird	ringneck	roble	roof	rotch	rubber	rum

rumba	rutting	safety	salinity	same	sansar	sarsenet
rumble	ruttish	safflower	saliva	samech	santonica	sartor
rumen	rutty	saffron	salivary	samek	santonin	sartorial
rumina	rye	safranin	salivate	samekh	santonine	sartorius
ruminant	rynd	safranine	sallet	samisen	sap	sash
ruminate	ryot	safrol	sallow	samite	sapadillo	sashay
rummage		safrole	sallowish	samlet	sapajou	saskatoon
rummer	**S**	sag	sallowy	samoan	sapanwood	sass
rummy		saga	sally	samp	saphead	sassaby
rumor	sabadilla	sagacious	salmi	sampan	saphena	sassafras
rump	sabbat	sagacity	salmis	samphire	saphenae	satang
rumple	saber	sagaman	salmon	sample	saphenous	satanic
run	sabicu	sagamore	salmonoid	sanative	sapid	satanical
runagate	sabine	saganash	salol	sanatory	sapidity	satchel
runcinate	sable	sage	salon	sanbenito	sapience	sate
rundle	sabotage	sagebrush	saloon	sanctify	sapiency	sateen
rundlet	saboteur	saggar	salpa	sanction	sapient	satellite
runlet	sabulose	saggard	salpian	sanctity	sapless	satiable
rune	sabulous	sagger	salpid	sanctuary	sapling	satiably
runic	sac	sagittal	salpiform	sanctum	sapodilla	satiate
rung	sacaton	sagittate	salpinx	sand	saponify	satiation
runnel	saccate	sago	salpinges	sandal	saponin	satiety
runt	saccharic	saguaro	salsify	sandaled	saponine	satin
runty	saccharin	saguaros	salsilla	sandarac	saponite	satinet
runway	sacculate	sagum	salt	sandarach	sapor	satinette
rupee	saccule	sagy	saltant	sandbag	saporific	satinpod
rupture	sacculi	said	saltation	sandbar	saporous	satinwood
rural	sacculus	saiga	saltatory	sandblast	sapota	satiny
ruralism	sachem	sail	saltern	sandblind	sapour	satire
ruralist	sachet	sailboat	saltier	sandbox	sapphire	satiric
rurality	sack	sailcloth	saltire	sandbur	sappy	satirical
ruralize	sackbut	sailfish	saltish	sandburr	sapraemia	satirist
ruse	sackcloth	sainfoin	saltlick	sandcrack	sapremia	satirize
rush	sackful	saintfoin	saltpan	sandeel	sapremic	satisfy
rushlight	sacque	saint	saltpeter	sandman	saprolite	satrap
rushy	sacral	sainthood	saltpetre	sandpaper	sapsago	satrapy
rusine	sacrament	saith	saltworks	sandpiper	sapsucker	satrapate
rusk	sacraria	sajou	saltwort	sandpeep	sapwood	saturant
russet	sacrarium	sake	salty	sandstone	saraband	saturate
russety	sacred	saker	salubrity	sandstorm	sarabande	saturable
rust	sacrifice	salaam	saluki	sandwich	sarcasm	saturnid
rustic	sacrilege	salacious	salutary	sandwort	sarcastic	saturnine
rustical	sacrist	salacity	salute	sandy	sarcenet	saturnism
rusticate	sacristan	salad	salvable	sane	sarcocarp	satyr
rusticity	sacristy	salary	salvage	sanforize	sarcoma	satyric
rustle	sacra	sale	salvation	sangaree	sarcomata	satyrical
rusty	sacrum	saleratus	salve	sanguine	sarcous	sauce
rut	sad	salesman	salvia	sanicle	sard	saucepan
rutabaga	sadden	salicin	salvo	sanies	sardine	saucer
rutaceous	saddle	salicine	salvos	sanious	sardius	saucy
ruth	saddlebow	salicylic	salvoes	sanitaria	sardonic	sauger
ruthenic	saddlery	salience	salvor	sanitary	sardonyx	saunter
ruthenium	sadism	saliency	samara	sanitate	sargasso	saurel
ruthful	sadist	salient	samarium	sanitize	sargassum	saurian
ruthless	sadistic	salify	sambuca	sanity	sarment	sauropod
rutilant	safari	salimeter	sambuke	sannop	sarmenta	saury
rutilated	safe	salina	sambar	sannup	sarmentum	sausage
rutile	safeguard	saline	sambur	sans	sarsar	sauterne

sautoir	scalenus	scaur	schuyt	scoopful	scrim	scutter
savage	scall	scavenge	schwa	scoot	scrimmage	scuttle
savagery	scalled	scenari	sciaenid	scope	scrimp	scuta
savagedom	scallion	scenario	sciaenoid	scopoline	scrimpy	scutum
savagism	scallop	scenarios	sciamachy	scopulate	scrimshaw	scythe
savanna	scalp	scenarist	sciatic	scorbutic	scrip	sea
savannah	scalpel	scend	sciatica	scorbutus	script	seaboard
savant	scaly	scene	science	scorch	scripture	seafarer
save	scamble	scenery	sciential	scordato	scrive	seafaring
savin	scammony	scenic	scientism	score	scrivello	seal
savior	scamp	scenical	scientist	scoria	scrivener	sealery
saviour	scamper	scent	scilicet	scoriae	scrod	seam
savor	scampish	scentless	scimetar	scorify	scrofula	seaman
savour	scampy	scepter	scimitar	scoriform	scroll	seamless
savorous	scan	sceptic	scimiter	scorn	scroop	seamster
savorless	scandal	sceptical	scincoid	scornful	scrota	seamy
savory	scandent	sceptre	scintilla	scorpioid	scrotum	seance
savoy	scandia	schappe	sciolism	scorpion	scrotal	seaplane
saw	scandic	schatchen	sciolist	scotch`	scrub	seaport
sawn	scandium	schadchan	sciolous	scoter	scrubby	seaquake
sawbuck	scansion	schedule	sciomachy	scotfree	scrubland	sear
sawdust	scant	scheelite	scion	scotia	scruff	search
sawfish	scantling	scheik	sciophyte	scotoma	scrum	seascape
sawfly	scanty	schema	scirrhi	scotomata	scrummage	seashore
sawgrass	scape	schemata	scirrhoid	scotopia	scrunch	seasick
sawhorse	scapegoat	scheme	scirrhous	scoundrel	scruple	seaside
sawmill	scaphoid	schematic	scirrhus	scour	scrutiny	season
sawpit	scapolite	scherzi	scissile	scourge	scud	seasonal
sawyer	scapose	scherzo	scission	scourings	scudi	seasoning
sax	scapula	scherzos	scissor	scouse	scudo	seat
saxatile	scapulae	schilling	scissure	scout	scuff	seatstone
saxhorn	scapular	schism	sciurine	scow	scuffle	seawan
saxifrage	scapulary	schist	sciuroid	scowl	scull	seawant
saxophone	scar	schistose	sclera	scowler	scullery	seaward
saxtuba	scarab	schistous	sclerite	scrag	scullion	seawards
say	scarabee	schizont	scleritic	scraggy	sculpin	seaware
says	scarabaei	schizoid	scleritis	scramble	sculptor	seaway
scab	scarabeus	schizopod	scleroid	scrap	sculpture	seaweed
scabby	scaraboid	schliere	scleroma	scrapbook	scum	seaworthy
scabbard	scarce	schlieren	sclerosal	scrape	scumble	sebaceous
scabbling	scarcity	schlieric	sclerosed	scrapple	scummer	sebacic
scabies	scare	schnapper	sclerosis	scrappy	scummy	seborrhea
scabietic	scarecrow	schnapps	sclerotic	scratch	scup	sebum
scabiosa	scarehead	schnaps	sclerous	scratchy	scuppaug	secant
scabious	scarf	schnauzer	scoff	scrawl	scupper	secede
scabrous	scarfskin	scholar	scold	scrawny	scurf	secern
scaffold	scarify	scholarch	scolecite	screak	scurfy	secession
scaglia	scariose	scholia	scolex	scream	scurrile	seck
scagliola	scarious	scholiast	scoleces	scree	scurril	seckel
scalade	scarlet	scholium	scolices	screech	scurry	seclude
scalado	scarpetti	scholiums	scolioma	screechy	scurvy	seclusion
scalage	scarves	school	scoliosis	screed	scutage	seclusive
scalar	scat	schoolboy	scoliotic	screen	scutate	second
scald	scathe	schooling	scollop	screw	scutch	secondary
scaldic	scathless	schoolman	scombroid	screwbean	scutcheon	seconde
scale	scatology	schooner	sconce	scribble	scutella	secondine
scalene	scatter	schorl	scone	scribal	scutellar	secrecy
scalenous	scaup	schuit	scoop	scribe	scutiform	secret

secretary	seggar	semester	sentient	serail	servile	sextile
secrete	segment	semestral	sentiment	seral	servility	sexton
secretin	segmental	semibreve	sentinel	serape	servitor	sextuple
secretion	sego	semicolon	sentry	seraph	servitude	sextuplet
secretive	segregate	semidome	sepal	seraphim	sesame	sexual
secretory	seicento	semifinal	sepaline	seraphina	sesamoid	sexuality
sect	seiche	semifluid	sepalous	seraphine	sessile	shabbily
sectarian	seignior	semilunar	separable	serenade	sessility	shabby
sectary	seigneur	semimute	separata	serene	session	shack
sectarist	seigniory	seminal	separate	serenity	sessional	shackle
sectile	seine	seminar	separator	serf	sesspool	shacko
sectility	seise	seminary	separatum	serfdom	sesterce	shad
section	seisin	semiology	sepia	serfhood	sestet	shadberry
sectional	seismal	semiotic	sepiolite	serge	sestia	shadbush
sector	seismic	semirigid	sepoy	sergeant	sestina	shadblow
secular	seismical	semiround	sepsis	sergeancy	set	shaddock
secund	seismotic	semitone	sept	serjeant	seta	shade
secundine	seismism	semitonic	septa	serial	setae	shadeless
secure	seisor	semivowel	septaemia	seriate	setaceous	shadfly
security	seize	semolina	septal	seriatim	setback	shadoof
sedan	seizin	senary	septangle	seriation	setiform	shadow
sedate	seizure	scnate	septaria	sericeous	seton	shadowy
sedative	sejant	senator	septarian	seriema	setose	shadrach
sedentary	sejeant	send	septarium	series	setscrew	shaduf
sedge	selachian	sendal	septate	serif	settee	shady
sedged	selachoid	sendaline	septemia	serin	settle	shaft
sedgy	selah	senega	septemvir	serine	seven	shag
sedile	selamik	seneka	septenary	serious	sevenfold	shagbark
sedilia	seldom	senescent	septenate	sermon	seventeen	shaggy
sedilium	select	seneschal	septet	sermonic	seventh	shagreen
sediment	selectee	senile	septette	sermonize	seventhly	shah
sedition	selection	senility	septic	serology	seventy	shaik
seditious	selective	senior	septicide	seroon	sever	shake
seduce	selectman	seniority	septicity	serosity	several	shako
seduction	selenate	senna	septime	serotinal	severance	shaky
seductive	selenic	sennet	septule	serotine	severe	shale
sedulity	selenious	sennit	septum	serous	severity	shall
sedulous	selenite	senor	sepulcher	serpent	sew	shalloon
sedum	selenium	senora	sepulchre	serpentine	sewage	shallop
see	self	senorita	sepulture	serpigo	sewan	shallot
seecatch	selfheal	sensate	sequacity	serranoid	sewar	shallow
seed	selfhood	sensated	sequel	serrate	sewellel	shaly
seedcake	selfish	sensation	sequela	serrated	sewer	sham
seedcase	selfless	sense	sequelae	serration	sewerage	shammer
seedless	sell	senseless	sequence	serrature	sewn	shaman
seedling	sellinger	sensitive	sequency	serrefile	sex	shamanic
seedman	selvage	sensitize	sequent	serried	sexangle	shamble
seedsman	semanteme	sensor	sequester	serriform	sexangled	shame
seedy	semantic	sensoria	sequestra	serrulate	sexennial	shameful
seek	semantics	sensorial	sequin	serry	sexfid	shameless
seel	semaphore	sensorium	sequoia	serum	sexifid	shammy
seem	sematic	sensory	ser	serums	sexless	shamois
seep	semblable	sensual	sera	serval	sext	shampoo
seepage	semblably	sensuous	serac	servant	sextan	shamrock
seer	semblance	sent	serafile	serve	sextant	shanghai
seeress	semble	sentence	seraglio	service	sextarius	shank
seethe	semeiotic	sentience	serai	serviette	sextet	shanty
segar	semen	sentiency			sextette	shantyman

shape	sherif	shivy	shrike	sideburns	silicate	simulate
shapeless	sheriff	shoal	shrill	sidecar	siliceous	simurg
shard	sheroot	shoat	shrimp	sidelight	silicic	sin
share	sherry	shock	shrine	sideline	silicide	sinalbin
shark	shewbread	shod	shrink	sideling	silicify	sinapin
sharkskin	shewer	shoddy	shrinkage	sidelong	silicle	sinapine
sharp	sheyk	shoe	shrivel	sidepiece	silicon	sinapism
sharpen	shield	shoebill	shroud	siderite	silicosis	since
sharpie	shieling	shoeblack	shrove	sideritic	siliqua	sincere
shatter	shier	shoehorn	shrub	siderosis	silique	sincerity
shave	shift	shoemaker	shrubbery	sideswipe	siliquose	sinciput
shaveling	shiftless	shogun	shrubby	sidetrack	siliquous	sine
shawl	shifty	shogunate	shrug	sidewalk	silk	sinecure
shawm	shikaree	shone	shrunk	sideward	silkalene	sinew
shay	shikari	shoo	shrunken	sidewards	silkaline	sinewless
she	shikarree	shook	shuck	sideway	silken	sinewy
shea	shill	shoot	shudder	sideways	silkman	sing
sheaf	shillala	shop	shuffle	sidewise	silkweed	singe
shear	shillalah	shore	shun	siding	silkworm	single
shears	shillelah	shoreless	shunpike	sidle	silky	singlet
sheatfish	shillaly	shorl	shunt	siege	sill	singleton
sheath	shilling	short	shut	sienna	sillabub	singsong
sheathe	shily	shortage	shutdown	sierra	silly	singspiel
sheave	shim	shortcake	shutoff	siesta	silo	singular
sheaves	shimmer	shorten	shutout	sieur	silos	sinigrin
shed	shimmery	shorthand	shuttle	sieve	silt	sinister
sheen	shimmy	shorthorn	shy	sifaka	silty	sinistrad
sheeny	shin	shortia	shyster	siffle	silurid	sinistral
sheep	shine	shorting	si	sift	siluroid	sink
sheepcote	shingle	shortish	sialid	sigh	silva	sinkhole
sheepfold	shinleaf	shortstop	sialidan	sight	silvan	sinless
sheepish	shinney	shot	sialogog	sightless	silver	sinter
sheepskin	shinny	shote	sialoid	sightseer	silvern	sinuate
sheer	shiny	shotgun	sib	sigil	silvery	sinuosity
sheers	ship	shotten	sibb	sigillary	simarouba	sinuous
sheet	shipboard	should	sibilant	sigma	simaruba	sinus
sheeting	shipload	shoulder	sibilance	sigmate	simian	sinusitis
sheik	shipman	shout	sibilancy	sigmatism	similar	sinuitis
shekel	shipmate	shove	sibilate	sigmoid	simile	sip
sheldrake	shipment	shovel	sibling	sign	simioid	siphon
shelf	shippable	show	sibyl	signal	simious	siphonage
shell	shipshape	showbill	sibyllic	signalize	simitar	sippet
shellac	shipway	showboat	sibylline	signalman	simiter	sir
shellack	shipworm	showbread	sic	signatory	simlin	sirdar
shellback	shipwreck	showcase	siccative	signature	simmer	sire
shellbark	shipyard	showdown	sick	signboard	simoinac	siren
shellfire	shire	showery	sickbay	signet	simony	sirenian
shellfish	shirk	shown	sickbed	signify	simoom	siriasis
shellheap	shirr	showy	sicken	signior	simoon	sirloin
shellhole	shirt	shrank	sickish	signor	simper	sirocco
shelly	shirting	shrapnel	sickle	signory	simple	sirrah
shelter	shist	shred	sicklist	signpost	simpleton	sirup
shelve	shistic	shrew	sid	silage	simplex	sirupy
shelvy	shiv	shrewd	sidhe	silence	simplify	sisal
shend	shivaree	shrewish	siddur	silent	simply	siscowet
shepherd	shive	shriek	side	silesia	simulacra	siskawet
sherbet	shiver	shrieval	sideband	silex	simulant	siskiwit
shereef	shivery	shrift	sideboard	silica	simular	siskin

siss	skiff	slash	slogan	smearcase	snare	soakage
sister	skijoring	slat	sloid	smeary	snarl	soaky
sistroid	skilful	slate	slojd	smeath	snatch	soap
sistra	skillful	slattern	sloop	smee	snatchy	soapbark
sistrum	skill	slaty	slop	smell	snath	soapberry
sistrums	skilless	slaughter	slope	smelt	snathe	soapbox
sit	skillet	slave	sloppy	smeltery	sneak	soapstone
site	skilling	slavery	slopwork	smew	sneaky	soapsuds
sitfast	skim	slavish	slosh	smilax	snecked	soapwort
situate	skimpy	slavocrat	sloshy	smile	sneer	soapy
situation	skin	slaw	slot	smirch	sneeze	soar
six	skinflint	slay	sloth	smirk	snell	sob
sixfold	skingame	sleave	slothbear	smite	snicker	sobeit
sixpence	skink	sleazy	slothful	smith	sniff	sober
sixpenny	skinless	sled	slough	smithers	sniffle	sobriety
sixscore	skinny	sledge	sloughy	smithery	snifter	sobriquet
sixteen	skip	sleek	sloven	smithy	snigger	socage
sixteenmo	skipjack	sleep	slow	smitten	snip	sociable
sixteenth	skippet	sleepless	slowworm	smock	snipe	sociably
sixth	skirmish	sleepy	sloyd	smog	snippet	social
sixtieth	skirr	sleet	slub	smoke	snippy	socialism
sixty	skirret	sleety	sludge	smokeless	snits	socialist
sizable	skirt	sleeve	sludgy	smokepot	snivel	socialite
sizar	skit	sleigh	slue	smoky	snob	sociality
sizarship	skittish	sleight	slug	smolder	snobbery	socialize
size	skittle	slender	sluggard	smolt	snobbish	society
sizy	skive	sleuth	sluggish	smooch	snood	sociologic
sizz	skoal	slew	sluice	smooth	snore	sociology
sizzle	skua	slice	sluiceway	smoothen	snort	socket
sjambok	skulk	slick	slum	smote	snot	socle
skald	skull	slidden	slumber	smother	snotty	socman
skat	skullcap	slide	slumbery	smothery	snout	sockman
skate	skunk	slideknot	slumbrous	smudge	snow	sod
skatol	skunkweed	slight	slumgum	smudgy	snowball	soda
skatole	sky	slily	slump	smug	snowberry	sodalite
skean	skyey	slim	slungshot	smuggle	snowbird	sodality
skee	skylark	slime	slunk	smut	snowbroth	sodden
skeen	skylight	slimily	slur	smutch	snowbush	sodium
skeet	skyrocket	slimy	slurry	smutchy	snowdrift	sodomite
skeg	skysail	sling	slush	smutty	snowdrop	sodomy
skein	skyward	slingshot	slut	snack	snowfall	soever
skeletal	slab	slink	sluttish	snaffle	snowflake	sofa
skeleton	slabby	slip	sly	snag	snowplow	soffit
skelp	slack	slipcover	slyboots	snaggy	snowshed	soft
skep	slacken	slipknot	smack	snail	snowshoe	soften
skeptic	slag	slippage	small	snake	snowstorm	softhead
skeptical	slaggy	slipper	smallage	snakebird	snowsuit	soggy
sketch	slain	slippery	smallish	snakehead	snowwhite	soil
sketchy	slake	slipshod	smallpox	snakeroot	snowy	soilage
skew	slalom	slipslop	smalt	snakeweed	snub	soilure
skewbald	slam	slit	smaltine	snaky	snuff	soja
skewer	slander	slither	smaltite	snap	snuffbox	sojourn
ski	slang	slithery	smart	snapback	snuffle	soke
skiagraph	slant	sliver	smarten	snappish	snuffy	sokeman
skiascope	slantwise	slob	smartweed	snappy	snug	sol
skiascopy	slap	slobber	smash	snapshot	snuggery	solace
skid	slapjack	slobbery	smatter	snapweed	snuggle	soles
skidway	slapstick	sloe	smear	snoak	soak	solan

soland
solano
solanum
solar
solaria
solarism
solarium
solarize
solatia
solatium
sold
solder
soldier
soldiery
soldi
soldo
sole
solecism
solecist
solecistic
solecize
solemn
solemnity
solemnize
solenoid
soleret
solfatara
solfeggi
solfeggio
solferino
soli
solicit
solid
solidago
solidary
solideme
solidi
solidify
solidity
solidus
soliloquy
solipsism
solipsist
solitaire
solitary
solitude
solleret
solmizate
solo
solos
solstice
soluble
solubly
solum
solute
solution
solutive
solvation

solve
solvency
solvent
soma
somatic
somatics
somatism
somatist
somber
sombre
sombrero
some
somebody
somehow
someone
somerset
something
sometime
sometimes
someway
someways
somewhat
somewhen
somewhere
somewhy
somewise
somital
somite
somitic
somnific
somnolent
son
sonance
sonant
sonar
sonata
sonatina
sonatine
sonder
song
songbird
songful
songster
sonic
sonnet
sonneteer
sonority
sonorous
sonship
soochong
soon
soot
soothe
soothfast
soothsay
sooty
sop
sophism

sophist
sophister
sophistic
sophistry
sophomore
sopor
soporific
soppy
soprani
soprano
sopranos
sora
sorbitol
sorbose
sorcerer
sorceress
sorcerous
sorcery
sordid
sore
sorede
soredia
soredium
sorel
sorghum
sori
soricine
sorites
soritical
sorority
sorosis
sorption
sorrel
sorrow
sorrowful
sorry
sort
sortie
sorus
sot
sotol
sottish
sou
souari
soubrette
souchong
souffle
sough
sought
soul
souled
soulful
soulless
sound
soundbox
soup
sour

source
sourcrout
sourdine
sourgum
souse
south
southeast
souther
southerly
southern
southing
southron
southward
southwest
souwester
souvenir
sovran
sovranty
sovereign
soviet
sovietdom
sovietism
sovietist
sovietize
sow
sowther
soy
soya
soybean
sozin
sozine
spa
space
spacial
spacious
spade
spadeful
spadefish
spadices
spadix
spaghetti
spagiric
spagyric
spahee
spait
spall
spalpeen
span
spandrel
spanaemia
spanemia
spanemic
spangle
spaniel
spank
spanless
spar
spare

sparerib
sparge
spark
sparkish
sparkle
sparling
sparoid
sparrow
sparry
sparse
sparsity
sparteine
spasm
spasmodic
spastic
spate
spathal
spathe
spathic
spathose
spatial
spatter
spatula
spatular
spatulate
spavin
spawn
spay
speak
spear
spearfish
spearhead
spearman
spearmint
spearsman
spearwort
special
specialty
specie
species
specific
specify
specimen
specious
speck
speckle
spectacle
spectator
specter
spectre
spectra
spectral
spectrum
specula
specular
speculate
speculum
speculums

speech
speechify
speed
speedster
speedway
speedwell
speedy
speise
speiss
spelaean
spelean
spell
spellbind
spelt
spelter
spencer
spend
spent
sperm
spermary
spermatia
spermatic
spermatid
spermic
spermine
spermism
spew
sphagnum
sphagnous
sphene
sphenic
sphenodon
sphenoid
spheral
sphere
spheric
spherical
spherics
spheroid
spherular
spherule
sphery
sphincter
sphinges
sphinx
sphinxes
sphygmic
sphygmoid
sphygmus
spica
spicae
spical
spicate
spice
spicebush
spicewood
spicery
spicula

spicular
spiculate
spicule
spiculum
spicy
spider
spidery
spiegel
spigelia
spigot
spike
spikelet
spikenard
spiky
spile
spill
spillage
spillikin
spillway
spilosite
spilth
spin
spinach
spinage
spinal
spinate
spindle
spindrift
spine
spinel
spineless
spinet
spinifex
spinnaker
spinneret
spinnery
spinney
spinny
spinose
spinosity
spinous
spinster
spinula
spinule
spinulose
spiny
spiracle
spiraea
spirea
spiral
spirant
spire
spirem
spireme
spirilla
spirillum
spirit
spiritism

spiritist	sponsion	sprit	squeak	stallion	statical	stelar
spiritous	sponson	sprite	squeaky	stalwart	statics	stele
spiritual	sponsor	spritsail	squeal	stamen	station	stelene
spirituel	spook	sprocket	squeamish	stamina	stationer	steles
spiritus	spooky	sprout	squeegee	staminal	statism	stelic
spirogyra	spookily	spruce	squeeze	staminate	statist	stellar
spiroid	spookish	sprue	squelch	stamineal	statistic	stellate
spirula	spool	spry	squib	staminode	stator	stellular
spiry	spoon	spud	squid	staminody	statuary	stem
spissated	spoonbill	spume	squilgee	stammel	statue	stemless
spit	spoonful	spumous	squill	stammer	statuette	stemson
spitball	spoor	spumy	squilla	stamp	stature	stench
spite	sporadial	spumone	squinch	stampede	status	stencil
spittle	sporadic	spumoni	squint	stanch	statute	stenosis
spittoon	sporangia	spunk	squire	stanchion	statutory	stenotype
spitz	spore	spur	squirelet	stand	staunch	stenotypy
splash	sporidia	spurge	squirm	standard	stave	stentor
splashy	sporidium	spurious	squirmy	standish	stay	step
splatter	sporocarp	spurn	squirrel	standpipe	staysail	steppe
splay	sporocyst	spurrey	squirt	stanhope	stead	steradian
splayfoot	sporocyte	spurry	stab	staniel	steadfast	stere
spleen	sporogony	spurt	stabile	stannary	steady	stereome
spleenful	sporophyl	sputa	stability	stannel	steak	steric
spleenish	sporozoan	sputter	stabilize	stannic	steal	sterical
spleeny	sporran	sputum	stable	stannous	stealage	sterile
splendent	sport	spy	stableman	stannum	stealth	sterility
splendid	sportful	spyglass	stably	stanza	stealthy	sterilize
splendor	sportive	squab	staccato	stanzaic	steam	sterlet
splenetic	sportsman	squabbish	stack	stapedial	steamship	sterling
splenia	sporty	squabby	stacte	stapelia	steamy	stern
splenial	sporulate	squabble	stadia	stapes	steapsin	sterna
splenic	sporule	squad	stadium	staple	stearate	sternal
splenii	spot	squadron	stadiums	star	stearic	sternmost
splenium	spotless	squail	staff	starboard	stearin	sternpost
splenius	spotlight	squalid	stag	starch	stearine	sternson
splice	spotty	squall	stage	starchy	stearrhea	sternum
spline	spousal	squalor	staggard	stare	steatite	sternums
splint	spouse	squalus	staggart	starfish	stedfast	sternward
splinter	spout	squama	stagger	stargrass	steed	sternway
splintery	sprag	squamae	staghound	stark	steel	steroid
split	sprain	squamate	stagnancy	starless	steelhead	steroi
splotch	sprang	squamose	stagnant	starlight	steely	stertor
splotchy	sprat	squamosal	stagnate	starlike	steelyard	sterule
splutter	sprawl	squamous	stagy	starlit	steenbok	stet
spodumene	spray	squander	stagey	starling	steep	stevedore
spoil	spread	squantum	staid	starnose	steepen	stew
spoilage	spree	square	stain	starry	steeple	steward
spoilsman	sprig	squarrose	stainless	starshell	steer	sthenia
spoke	spriggy	squarrous	stair	start	steerage	sthenic
spoken	spright	squash	staircase	startle	steersman	stibial
spokesman	spring	squashy	stairway	starve	steeve	stibium
spoliator	springal	squat	stake	starwort	stegomyia	stibnite
spondaic	springald	squatty	stale	stasis	stein	stich
spondee	springbok	squaw	stalemate	state	steinbok	stichic
sponge	springe	squawbush	stalk	statement	stela	stichwort
spongin	springy	squawfish	stalkless	stateroom	stelae	stick
spongy	sprinkle	squawk	stalky	statesman	stelai	stickle
sponsal	sprint	squawroot	stall	static		

stickpin	stithy	stopcock	stream	stroud	stylize	sublime
stickseed	stiver	stope	streamlet	structure	stylobate	sublimity
stickweed	stoa	stopgap	street	struggle	styloid	sublunar
sticky	stoae	stoppage	strength	strum	stylolite	sublunary
stiff	stoas	stopple	strenuous	struma	stylus	submarine
stiffen	stoat	stopwatch	stress	strumae	stymie	submental
stifle	stob	storage	stretch	strumatic	stypsis	submentum
stigma	stock	storax	stretta	strumose	styptic	submerge
stigmas	stockade	store	strettas	strumous	styptical	submicron
stigmata	stockinet	storeroom	strette	strumpet	styrene	submine
stigmatic	stockish	storey	stretti	strut	styrolene	submission
stilb	stockman	storiette	stretto	strychnia	stythe	submissive
stilbene	stockpot	stork	strettos	strychnin	suability	submit
stilbite	stockwork	storksbill	strew	stub	suasion	submittal
stile	stocky	storm	stria	stubble	suasive	submontane
stiletto	stockyard	stormbelt	striae	stubborn	suasory	subnormal
stilettos	stodge	stormy	striate	stubby	suave	suboceanic
stilet	stodgy	story	striation	stucco	suavity	suborder
stilette	stogie	stoss	striature	stuccoes	subacute	subordinal
still	stogy	stotinka	stricken	stuccos	subaerial	suborn
stillborn	stoic	stotinki	strickle	studding	subalpine	suboxide
stilt	stoical	stoup	strict	student	subaltern	subpena
stilted	stoicism	stout	striction	studfish	subarctic	subphylum
stimulant	stoke	stove	stricture	studio	subarea	subplinth
stimulate	stokehold	stow	stride	studwork	subarid	subpoena
stimuli	stokehole	stowage	stridence	study	subatomic	subramose
stimulus	stole	stowp	stridency	stuff	subcellar	subregion
stimy	stoled	strabism	strident	stuffy	subclimax	subrogate
sting	stolid	straddle	strife	stull	subdeacon	subscribe
stingaree	stolidity	straggle	strigil	stultify	subdean	subscript
stinge	stolon	straight	strigose	stum	subdepot	subserve
stingy	stoma	strain	strike	stumble	subdivide	subside
stink	stomach	strait	string	stump	subdual	subsidize
stinkard	stomachal	straiten	stringent	stumpage	subdue	subsidy
stinkball	stomacher	strake	stringhalt	stumpy	suber	subsist
stinkbomb	stomachic	stramony	stringy	stun	subereous	subsistent
stinkpot	stomachy	strand	strip	stunsail	suberic	subsoil
stinkbug	stomata	strange	stripe	stunt	suberin	subsolar
stinkhorn	stomatal	strangle	stripling	stupa	suberine	subsonic
stinkweed	stomatic	strangury	stripy	stupe	suberize	substance
stinkwood	stomadaea	strap	strive	stupefy	suberose	substrata
stint	stomodeum	strapless	strobic	stupid	suberous	substrate
stipe	stomodea	strappado	strobil	stupidity	subfamily	subsume
stipel	stomodeal	strass	strobile	stupor	subgenus	subtenant
stipend	stone	strata	stroke	stuporous	subgroup	subtend
stipes	stonechat	stratagem	stroll	stupp	subhead	subtense
stipiform	stonecrop	stratal	stroma	sturdy	subhumid	subtile
stipitate	stonewall	strategic	stromatic	sturgeon	subindex	subtility
stipple	stoneware	strategy	strong	stutter	subinfeud	subtilism
stipular	stonework	stratify	strongyl	sty	subjacent	subtilize
stipulate	stonewort	stratum	strongyle	stylar	subject	subtilty
stipule	stonish	stratums	strontia	style	subjoin	subtitle
stir	stony	stratus	strontian	stylet	subjugate	subtle
stirabout	stood	straw	strontic	styliform	sublation	subtlety
stirk	stook	strawy	strontium	stylish	sublease	subtly
stirps	stool	stray	strop	stylist	sublet	subtonic
stirup	stoop	streak	strophe	stylistic	sublethal	subtorrid
stitch	stop	streaky	strophic	stylite	sublimate	subtract

subtropic
subulate
suburban
subvene
subversal
subvert
subway
succeed
succentor
success
successor
succinate
succinct
succinic
succor
succory
succotash
succour
succubi
succubus
succulent
succumb
succuss
such
suck
suckfish
suckle
sucre
sucrose
suction
suctorial
sudan
sudaria
sudarium
sudary
sudation
sudatory
sudd
sudden
sudor
sudorific
suds
sudsy
sue
suede
suet
suety
suffari
suffer
suffice
suffix
suffixal
suffixion
suffocate
suffragan
suffrage
suffrutex
suffuse

suffusive
suffusion
sufism
sugar
sugarbird
sugarcane
sugarplum
sugary
suggest
suicidal
suicide
suint
suit
suitcase
suite
suitor
sukiyaki
sulcate
sulcated
sulci
sulcus
sulfate
sulfatize
sulfid
sulfite
sulfonal
sulfonate
sulfone
sulfonic
sulfonium
sulfonyl
sulfur
sulfurate
sulfuret
sulfuric
sulfurize
sulfurous
sulfury
sulfuryl
sulk
sulky
sullage
sullen
sully
sulphite
sulphitic
sultan
sultana
sultaness
sultanate
sultry
sum
sumac
sumless
summarist
summarize
summary
summation

summer
summerset
summit
summital
summon
summons
sump
sumpter
sumptuary
sumptuous
sumpweed
sun
sunbeam
sunbird
sunbonnet
sunbow
sunburn
sunburnt
sunburned
sunburst
sundae
sunder
sundew
sundial
sundrops
sundry
sunfish
sunflower
sunglass
sunglow
sunken
sunless
sunlight
sunny
sunrise
sunset
sunshade
sunshine
sunshiny
sunspot
sunstone
sunstroke
sunstruck
sunward
sunwards
sunwise
sup
super
superable
superadd
superb
supercool
superego
superfine
superfuse
superheat
superior
supermale

superman
supernal
superpose
supersede
supersex
supertax
supervene
supervise
supinate
supine
supper
supplant
supple
suppliant
supply
support
supposal
suppose
suppress
suppurate
supremacy
supreme
sura
surah
sural
surbase
surbased
surcease
surcharge
surcingle
surcoat
surculose
surd
sure
sureness
surety
surf
surfy
surface
surfbird
surfboard
surfboat
surfeit
surficial
surfer
surge
surgy
surgeon
surgeoncy
surgery
surgical
suricate
surloin
surly
surmise
surmount
surmullet
surname

surpass
surplice
surplus
surprint
surprisal
surprise
surprizal
surprize
surrender
surrey
surrogate
surround
surtax
surtout
survey
survival
survive
suslik
suspect
suspend
suspense
suspensor
suspicion
suspire
sustain
susurrant
susurrate
susurrus
sutler
sutta
suttee
sutteeism
suttle
sutural
suture
suzerain
svaraj
svarajism
svarajist
svelte
swab
swaddle
swagbelly
swage
swagger
swagman
swail
swain
swainish
swale
swallow
swami
swamy
swamp
swampy
swampish
swan
swanherd

swannery
swanskin
swap
swaraj
sward
swarm
swart
swarth
swarthy
swarty
swash
swastica
swastika
swat
swatch
swath
swathe
sway
swayback
sweal
swear
sweat
sweaty
sweatband
sweatbox
sweatshop
sweep
sweepback
sweepy
sweet
sweeten
sweetflag
sweetgale
sweetgum
sweeting
sweetish
sweetmeat
sweets
sweetsop
swell
swellbox
swellfish
swelter
sweltry
sweptback
swerve
swift
swifter
swig
swill
swim
swimmeret
swindle
swine
swineherd
swinepox
swing
swinge

swingle
swiple
swinish
swipple
swirl
swirlie
swirly
swish
switch
switchman
swivel
swizzle
swob
swollen
swoon
swoop
sword
swordbill
swordfish
swordknot
swordman
swordplay
swordsman
swot
swounds
swouns
sybarite
sybo
syboes
sycamine
sycamore
sycomore
sycee
sycon
syconia
syconium
sycophant
sycosis
syenite
syenitic
syenyte
syllabary
syllabi
syllabic
syllabify
syllabism
syllabist
syllabize
syllable
syllabub
syllabus
syllepses
syllepsis
sylleptic
syllogism
syllogize
sylph
sylphid

sylphish	syncrasy	syrphid	tad	tamandua	tapestry	tasteful
sylphlike	syncrisis	systalic	tadpole	tamarack	tapeta	tasteless
sylphy	syndactyl	system	tael	tamarin	tapetum	tasty
sylva	syndesis	systemic	taenia	tamarind	tapeworm	tat
sylvae	syndetic	systole	tafferel	tamarisk	tapidero	tatoo
sylvan	syndic	systolic	taffeta	tamasha	tapioca	tatouay
sylvanite	syndical	syzygy	taffrail	tambour	tapir	tattle
sylvas	syndicate	syzygial	taffy	tambourin	tapis	tau
sylvin	syndrome		tag	tame	tappet	taught
sylvine	syndromic	**T**	tahsildar	tameless	taproom	taunt
sylvinite	synecious	tab	taiga	tamis	taproot	taupe
sylvite	syneresis	tabanid	tail	tamp	tapster	taurine
symbion	synergia	tabard	tailboard	tampala	tar	taut
symbiont	synergic	tabby	tailfirst	tampan	tarantas	tautaug
symbiosis	synergism	tabes	tailor	tampion	tarantass	tauten
symbiotic	synergist	tabescent	tailpiece	tampon	tarantism	tautog
symbol	synergy	tabetic	tailskid	tan	tarantula	tautology
symbolic	synesis	tablature	tailspin	tanager	taraxacum	tautonym
symbolics	synezisis	table	tailstock	tanbark	tarboosh	tautonymy
symbolism	syngamic	tableau	tain	tandem	tarbush	tavern
symbolist	syngamous	tableaus	taint	tang	tardy	taw
symbolize	syngamy	tableaux	take	tangelo	tare	tawdry
symbology	synizesis	tableland	talapoin	tangence	targ	tawny
symmetric	synod	tablet	talar	tangency	targe	tax
symmetry	synodal	tableware	talbot	tangent	target	taxaceous
sympathin	synodical	tabloid	talc	tangental	targeteer	taxation
sympathy	synodic	taboo	talcose	tangerine	tariff	taxi
symphonic	synonym	tabor	talcum	tangible	tarlatan	taxiarch
symphony	synonyme	taboret	tale	tangle	tarn	taxicab
symphyses	synonymic	taborin	talent	tangly	tarnish	taxidermy
symphysis	synonymy	taborine	talented	tango	taro	taximeter
sympodia	synopses	tabour	taler	tangos	taros	taxin
sympodial	synopsis	tabouret	talesman	tangram	tarot	taxine
sympodium	synoptic	tabourine	tali	tanist	tarpaulin	taxiplane
symposia	synovia	tabu	talion	tanistry	tarpon	taxis
symposiac	synovial	tabular	taliped	tank	tarragon	taxite
symposial	synovitis	tabulate	talipes	tankage	tarry	taxitic
symposion	syntactic	tacamahac	talipot	tankard	tarsal	taxonomer
symposium	syntax	tace	talisman	tannage	tarsier	taxonomic
symptom	syntheses	tachinid	talk	tannate	tarsi	taxonomy
synagog	synthesis	tachiol	talkative	tannery	tarsus	taxpayer
synagogal	synthetic	tachylyte	tall	tannic	tart	taxy
synagogue	syntonic	tacit	tallage	tannin	tartan	tchick
synalepha	syntonize	taciturn	tallish	tanrec	tartar	teabag
synalgia	syntony	tack	tallith	tansy	tartaric	teaball
synalgic	synura	tackle	tallol	tantalate	tartarize	teaberry
synapse	synurae	tacky	tallow	tantalic	tartarous	teach
synapsis	sypher	tact	tallowy	tantalite	tartlet	teacup
synaptic	syphilis	tactful	tally	tantalize	tartrate	teacupful
synaxis	syphiloid	tackey	tallyho	tantalum	tartufe	teak
syncarp	syphilous	tactic	tallyman	tantara	tartuffe	teakettle
syncarpia	syphon	tactical	talon	tantivy	tasimeter	teal
synclinal	syren	tactician	taluk	tap	tasimetry	team
syncline	syringa	tactile	talus	tapa	task	teamster
syncopal	syringe	tactility	tam	tapadera	tasse	teamwork
syncopate	syrinx	taction	tamal	tapadero	tassel	teapot
syncope	syringeal	tactless	tamale	tape	tasset	teapoy
syncopic	syrphian	tactual	tamandu	tapeline	taste	tear

teardrop	telephony	tenacy	tepid	terrorism	thalassic	theogonic
tearless	telephote	tenant	tepidity	terrorist	thaler	theogony
teary	telephoto	tenantry	tepidaria	terrorize	thalli	theolog
tearful	telescope	tench	teraph	terry	thallic	theologic
tease	telescopy	tend	teraphim	terse	thallin	theologue
teasel	telestich	tendency	teratism	tertial	thalline	theology
teaspoon	teletype	tendinous	teratoid	tertian	thallium	theomachy
teat	televise	tendon	terbia	tertiary	thalloid	theopathy
teazel	telfer	tendril	terbic	tervalent	thallous	theophany
teazle	telford	tenebrae	terbium	terzarima	thallus	theorbo
technic	telial	tenebrous	tercel	terzerime	thalluses	theorem
technical	telic	tenement	tercelet	tessera	than	theoremic
technique	telically	tenendum	tercet	tesserae	thanage	theoretic
technism	telium	tenesmic	terebene	test	thanatoid	theorist
techy	tell	tenesmus	terebic	testa	thane	theorize
tectonic	telltale	tenet	terebinth	testae	thank	theory
tectonics	tellurate	tenfold	teredo	testacean	thankful	theosophy
tectrices	tellurian	tenia	terete	testacy	thankless	therapist
tectrix	telluric	teniacide	terfa	testament	that	therapy
ted	telluride	teniafuge	tergal	testate	thatch	there
teddy	telluret	teniasis	tergum	testatrix	thatchy	thereat
tedious	tellurid	tennis	term	testes	thaw	thereby
tedium	tellurite	tenon	termagant	testicle	the	therefor
tee	tellurium	tenonitis	termer	testify	theaceous	therefore
teem	tellurize	tenor	terminal	testimony	thearchic	therefrom
teens	tellurous	tenorite	terminate	testis	thearchy	therein
teepee	teloblast	tenotomy	terminer	testudo	theater	thereinto
teeter	telophase	tenpenny	termini	testy	theatre	thereof
teeth	telpher	tenpins	terminism	tetanic	theatric	thereon
teethe	telpheric	tenrec	terminus	tetanical	theatrics	thereto
teetotal	telson	tense	termite	tetanize	thebain	thereunto
teetotum	temblor	tensible	termless	tetanus	thebaine	thereupon
tegmen	temblors	tensile	termor	tetany	theca	therewith
tegmina	temblores	tensility	tern	tetchy	thecae	theriac
tegminal	temerity	tension	ternary	tether	thecal	theriaca
tegula	temper	tensional	ternate	tetotum	thecate	theriacal
tegulae	tempera	tensity	terne	tetracid	thee	therm
tegular	temperate	tensive	ternion	tetrad	theelin	therme
tegulated	tempest	tensor	terpene	tetragram	theelol	thermae
tegumen	templar	tent	terpineol	tetrapod	theft	thermal
tegument	template	tentless	terrace	tetrapody	thegn	thermic
teil	temple	tentacle	terrain	tetrarch	thein	thermion
tela	tempo	tentage	terrane	tetrarchy	theine	thermite
telae	temporal	tentation	terrapin	tetraseme	their	theroid
telamon	temporary	tentative	terraria	tetrode	theirs	theropod
telamones	temporize	tenth	terrarium	tetroxid	theism	thesauri
telegonic	tempt	tenues	terreen	tetroxide	thelitis	thesaurus
telegony	temptress	tenuis	terrene	tetryl	them	these
telegram	ten	tenuous	terret	tetter	theme	theses
telegraph	tenable	tenuity	terrible	text	thematic	thesis
telemark	tenably	tenure	terrier	textile	then	theta
telemater	tenace	tenurial	terrific	textual	thenage	thetic
telemetry	tenacious	teocalli	terrify	textuary	thenar	thetical
telemotor	tenacity	teosinte	terrigene	texture	thenal	theurgic
teleology	tenacula	tepee	terrine	textural	thence	theurgist
teleost	tenaculum	tepefy	territ	thalami	theocracy	theurgy
telepathy	tenaille	tephrite	territory	thalamic	theocrasy	thew
telephone	tenail	tephritic	terror	thalamus	theodicy	they

thiamin
thiamine
thiazin
thiazine
thiazole
thick
thicken
thicket
thickhead
thickskin
thickish
thickleaf
thickness
thief
thieve
thievery
thievish
thigh
thill
thimble
thin
thine
thing
think
thinnish
thiogen
thiol
thionic
thionin
thionine
thionyl
thiophen
thiophene
thiurea
third
thirl
thirlage
thirst
thirsty
thirteen
thirtieth
thirty
this
thistle
thither
thitherto
tho
thole
thong
thoraces
thoracic
thorax
thoraxes
thoria
thorite
thorium
thoric
thorn

thornback
thornbill
thornless
thorny
thoro
thoron
thorough
those
thou
though
thought
thousand
thraldom
thrall
thralldom
thrash
thread
threadfin
thready
threat
threaten
three
threefold
threesome
threnode
threnodic
threnody
thresh
threshold
threw
thrice
thrift
thrifty
thrill
thrips
thrive
thriven
throat
throaty
throb
throe
thrombin
thrombus
throne
throng
throttle
through
throve
throw
throwster
thru
thrum
thrummy
thrush
thrust
thud
thug
thuggee

thuggery
thuggish
thuja
thulia
thulium
thumb
thumbkin
thumbling
thumbnail
thumbnut
thumbtack
thump
thunder
thundrous
thurible
thurifer
thus
thuya
thwack
thwart
thy
thylacine
thyme
thymy
thymic
thymol
thymus
thyreoid
thyroid
thyroxin
thyrse
thyrsoid
thyrsus
thyself
ti
tiara
tibia
tibiae
tibial
tibias
tic
tical
tick
ticket
tickle
ticklish
tickseed
tidal
tidbit
tide
tideless
tideland
tiderip
tidewater
tideway
tidings
tidy
tidytips

tie
tier
tierce
tiff
tiffany
tiger
tigerish
tight
tighten
tightrope
tights
tiglic
tiglinic
tigrish
tike
til
tilbury
tilde
tile
tilefish
till
tillage
tilt
tilth
tiltyard
timarau
timbal
timbale
timber
timbre
timbrel
time
timeless
timema
timepiece
timid
timidity
timing
timocracy
timorous
timothy
timpani
timpanist
timpano
timpanum
tin
tinamou
tincal
tinct
tincture
tinder
tindery
tinderbox
tine
tinea
tineid
tinfoil
ting

tinge
tingle
tink
tinker
tinkle
tinnitus
tinny
tinsel
tinsmith
tinstone
tint
tintype
tinware
tinwork
tiny
tip
tipcart
tipcat
tipi
tippet
tipple
tipstaff
tipstaffs
tipstaves
tipsy
tiptoe
tirade
tire
tireless
tiresome
tiro
tisane
tissue
tit
titan
titaness
titanate
titanic
titanite
titanium
titanous
titbit
titer
tithable
tithe
tither
titi
titian
titillant
titillate
titlark
title
titmouse
titrate
titration
titre
titter
tittle

titular
titulary
tittup
tivy
tmesis
to
toad
toadfish
toadflax
toadstone
toadstool
toady
toadyish
toadyism
toast
tobacco
tobaccos
tobaccoes
toboggan
toby
toccata
tocology
tocsin
tod
today
toddle
toddy
tody
toe
toehold
toenail
toffee
toffy
toga
togae
togas
togated
together
toggle
toil
toile
toilet
toiletry
toilette
toilful
toilsome
token
tokology
tolane
told
tole
toledo
tolerable
tolerably
tolerance
tolerant
tolerate
tolidin

tolidine
toll
tollage
tollgate
tollhouse
tolu
toluate
toluene
toluic
toluid
toluide
toluidine
toluol
toluole
toluyl
tolyl
tom
tomahawk
tomalley
tomally
toman
tomato
tomb
tombac
tomback
tombak
tomboy
tomboyish
tombstone
tomcat
tomcod
tome
tomenta
tomentose
tomentous
tomentum
tomfool
tomfulla
tomorrow
tompion
tomtit
ton
tonal
tonality
tone
toneless
tong
tongue
tonic
tonicity
tonight
tonite
tonnage
tonneau
tonneaus
tonneaux
tonograph
tonometer

tonometry
tonoscope
tonsil
tonsilar
tonsillar
tonsorial
tonsure
tontine
tonus
too
tool
toon
toot
tooth
toothache
toothless
toothpick
toothsome
toothwort
tootle
top
topaz
topboot
tope
topek
toph
tophe
tophamper
topheavy
tophi
tophus
topiary
topic
topical
topknot
topmast
topmost
topology
toponym
toponymic
toponymy
topotype
topple
topsail
topside
topsoil
topstone
toque
toquet
tora
torah
torc
torch
torchwood
tore
toreador
toreutic
toreutics

tori
toric
torment
tormentil
torn
tornadic
tornado
tornadoes
tornados
toroid
toroidal
torose
torous
torosity
torpedo
torpedoes
torpedos
torpid
torpidity
torpor
torquate
torque
torreador
torrefy
torrify
torrent
torrid
torridity
torsade
torsi
torsion
torsional
torso
torsos
tort
tortile
tortility
tortilla
tortious
tortoise
tortricid
tortuous
torture
torulose
torulous
torus
tory
toss
tosspot
total
totality
totalize
totamism
totaquina
totem
totemic
totemism
totemist

totter
tottery
toucan
touch
touchback
touchdown
touchhole
touchwood
touchy
tough
toughen
toupee
tour
touraco
tourist
touristic
tourmalin
tourney
tournure
tousle
touzle
tow
towage
toward
towards
towboat
towel
tower
towery
towhead
towhee
towline
town
townfolk
township
townsman
towpath
towrope
towy
toxemia
toxaemic
toxemic
toxic
toxical
toxicant
toxicity
toxicoses
toxicosis
toxin
toxine
toxophil
toxophile
toy
toyish
toyon
trabeate
trabeated
trabecula

trace
tracery
trachea
tracheae
tracheal
tracheid
trachoma
trachyte
trachytic
track
trackage
trackless
trackman
trackmeet
trackway
tract
tractate
tractile
traction
tractive
tractor
tractus
trade
tradesfolk
tradesman
tradition
traditor
traduce
traffic
tragedian
tragedy
tragi
tragic
tragical
tragopan
tragus
trail
train
trainless
trainband
trainee
trainman
traipse
trait
traitor
traitress
traject
tram
trame
tramel
tramell
trammel
tramp
trample
trampolin
tramroad
trance
tranquil

transact
transcend
transect
transept
transeunt
transfer
transflux
transform
transfuse
tranship
transient
transit
translate
translunar
transmit
transom
transpire
transport
transpose
transude
trap
trapes
trapeze
trapezia
trapezium
trapezoid
trapfall
trappean
trappist
trappose
trappous
trash
trashy
trashily
trasko
trass
trauma
traumas
traumata
traumatic
travail
travel
travelog
traversal
traverse
travertin
travesty
travois
travoise
travoises
trawl
tray
treachery
treacle
treacly
tread
treadle
treadmill

treadway
treason
treasure
treasury
treat
treatise
treaty
treble
trebuchet
treddle
tree
trefoil
trehala
trehalose
treillage
trek
trellis
trematode
trematoid
tremble
tremetol
tremolite
tremor
tremulant
tremulent
tremulous
trench
trenchant
trend
trepan
trepang
trepanize
trephine
treponeme
trespass
tress
tressure
tressour
trestle
tret
trevet
trevis
trey
triable
triacid
triad
triadic
triagonal
trial
triamorph
triangle
triarchy
triatic
triatomic
triaxial
triazine
triazoic
triazole

tribasic
tribal
tribe
tribesman
tribrach
tribunal
tribunate
tribunary
tribune
tributary
tribute
trice
triceps
trichina
trichinae
trichite
trichitic
trichoid
trichoma
trichome
trichomic
trichosis
trichroic
trichrome
trick
trickery
trickish
trickle
tricklet
trickster
tricksy
tricky
triclinia
triclinic
tricolor
tricolour
tricorn
tricot
tricrotic
tricuspid
tricycle
tricyclic
tridactyl
trident
triennial
trierarch
trieteric
trifacial
trifid
trifle
trifold
trifolium
triforia
triforial
triforium
triform
trig
trigemini

trigger
triglyph
trigon
trigonal
trigonous
trigraph
trihedral
trihedron
trihybrid
trihydric
trijugate
trijugous
trilby
trilinear
trill
trillion
trillium
trilobate
trilobal
trilobed
trilobite
trilogy
trim
trimerous
trimester
trimeter
trimetric
trimorph
trinal
trinary
trination
trindle
trine
trinity
trinket
trinodal
trinomial
trintle
trionymal
trio
trios
triode
triocious
triolet
trioxid
trioxide
trip
tripe
tripedal
triphase
triplane
triple
triplet
triplex
triplite
triploid
triploidy
tripod

tripodal
tripodial
tripodic
tripody
tripoli
tripos
trippet
triptote
triptych
triptyca
triradial
trireme
trisect
triseme
trisemic
triserial
triscele
triskele
trismic
trismus
trisporic
trisporus
tristich
trisulfid
trite
tritheism
tritheist
trithing
triton
tritone
triturate
triumph
triumphal
triumvir
triumviri
triumvirs
triune
triunity
trivalent
trivalve
trivel
trivet
trivia
trivial
trivium
triweekly
trocar
trocha
trochaic
trochal
trochar
troche
trochee
trochil
trochili
trochilic
trochilos
trochilus

trochlea
trochlear
trochoid
trodden
trogon
troll
trold
trolley
trolly
trollop
trollopy
trombone
trommel
tromp
trompe
troop
troopial
troopship
troostite
tropaeum
tropaion
troparia
troparion
trope
trophic
trophical
trophied
trophy
tropic
tropical
tropin
tropine
tropism
tropist
tropistic
tropology
trot
troth
trotyl
trouble
troublous
trough
trounce
troupe
troupial
trousers
trousse
trousseau
trout
trouvere
trouveur
trover
trow
trowel
troy
truancy
truant
truantry

truce
truck
truckage
truckhead
truckle
truckman
truculent
trudge
trudgen
true
trueblue
truelove
truffle
truism
trull
truly
trump
trumpery
trumpet
truncate
truncheon
trundle
trunk
trunkfish
trunnel
trunnion
truss
trust
trustee
trustful
trusty
truth
truthless
truthful
try
tryma
trypsin
tryptic
tryst
tryste
tryster
tsar
tsarina
tsetse
tsunami
tuatara
tuatera
tub
tuba
tubae
tubal
tubas
tubate
tubby
tube
tuber
tubercle
tuberoid

tuberose
tubiform
tubular
tubulate
tubule
tubulose
tubulous
tubulure
tuck
tuckahoe
tucket
tufa
tufaceous
tuff
tuft
tufty
tug
tugboat
tuille
tuition
tuitional
tularemia
tule
tulip
tuliptree
tulipwood
tulle
tumble
tumblebug
tumbrel
tumbril
tumefy
tumescent
tumid
tumidity
tumor
tumular
tumuli
tumulose
tumulous
tumult
tumulus
tun
tuna
tundra
tune
tuneful
tungsten
tungstic
tungstite
tunic
tunica
tunicae
tunicate
tunicated
tunicle
tunket
tunnel

tunny
tup
tupelo
tupelos
tuque
turacou
turban
turbaned
turbary
turbeth
turbith
turbid
turbidity
turbinal
turbinate
turbine
turbit
turbot
turbulent
turdiform
turdine
tureen
turf
turfs
turves
turfman
turfy
turgent
turgid
turgidity
turgite
turgor
turkey
turkois
turmaline
turmeric
turmoil
turn
turncoat
turnery
turnhall
turnip
turnix
turnkey
turnout
turnover
turnpike
turnsole
turnspit
turnstile
turnstone
turntable
turnup
turpeth
turpitude
turquoise
turrel
turret

turreted
turrical
turrilite
turtle
turtlepeg
tush
tushed
tusk
tusked
tusker
tussah
tussar
tusseh
tusser
tussore
tussur
tussle
tussock
tussocky
tussuck
tut
tutelage
tutelar
tutelary
tutenag
tutenague
tutor
tutorage
tutorial
tutorship
tutti
tutty
tuxedo
tuyere
twaddle
twain
twang
twangy
twangle
twanky
twattle
twablade
tweak
tweaky
tweed
tweedle
tweese
tweet
tweeze
tweezers
twelfth
twelve
twelvemo
twentieth
twenty
twibil
twibill
twicer

twiddle	tzar	umbrae	uncertain	underhung	unfit	unionize
twier	tzarina	umbrage	unchain	underlaid	unfix	uniparous
twig	tzetze	umbrella	uncharged	underlay	unfledged	uniplanar
twigless		umbrette	unchurch	underlet	unfleshly	unipolar
twiggen	**U**	umlaut	uncial	underlie	unfold	unique
twilight	ubiquity	umpirage	unciform	underline	unformed	unisexual
twill	udder	umpire	uncinal	underling	unfounded	unison
twilled	udometer	unable	uncinate	undermine	unfrock	unisonal
twin	udometric	unadvised	uncivil	undermost	unfumed	unisonant
twinberry	udometry	unalloyed	unclad	underpass	unfunded	unisonous
twine	ugh	unanimity	unclasp	underpay	unfurl	unit
twinge	uglify	unanimous	uncle	underpin	ungainly	unitary
twinkle	ugly	unapt	unclean	underplot	ungifted	unite
twirl	uhlan	unargued	unclench	underprop	ungodly	unitive
twist	uintahite	unarm	unclew	underrate	ungotten	unity
twit	uintaite	unau	unclinch	underrun	ungual	univalent
twitch	ukase	unaware	uncloak	undersea	unguard	univalvate
two	ukulele	unawares	unclose	undersell	unguent	univalve
twofold	ulan	unbacked	uncock	underset	unguiform	universal
twopence	ulcer	unbaked	uncoil	undershot	unguinous	universe
twopenny	ulcerate	unbalance	uncoined	underside	ungues	univocal
twyblade	ulcerous	unbar	uncommon	undersign	unguis	unjust
twyere	ulema	unbarbed	unconcern	undersoil	ungula	unkempt
tycoon	ullage	unbear	uncork	undersong	ungulae	unkennel
tyke	ulmaceous	unbeknown	uncounted	underspin	ungular	unkind
tymbal	ulna	unbelief	uncouple	undertake	ungulate	unknown
tympan	ulnar	unbelt	uncouth	undertint	unhair	unlabored
tympana	ulster	unbend	uncover	undertone	unhallow	unlace
tympani	ulterior	unbiased	uncreate	undertook	unhand	unlade
tympanic	ultima	unbiassed	unction	undertow	unhandy	unlaid
tympanist	ultimata	unbid	unctuous	undervest	unhappy	unlatch
tympanum	ultimate	unbidden	uncut	underwear	unharness	unlawful
tympany	ultimatum	unbind	undamped	underwent	unhat	unlay
typal	ultra	unbitted	undaunted	underwing	unhealthy	unlead
type	ultraism	unblessed	unde	underwood	unheard	unlearn
typha	ultraist	unbloody	undee	underwork	unhelm	unleash
typhlitic	ululant	unbodied	undecagon	undine	unhinge	unless
typhlitis	ululate	unbolt	undeceive	undo	unhitch	unlike
typhlosis	ululation	unboned	undecided	undraw	unholy	unlimber
typhoid	umbel	unbonnet	undecked	undress	unhook	unlimited
typhoidal	umbellar	unborn	undecuple	undue	unhoped	unlisted
typhoidin	umbellate	unbosom	under	undulant	unhorse	unlive
typhoon	umbellet	unbounded	underbid	undulate	unhurried	unload
typhose	umbellule	unbowed	underbred	undulous	unhusk	unlock
typhus	umber	unbrace	underbush	unduly	uniaxial	unlooked
typhous	umbery	unbred	underbuy	undying	unicolor	unloose
typical	umbilical	unbridled	underclay	unearned	unicorn	unloosen
typic	umbilici	unbroken	undercool	unearth	unicycle	unlovely
typify	umbilicus	unbroke	undercut	uneasy	unideaed	unlucky
typist	umbles	unbuckle	underdo	unequal	unifiable	unmake
typology	umbo	unbuild	underdone	unerring	unific	unman
tyrannic	umbones	unburden	underdose	uneven	unifilar	unmarked
tyrannize	umbonic	unbutton	underfeed	uneventful	uniform	unmask
tyrannous	umbonal	uncaged	underfoot	unfailing	unify	unmeaning
tyranny	umbonate	uncalled	underfur	unfair	unijugate	unmeet
tyrant	umbonated	uncanny	undergird	unfasten	union	unmew
tyro	umbos	uncap	undergo	unfeeling	unionism	unmindful
tyrosine	umbra	uncaused	underhand	unfeigned	unionist	unmiter

unmitre
unmoor
unmoral
unmortise
unmuffle
unnatural
unnerve
unpack
unpaid
unpaired
unpeg
unpeople
unpick
unpin
unplumbed
unpoised
unpolitic
unpolled
unpopular
unpriced
unprizable
unquiet
unravel
unread
unready
unreal
unreality
unreason
unreel
unreeved
unreserve
unrest
unriddle
unrifled
unrig
unrip
unripe
unrivaled
unroll
unroot
unruffled
unrove
unruly
unsaddle
unsaid
unsavory
unsay
unscathed
unscrew
unseal
unseam
unseat
unseemly
unseen
unsettle
unsex
unshackle
unshaped

unshapen
unsheathe
unship
unsighted
unsightly
unskilful
unskilled
unsling
unsnap
unsnarl
unsolder
unsound
unsparing
unspeak
unsphere
unspotted
unstable
unstate
unsteel
unstep
unstopped
unstowed
unstrap
unstring
unstriped
unstrung
unstudied
unsung
unswathe
unswear
untangle
untaught
unteach
untenable
untented
unthanked
unthink
unthread
untidy
untie
until
untimely
untitled
unto
untold
untoward
untread
untried
untrimmed
untrod
untrodden
untrue
untruly
untruss
untruth
untutored
untwine
untwist

unused
unusual
unvalued
unveil
unvoiced
unwary
unwearied
unwelcome
unwell
unwept
unwieldy
unwilled
unwilling
unwind
unwise
unwish
unwitting
unwonted
unworldly
unworthy
unwrap
unwrinkle
unwritten
unyoke
unyoked
up
upas
upbeat
upbraid
upcast
upgrade
upgrowth
upheaval
upheave
uphill
uphold
upholster
uphroe
upkeep
upland
uplift
upmost
upon
uppercut
uppermost
upraise
uprear
upright
uprise
uprising
uproar
uproot
uprouse
upset
upshot
upside
upsilon
upspring

upstage
upstairs
upstart
upstroke
upsweep
upswing
uptake
upthrow
upthrust
upturn
upward
uraemia
uraeus
uralite
uralitic
uranic
uraninite
uranite
uranitic
uranium
uranology
uranous
uranyl
urare
urari
urate
urbacity
urban
urbane
urbanity
urbanize
urceolate
urchin
urea
ureal
urease
uredo
ureide
uremia
uraemic
uremic
ureter
ureteral
ureteric
urethan
urethane
urethra
urethral
uretic
urge
urgency
urgent
uric
urinal
urinary
urinate
urination
urine

urinaemia
urinemia
urinemic
urinaemic
urinose
urinous
urn
urochord
urochrome
urochs
urogenous
urolith
urolithic
urologic
urologist
urology
uropod
uropodal
uropodous
uropygial
uropygium
uroscopic
uroscopy
ursiform
ursine
urticaria
urticate
urus
urushiol
us
usable
usably
useable
usage
usance
usaunce
use
useful
useless
usher
usquabae
usque
usquebae
ustion
ustulate
usual
usufruct
usurer
usurious
usurp
usury
ut
utensil
uterine
uteritis
uterus
utile
utility

utilize
utmost
utopia
utopian
utricle
utricular
utriculi
utriculus
utter
uttermost
uva
uvarovite
uvea
uveal
uveous
uvula
uvular
uvulitis
uxorial
uxoricide
uxorious

V

vacancy
vacant
vacate
vacation
vaccina
vaccinal
vaccinate
vaccine
vaccinia
vacillate
vacillant
vacua
vacuity
vacuole
vacuous
vacuum
vagabond
vagary
vagi
vagina
vaginae
vaginal
vaginate
vaginitis
vagitus
vagotonia
vagotonic
vagrancy
vagrant
vague
vagus
vain
vainglory
vair
valance

valanced
vale
valence
valency
valencia
valentine
valerian
valeric
valet
valgus
valiant
valiance
valiancy
valid
validate
validity
valise
valkyr
valkyrian
valkyrie
vallation
vallatory
vallecula
valley
valonia
valor
valorize
valorous
valour
valuation
value
valueless
valvate
valval
valvar
valve
valveless
valvelet
valvula
valvular
valvule
vambrace
vamp
vampire
vampiric
vampirish
vampirism
van
vanadate
vanadiate
vanadic
vanadium
vanadous
vanadious
vandal
vandalic
vandalism
vane

vang	vasculous	velours	veranda	veronica	vesuvian	vicious
vanguard	vasculum	velum	verandah	verruca	vetch	victim
vanilla	vase	velure	verano	verrucae	vetchling	victimize
vanillic	vasomotor	velvet	veratric	verrucano	veteran	victor
vanillin	vassal	velveteen	veratrine	verrucose	vetiver	victoria
vanilline	vassalage	velvety	veratria	verrucous	veto	victory
vanish	vassalize	vena	veratrin	versant	vetoes	victual
vanity	vast	venae	veratrina	versatile	vex	vicuna
vanquish	vastitude	venal	veratrize	verse	vexation	vicugna
vantage	vastation	venality	veratrum	versicle	vexatious	vide
vantbrace	vastity	venatic	verb	versify	vexil	videlicet
vanward	vat	venatical	verbal	version	vexilla	video
vapid	vatic	venation	verbalism	verso	vexillar	vidette
vapidity	vatical	vend	verbalist	verst	vexillary	viduage
vapor	vaticide	vendace	verbalize	versus	vexillate	vie
vaporific	vaticinal	vendee	verbatim	vert	vexillum	view
vaporish	vault	vendetta	verbena	vertebra	via	viewless
vaporize	vaunt	vendettas	verbiage	vertebrae	viable	viewpoint
vaporous	veal	vendible	verbify	vertebras	viability	vigesimal
vapory	vection	vendibly	verbose	vertebral	viaduct	vigil
vapour	vector	vendis	verbosity	vertex	viagraph	vigilance
vaquero	vectorial	vendition	verdancy	vertexes	vial	vigilant
vaqueros	vedette	vendue	verdant	vertical	viand	vigilante
var	vee	veneer	verderer	vertices	viatic	vignette
vara	veer	venerable	verderor	verticil	viatical	vignettist
varanian	veery	venerate	verdict	verticity	viaticum	vigor
varanid	vegetable	venereal	verdigris	vertigo	viator	vigorous
variance	vegetably	venery	verdin	vertigoes	viatores	viking
variant	vegetal	vengeance	verditer	vervain	vibrancy	vilayet
variation	vegetant	vengeful	verdure	verve	vibrant	vile
varicella	vegetate	venial	verdurous	vervet	vibrate	vilify
varices	vegetist	veniality	verecund	very	vibratile	vilipend
varicose	vegetism	venially	verge	vesica	vibration	vill
varicosis	vegetive	venire	verdic	vesicae	vibrator	villa
variegate	vehemence	venison	verdical	vesical	vibratory	villadom
varietal	vehemency	venom	verify	vesicant	vibrative	village
variety	vehement	venomous	verily	vesicate	vibrio	villager
variform	vehicle	venose	verism	vesicle	vibrioid	villain
variola	vehicular	venosity	verist	vesicula	vibrissa	villainy
variolar	veil	venous	veristic	vesiculae	vibrissae	villanage
variolate	vein	vent	veritable	vesicular	viburnum	villatic
variole	veinless	ventage	verity	vesiculate	vicar	villein
variolite	veinlet	ventail	verjuice	vesper	vicarage	villenage
varioloid	veinstone	ventiduct	vermeil	vesperal	vicarial	villiform
variolous	veiny	ventilate	vermicide	vespiary	vicariate	villosity
variorum	velamen	ventrad	vermiform	vespid	vicarious	villous
various	velamenta	ventral	vermifuge	vessel	vicarship	villus
varix	velamina	ventricle	vermilion	vest	vice	vim
varletry	velar	venture	vermin	vesta	vicegeral	vimen
varmint	velarize	venturous	verminate	vestal	vicenary	viminal
varmintry	velate	venue	verminous	vestee	vicennial	vimineous
varnish	velation	venular	vermouth	vestibule	viceregal	vina
varus	velites	venule	vermuth	vestige	viceroy	vinaceous
varve	velleity	venulose	vernal	vestigia	viceroyal	vincible
vary	vellicate	venulous	vernalize	vestment	vicinage	vincula
vascula	vellum	venus	vernation	vestry	vicinal	vinculum
vascular	velocity	veracious	vernicose	vestryman	vicinism	vindicate
vasculose	velodrome	veracity	vernier	vesture	vicinity	vine

vinegar	virtuoso	vitriol	volition	vulcanian	waistcoat	wardrobe
vinegary	virtuosos	vitriolic	volitive	vulcanic	waister	wardroom
vinery	virtuous	vitta	volley	vulcanite	waisting	wardship
vineyard	virulence	vittae	volplane	vulcanize	waistline	ware
vinic	virulent	vittate	volt	vulgar	wait	warehouse
vinometer	virus	vituline	voltage	vulgarian	waitress	wareroom
vinosity	visa	viva	voltaic	vulgarism	waive	warfare
vinous	visaed	vivace	voltaism	vulgarity	waiver	warhead
vintage	visage	vivacious	voltigeur	vulgarise	wakanda	warison
vintner	visard	vivacity	voltmeter	vulgarize	wake	warlike
viny	viscacha	vivaria	voluble	vulgate	wakeful	warlock
vinyl	viscera	vivarium	volume	vulnerary	wakeless	warm
viol	visceral	vivariums	volumed	vulpicide	waken	warmish
viola	viscid	vivary	volumeter	vulpine	wakerobin	warmth
violable	viscidity	viverrine	volumetry	vulpinite	waldgrave	warn
violably	viscoidal	vives	voluntary	vulture	wale	warp
violate	viscose	vivid	volunteer	vulturine	walk	warpath
violation	viscosity	vivify	volute	vulturous	walkway	warplane
violative	viscount	vivisect	volution	vulva	walkyrie	warragal
violence	viscounty	vixen	volva	vulvae	wall	warrigal
violent	viscous	vizard	volvuli		wallabies	warrant
violet	viscus	vizier	volvulus	**W**	wallaby	warrantee
violin	vise	vizir	vomer	wabble	wallet	warranty
violinist	visible	vizierate	vomerine	wabbly	wallop	warren
violist	vision	vizirate	vomica	wacke	wallow	warrior
violone	visional	vizirship	vomicae	wad	walnut	warsaw
viosterol	visionary	vizor	vomit	waddle	walrus	warship
viper	visit	vocable	vomitive	waddy	waltz	wart
viperine	visitant	vocal	vomito	wade	wampum	warthog
viperish	visor	vocalic	vomitory	wadi	wammus	warty
viperous	vista	vocalism	voodoo	wadset	wampus	wary
virago	visual	vocalist	voodooism	wady	wamus	was
viragoes	visuality	vocalize	voracious	wafer	wan	wash
viragos	visualism	vocation	voracity	waffle	wand	washboard
virelai	visualize	vocative	vortex	waft	wander	washcloth
virelay	visualist	voces	vortexes	waftage	wanderoo	washerman
vireo	vitaceous	vodka	vortical	wafture	wane	washrag
vireonine	vital	vogue	vortices	wag	waney	washstand
virescent	vitalism	voice	vorticose	wage	wangle	washwoman
virga	vitalist	voiceful	votaress	waggery	wangan	washy
virgate	vitality	voiceless	votarist	waggish	wangun	wasp
virgin	vitalize	void	votary	waggle	wanigan	waspish
virginal	vitals	voidance	vote	waggly	wannigan	waspy
virginity	vitamin	voile	votive	wagon	wanion	wassail
virginium	vitamine	volant	votress	wagonage	wanning	wastage
virgulate	vitaminic	volar	vouch	wagonet	want	waste
virgule	vitascope	volatile	vouchee	wagonette	wantage	wasteful
viridian	vitellin	volcanic	vouchsafe	wagsome	wanton	wastrel
viridity	vitelline	volcanism	voussoir	wagtail	wany	wat
virile	vitellus	volcanist	vow	wahconda	wapentake	watap
virilism	vitiable	volcanize	vowel	wahoo	wapiti	watape
virility	vitiate	volcano	vowelize	waif	war	watch
virology	vitiation	volcanoes	vox	wail	warble	watchcase
virosis	vitiligo	volcanos	voyage	wailful	warblefly	watchcry
virtu	vitreous	vole	vug	wain	ward	watchdog
virtual	vitric	volery	vugg	wainscot	warden	watchful
virtue	vitriform	volitant	vuggy	waist	wardenry	watchman
virtuosi	vitrify	volitient	vugh	waistband	wardress	watchword

water	wealth	wergelt	whereupon	whit	wieldable	window
waterback	wealthy	wernerite	wherever	white	wieldy	windpipe
waterbuck	wean	werwolf	wherewith	whitebait	wiener	windrow
waterfall	weanling	west	wherry	whitecap	wife	windsock
waterflea	weapon	wester	wherve	whitefish	wifedom	windstorm
watergum	wear	western	whet	whitegum	wifehood	windward
waterish	weariful	westerner	whether	whiten	wifeless	windy
waterless	weariless	westing	whetslate	whitetail	wig	wine
waterlily	wearisome	westward	whetstone	whitewash	wigan	wineglass
watermark	weary	wet	whew	whiteweed	wigeon	winery
waternut	weasand	wether	whey	whitewood	wiggery	wing
watershed	weasel	whack	wheyey	whither	wiggle	wingback
waterside	weather	whale	which	whiting	wiggly	wingbow
waterway	weave	whaleback	whichever	whitish	wight	wingless
waterweed	web	whaleboat	whicker	whitlow	wigwag	winglet
watery	webby	whalebone	whiff	whittle	wigwam	wingy
watt	webworm	whaleman	whiffle	whiz	wikiup	wink
wattage	wed	whang	whifflery	whizz	wild	winkle
wattle	wedge	whangee	while	whoa	wildcat	winnow
wattless	wedgie	wharf	whiles	whoever	wildfire	winsome
wattmeter	wedgy	wharfs	whilom	whole	wildfowl	winter
waul	wedlock	wharfage	whilst	wholesale	wilding	winterish
wave	wee	wharve	whim	wholesome	wildlife	wintery
waveless	weed	wharves	whimbrel	wholly	wildling	wintrily
wavelet	weedy	what	whimper	whom	wildwood	wintry
wavellite	week	whatever	whimsical	whomever	wile	winy
wavemeter	weekly	wheal	whimsey	whomso	wilful	winze
waver	ween	wheat	whimsy	whoop	will	wipe
wavey	weep	wheaten	whin	whoopee	willemite	wire
wavy	weet	wheatworm	whinchat	whopping	willet	wiredraw
wawl	weever	wheedle	whine	whore	willful	wireless
wax	weevil	wheel	whiny	whoredom	williwaw	wireman
waxberry	weft	wheelbase	whinny	whorish	willow	wirephoto
waxbill	weigela	wheelbug	whip	whorl	willower	wirework
waxen	weigh	wheelman	whipcord	whorled	willowish	wireworm
waxmyrtle	weight	wheelsman	whipgraft	whose	willowy	wirra
waxpalm	weighty	wheelwork	whiphand	whoso	willpower	wiry
waxweed	weir	wheeze	whippet	whosoever	willy	wisdom
waxwing	weird	wheezy	whipsaw	why	wilt	wise
waxwork	wejack	whelk	whipstall	whydah	wily	wiseacre
waxworker	weka	whelky	whipstock	wich	wimble	wish
waxy	welcome	whelm	whipworm	wick	wimple	wishbone
way	weld	whelp	whir	wicking	win	wishful
waybill	welfare	when	whirl	wicked	wince	wisp
wayfarer	welkin	whence	whirligig	wicker	winch	wispy
wayfaring	well	whenever	whirlpool	wicket	wind	wist
waylay	wellsite	where	whirlwind	wickiup	windage	wistaria
wayside	welsh	whereas	whish	wicopy	windbreak	wistful
wayward	welt	whereases	whisht	wide	windcone	wit
wayworm	welter	whereat	whisk	widen	windfall	witan
we	wen	whereby	whisker	widgeon	windflaw	witch
weak	wend	wherefore	whiskery	widow	windgall	witchery
weaken	wenish	wherefrom	whiskey	widower	windgalled	with
weakfish	weny	wherein	whisky	widowhood	windigo	withal
weakling	were	whereinto	whisper	width	windlass	withdraw
weakly	werewolf	whereof	whispery	widthway	windle	withe
weal	wergeld	whereon	whist	widthwise	windless	wither
weald	weregild	whereto	whistle	wield	windmill	witherite

withers
withhold
within
without
withstand
withy
witless
witling
witness
witticism
witty
wive
wivern
wives
wizard
wizardry
wizen
woad
woadwaxen
woald
wobble
wobegone
woe
woebegone
woeful
woesome
wocus
woful
wokas
wold
wolf
wolfbane
wolfberry
wolfhound
wolfish
wolfram
wolver
wolverene
wolverine
wolves
woman
womanhood
womanize
womankind
womb
wombat
womby
women
womenfolk
won
wonder
wonderful
wondrous
wont
woo
wood
woodbin
woodbine

woodblock
woodbober
woodchat·
woodchuck
woodcock
woodcraft
woodcut
wooden
woodhen
woodhouse
woodland
woodlark
woodman
woodnote
woodpile
woodprint
woodruff
woods
woodsia
woodwaxen
woodwind
woodwork
woodworm
woody
woof
wool
woolen
woolfell
woollen
woolly
wooly
woolpack
woolsack
woorali
woorari
word
wordage
wordbook
wordily
wording
wordless
wordy
work
workaday
workbag
workbench
workbox
workday
workfolk
workfolks
workhouse
workless
workman
workout
workroom
workshop
worktable
workweek

world
worldling
worm
wormhole
wormholed
wormil
wormroot
wormseed
wormwood
wormy
worry
worse
worsen
worship
worshipful
worst
worsted
wort
worth
worthless
worthy
worthies
wot
would
wound
wove
woven
wow
wrack
wraith
wrangle
wrap
wrapt
wrasse
wrath
wrathful
wrathy
wreak
wreath
wreathy
wreathe
wreck
wreckage
wreckful
wren
wrench
wrest
wrestle
wretch
wriggle
wriggly
wright
wring
wrinkle
wrinkly
wrist
wristband
wristlet

writ
write
writhe
wrong
wrongful
wrote
wroth
wrought
wrung
wry
wryneck
wulfenite
wych
wye
wyvern

X

xanthate
xanthein
xanthic
xanthin
xanthous
xebec
xenia
xenogamy
xenogenic
xenogeny
xenolith
xenon
xeroderma
xerophyte
xerosis
xerotic
xerotropic
xerus
xiphoid
xylan
xylem
xylene
xylic
xylidin
xylidine
xylograph
xyloid
xylol
xylophage
xylophone
xylose
xylotomy
xylyl
xylylene
xyst
xyster

Y

yacht
yachtman
yachtsman

yah
yahoo
yak
yam
yank
yanking
yapon
yard
yardage
yardarm
yardgrass
yardstick
yardwand
yarn
yarrow
yarrup
yashmac
yashmak
yasmak
yatagan
yataghan
yaup
yaupon
yaw
yawl
yawmeter
yawn
yawp
ycleped
yclept
ye
yea
yean
yeanling
year
yearbook
yearling
yearlong
yearn
yeast
yeasty
yell
yellow
yellowish
yellowy
yelp
yen
yeoman
yeomanly
yeomanry
yerba
yes
yeses
yesses
yesterday
yestereve
yestreen
yet

yew
yield
yip
yodel
yodle
yoga
yogh
yogee
yogi
yogin
yogurt
yoghurt
yoghourt
yoicks
yoke
yokefellow
yokel
yokemate
yolk
yolky
yon
yond
yonder
yonker
yore
you
young
youngish
youngling
youngster
younker
youpon
your
yours
yourself
youth
youthful
yowie
yperite
ytterbia
ytterbic
ytterbium
yttria
yttric
yttrium
yuan
yucca
yupon

Z

zacaton
zaffar
zaffer
zaffir
zaffre
zaibatsu
zain
zamia

zamindar
zanana
zany
zaptiah
zaptie
zaptieh
zaɪape
zaratite
zareba
zareeba
zarf
zax
zeal
zealot
zealotry
zealous
zebec
zebeck
zebra
zebrine
zebroid
zebrass
zebrawood
zebrula
zebrule
zebu
zecchin
zecchino
zechin
zecchini
zedoary
zein
zelotypia
zemindar
zemstvo
zenana
zendik
zenith
zeolite
zephyr
zero
zeroes
zeros
zest
zestful
zeta
zeugma
zibeline
zibelline
zibet
ziggurat
zigzag
zikkurat
zinc
zincate
zincic
zincify

zincite	zirconic	zombiism	zooidal	zoophilia	zorila	zyme
zincked	zirconium	zonal	zoolater	zoophobia	zoster	zymic
zincking	zither	zonary	zoolatry	zoophobic	zounds	zymogen
zincky	zittern	zonate	zoologic	zoophyte	zucchetta	zymogene
zincotype	zloty	zonation	zoology	zoophytic	zucchetto	zymogenic
zincous	zlotys	zone	zoologist	zooplasty	zwieback	zymologic
zinfandel	zoa	zoneless	zoom	zoosperm	zygoma	zymologist
zinkenite	zodiac	zonula	zoometric	zoospore	zygomatic	zymology
zinky	zodiacal	zonule	zoometry	zoosporic	zygophyte	zymolytic
zinnia	zoetrope	zoo	zoomorphy	zoosporous	zygosis	zymolysis
zip	zoetropic	zoochore	zoon	zooster	zygosperm	zymometer
zipper	zoic	zoogloea	zoonal	zootomic	zygospore	zymosis
zircon	zoisite	zoogloeae	zoons	zootomy	zygote	zymotic
zirconate	zombi	zoography	zoonomy	zootoxin	zygotic	zymurgy
zirconia	zombie	zooid	zoophile	zoril	zymase	

SWITCH WORDS

Frequently the same group of letters can spell two or more different words. This fact may be very important to you in playing word games. You have the letters that enable you to make the word NIGHT. But if you form instead the word THING with the same letters you may be able to place the H on a triple-letter-score square, thus increasing your score by 9 points. Whenever you try to form a word from some or all the tiles you have, see what other words you can make with the same letters.

This list illustrates groups of words where all the words in the group are formed from the same letters.

abed bade bead
abets bates baste beats beast
ache each
acres cares races scare
aids dais said
ales sale seal
amen mane mean name
amend maned named
angel angle glean
arid raid
aril lair liar rail
arise raise
ascot coast
aside ideas
aster rates stare tares tears
astir stair

bales blase sable
bared beard bread
below bowel elbow
bleating tangible
bleats stable tables
braid rabid
brief fiber
browse bowers

capers crapes pacers scrape recaps spacer
capes paces space scape
caret cater crate trace
cartel claret
cause sauce
chaste cheats scathe
cheater teacher
cited edict
cleat eclat
coil loci
coins icons scion sonic
corset sector
credit direct
crisp scrip

dale deal lade lead
dare dear read
danger gander garden ranged
dealer leader redeal
denied indeed
design signed singed
detail dilate tailed
diet edit tide tied
draws sward wards
drapes parsed spader spared spread

earth hater heart
east eats etas sate seat seta
elapse please
emit mite time item
emits smite times items
entrap parent
erring ringer
ester steer trees
ether there three

fares fears safer
faster strafe
field filed flied
file life lief
filer flier rifle lifer
finger fringe

garnets strange
girth right
glare lager large regal
gnat tang
granite tearing
groan organ orang

hares hears share shear
hewn when
hinge neigh
hoes hose shoe
horse hoser shore

inert inter niter nitre trine
inks kins sink skin
inset nites stein tines
itself stifle filets

laces scale
lame male meal
laves salve slave vales
leap pale peal plea
least slate stale steal tales
license silence
lilts still
limes miles slime smile
lose loes sloe sole
luster result

mate meat tame team
mason moans
master remats stream
meteor remote

nets tens sent
night thing
notes onset seton stone tones

orts rots sort tors
ought tough

pares pears rapes reaps spare
pastel plates pleats staple
parts sprat strap traps
paws swap wasp
pest pets step
pines snipe spine
paste pates spate tapes
pointer protein tropine
pores poser prose ropes spore
priest ripest spiter sprite stripe tripes

quote toque

rats star tars
relating triangle
respect spectre
reserve severer reverse
riot tiro trio
rites tires tries
rivets strive

saint satin stain
serve sever veers verse
sheet these
skate stake steak takes teaks

throw worth wroth

wider weird